So you really want to learn

LATIN
BOOK III

GALORE PARK

Published by Galore Park Publishing, 3 Crown Yard, Bedgebury Estate, Goudhurst, Kent TN17 2QZ

Text copyright © NRR Oulton 1999

Illustrations copyright © Ian Douglass 1999

Typography and layout by S&B Associates, Nymet Rowland, Crediton, Devon EX17 6AN

Printed and bound in Great Britain by Biddles Ltd, *www.biddles.co.uk*

ISBN 1 902984 02 1

First published 1999. Reprinted 2001, 2003

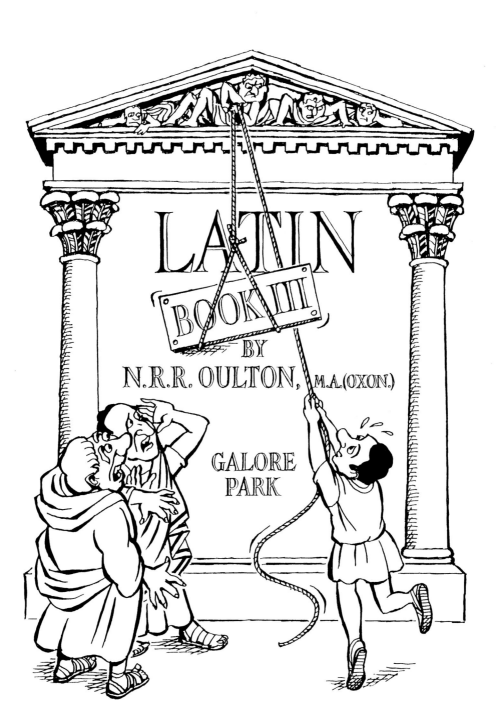

Contents

Acknowledgements

The author would like to thank the following, who have all contributed to the production of this book: Theo Zinn and Stephen Anderson, who read the proofs and pointed out its numerous faults with great tact and infinite patience – the errors that remain are, of course, entirely my own; the late C.G. Zumpt and his estimable translator, the late Rev. J. Kenrick, for hours of fun with grammatical niceties; Ian Douglass, for returning my call and creating the best set of Latin cartoons I have ever seen; Robert Parker, who fielded various obscure questions and responded with great speed and good humour; the girls of Tormead School, who saw the course through its trial period and greatly improved it by their constructive criticism and deadly eye for detail; the GCSE class of '98–99, who were the first full-blown guinea pigs and who all achieved A*s (bit of a plug, that); Honor Alleyne, who effectively commissioned the book and supported me through the whole process of production; Roland Smith for his ever-cheerful approach to the task of getting it down in print; Dennis Flynn for producing Arial Galore, the Latin font used throughout, silly accents and all; Bethany Brewer, for running the office at Galore Park and acting as the complete *sine quā nōn*; and the large number of colleagues who have shown their support for the project by buying truck loads of Books I and II.

PREFACE

So you made it through Books I and II? And you're not giving up, now that you've got this far? Well, here we go then, all the way up to GCSE level and beyond. Normal rules apply: grammar on the left, exercises on the right, and a slab of vocab. every chapter.

By now you will know how important it is to learn the grammar thoroughly. There is quite a lot more to be learnt, but the main task ahead of you now, once you've lapped up the remaining grammar, is to master the **syntax**, i.e. the way clauses are linked up together to form complex sentences.   Latin syntax involves a whole range of **constructions**, each one involving a little formula, such as "accusative and infinitive", or "*ut* + the subjunctive". Correct identification of the construction being used in a sentence is vital to accurate translation, both from Latin into English and the other way round. It may appear daunting at first but trust me, you will soon be *ut* + the subjunctive-ing with your eyes shut!

N.R.R.O
September 1999

GUIDE TO PRONUNCIATION

Vowels

The main problem with learning to pronounce Latin correctly lies in the vowels. The Romans, as Asterix is always telling us, were crazy and they pronounced their vowels as follows:

ă (short)	as in "cup"	ā (long)	as in "calf"
ĕ (short)	as in "set"	ē (long)	as in "stair"
ĭ (short)	as in "bit"	ī (long)	as in "bee"
ŏ (short)	as in "lot"	ō (long)	as in the French "*beau*"
ŭ (short)	as in "put"	ū (long)	as in "route"

In addition, where the letter *y* occurs in Latin, it represents the Greek letter *upsilon*, and should be pronounced like a French *u* in words such as "*lune*".

In this book, *long* vowels are marked with a macron (ā, ē, ī, ō, ū). If they are *not* marked, they are short. Occasionally a short vowel is marked as short (ă, ĕ, ĭ, ŏ, ŭ) if there is an incorrect tendency to pronounce the vowel long. For example the *o* in the Latin word *egŏ* is marked as short because so many people pronounce the word as if it were long.

Just occasionally a vowel may be marked as being both long *and* short. This is where a vowel is known to have been pronounced long in some places but short in others. In this book, for example, you will come across the words *quandŏ̄* and *homŏ̄*, the final '*o*'s of which are sometimes pronounced long, sometimes short. You will also find words such as *ubĭ̄* and *ibĭ̄*, the final '*i*'s of which may be either long or short.

A vowel is regularly pronounced long when followed by *ns* or *nf*. This rule even applies to the word *in* when this is followed by a word starting with *s* or *f*. E.g. *in agrō* but *īn silvā*.

Diphthongs

Where two vowels are pronounced as *one* sound (as in the English *boil*, or *wait*), this is called a **diphthong** and the resulting syllable will always be long. For example the *–ae* of the word *mēnsae* is a diphthong. Diphthongs, because they are *always* long, are not marked with a macron.

The most common diphthongs are:

ae	as in "eye"	*au*	as in "now"

but you may also find:

ei	as in "reign"	*oe*	as in "boil"
ui	as in French "*oui*"	*eu*	as in *e* and *u* said in one breath!

Vowel and syllable length

You need to learn the quantity of a *vowel* (i.e. whether it is long or short) to ensure that you pronounce the word correctly. But you also need to know the length of the *syllable* that the vowel is in. This is because Latin poetry was based on the subtle combination, not of herbs and spices, but of long and short syllables.

I don't want to put you off before you even start, but you should know that there is a difference between marking a *vowel* as long or short and saying that the syllable itself is long or short. A syllable is long:

  (a) if it contains a long vowel or diphthong; or
  (b) if it contains a vowel followed by two consonants.

For the purposes of this rule, *x* and *z* count as double consonants, as does the consonant *i* (see below) where this comes between two vowels (see Appendix on page 129). There is an exception to rule (b) which we won't bother with now. See page 104 for further details.

Consonants

- *c* is always *hard* as in "cot", never *soft* as in "century".
- *ch* is always as in "chorus", never as in "chips".
- *gn* is pronounced *ngn*, as in "hangnail".
- Latin has no letter *j*. Instead, the Romans used *i* as a consonant, pronounced as a *y* (thus *Iūlius Caesar*, pronounced Yulius).
- *m*, at the end of a word, is nasalised and reduced (i.e. only partially pronounced).
- *ph* is always a *hard p*, never a *soft f* (as in Philip).
- *r* is always rolled, on the tip of the tongue.
- *s* is always *s* as in "bus", never *z* as in "busy".
- *th* is always as in "Thomas", never as in "thistle".
- Just as *i* can be a vowel or a consonant, so it is with *u*. Consonant *u* is generally written as a *v* and is pronounced as a *w*. In some words, however, it is written as a *u*, as in the word *persuādeō*.
- *v* is in fact a consonant *u* (see above) and is pronounced as a *w*, never as a *v*.

Stress

Just as in English we have a particular way of stressing words, so they did in Latin. We, for example, say "potáto" (with the stress on the a). When we learn English words, we have to learn how to stress them. For the Romans, there was a simple rule, which could be applied to all words.

The Romans worked out how to stress a word by looking at its penultimate syllable. Syllables, as we have seen, are either long or short. They are long if they contain a long vowel or diphthong, or if they contain a short vowel followed by two consonants. They are short if they contain a short vowel which is *not* followed by two consonants. Using this information, a Latin word should be stressed as follows:

- The final syllable of a word should never be stressed (e.g. *ámō, ámās, ámat*, etc.).
- In a word of more than two syllables, if the penultimate syllable is long, stress it (e.g. *amātis* is stressed *amátis; amāvistis** is stressed *amāvístis).*
- If the penultimate syllable is short, stress the the one before it (e.g. *regitis* is stressed *régitis).*

* Note how the penultimate syllable of *amāvistis* is long because the *i*, although short, is followed by two consonants (*st*).

INTRODUCTION

In Book II we saw how Rome, having gained supremacy in Italy, turned her attention to matters outside Italy. Carthage, ancient home of Queen Dido, reared her ugly head and Rome became embroiled in a series of wars which was to occupy her for around 120 years. You may remember that, when Aeneas had left Dido and sailed on to Italy without her, she had put a curse on him, promising that their two peoples would always be at war and that one day, a Carthaginian warrior would rise from her ashes to avenge her. Virgil tells the story in Book IV of the *Aeneid* and, to give you a taste of what you will be able to read by the time you have finished this book, here it is in Latin:

"Tum vōs, ō Tyriī, stirpem et genus omne futūrum
exercēte odiīs; cinerīque haec mittite nostrō
mūnera: nūllus amor populīs, nec foedera suntō.
exoriāre aliquis nostrīs ex ossibus ultor,
quī face Dardaniōs ferrōque sequāre colōnōs.
nunc, ōlim, quōcunque dabunt sē tempore vīrēs,
lītora lītoribus contrāria, flūctibus undās
imprecor, arma armīs: pugnent ipsīque nepōtēsque."

"Then, O Tyrians (Carthaginians), harass his stock and his whole future race with hatred; grant this as an offering to my ashes: let there be no love between our peoples, no treaties. May someone arise from my bones as an avenger to pursue the Trojan colonists with fire and sword. Now, in the future, at whatever time strength will offer itself, I pray that our shores be set against their shores, our seas against their seas, our arms against their arms: let them fight, them and their descendants."

Pretty punchy stuff, I think you will agree, and of course it all came true. Carthage did pursue Aeneas's descendants, the Romans. In this book, we will see how the avenger did indeed materialise, in the form of Hannibal, and how he jolly nearly succeeded in bringing Rome down. But, as in all good tales, there was a twist and the Romans came out on top; which is why you are learning Latin, not Carthaginian!

So it came about that Rome took over the Mediterranean world, soaking up the old empire of Alexander the Great, and then moved north, led by the mighty Julius Caesar, into Gaul. The Roman Empire, as in the map on the right, was finally taking shape and we leave it with the emergence of the first Roman emperor, Augustus Caesar, in 27 B.C. Most of the Latin you read, at least in the early stages, will be Latin written at this time in Rome's history, the so-called "golden age" or "Augustan age". Virgil, Horace, Ovid, and Livy are all Augustan writers. Caesar, Cicero and Catullus are slightly earlier. Tacitus and Pliny are later. But the great thing is that, having mastered the material in this course, you will be ready to tackle these authors with confidence. If you really want to, that is!

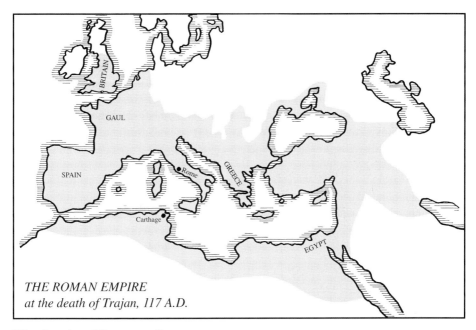

THE ROMAN EMPIRE
at the death of Trajan, 117 A.D.

Word order: "the worm"

In this book you will be learning to cope with increasingly complex sentences, made up of a large number of subordinate clauses. Breaking up these sentences into their component parts will be vital for you if you are not to be overwhelmed. However, before we begin, you need to know about "the worm". In a Latin sentence, you should try at all costs to avoid a situation known as a "worm". This is where complete sense may be found in a sentence **before you have reached the end**.

E.g. *cōnsul urbem bene regēbat quod sapiēns erat.*

In this sentence, perfect sense may be found in the words *cōnsul urbem bene regēbat*: "The consul ruled the city well". This leaves *quod sapiēns erat* hanging off the end; it is rather as if a worm has been chopped in half by a spade. The front half of the worm has wriggled off, separated from its back end. This situation can be avoided by altering the Latin word order as follows:

cōnsul, quod sapiēns erat, urbem bene regēbat = "the consul, because he was wise, ruled the city well".

In the new version, no sense can be found in the Latin until we reach the verb *regēbat*, which comes at the very end. If you tried to cut the sentence in two before reaching *regēbat*, the front end would make no sense. The "worm" has thus been avoided.

Try to remember this principle of Latin word order as you make your way through this book. It will help you both to understand some of the more complex sentences and ensure that the Latin you write yourself actually looks like Latin!

CHAPTER 1

Participles; compounds of sum; quīdam

Participles

Participles are adjectives, formed from verbs. Like normal adjectives, they agree with the noun or pronoun they describe in gender, case and number. In Latin there are three participles: present, future and past. We shall begin with the present participle.

Present participle

Present participles (which in English end in "–ing") are formed in Latin from the present stem, are always active and decline like *ingēns*. *Amō* and *moneō* add *-ns* to the present stem, the others add *-ēns*. Here they are, with their genitive singular forms:

amā-ns,	*monē-ns,*	*reg-ēns,*	*audi-ēns,*	*capi-ēns,*
amantis	*monentis*	*regentis*	*audientis*	*capientis*
Loving	Warning	Ruling	Hearing	Taking

	M.	F.	N.	M.	F.	N.
Nom.	*amāns*	*amāns*	*amāns*	*amantēs*	*amantēs*	*amantia*
Acc.	*amantem*	*amantem*	*amāns*	*amantēs*	*amantēs*	*amantia*
Gen.	*amantis*	*amantis*	*amantis*	*amantium*	*amantium*	*amantium*
Dat.	*amantī*	*amantī*	*amantī*	*amantibus*	*amantibus*	*amantibus*
Abl.	*amantī*	*amantī*	*amantī*	*amantibus*	*amantibus*	*amantibus*

Present participles may be said to describe what the nouns, with which they agree, are "doing".

E.g. The girl watched her mother **walking** in the garden =
  *puella mātrem in hortō **ambulantem** spectābat.*

In this example, the participle "walking" stands in place of a phrase such as *who was walking* and thus tells us what the mother was doing.

N.B. A present participle should not be used to stand in place of a causal clause (see page 62). Thus "feeling hungry, he decided to eat" becomes in Latin "because he felt hungry…".

Irregular participles

Most present participles are easy enough to form from the present stem, but the odd problem crops up here and there with the irregular verbs:

ferō: ferēns, ferentis. This is completely regular, just to keep you guessing!

eō: iēns, euntis. This is very silly!

possum: potēns, potentis exists as an adjective (= "powerful") but must not be used as a participle.

sum: no participle exists. There is, thus, no Latin word for "being".

Take care with that very silly-looking participle from *eō*.

E.g. We watched the boy going into the field = *puerum spectāvimus in agrum **euntem**.*

So you really want to learn Latin…

Exercise 1. 1
Study the information on the left-hand page about present participles. Give the nominative masculine singular and genitive masculine singular of the following participles:

1. Calling
2. Fighting
3. Remaining
4. Learning
5. Going

6. Dragging
7. Turning
8. Conquering
9. Completing
10. Playing

Exercise 1. 2
Translate into English:

1. *nāvēs in portum nāvigantēs spectābat.*
2. *Gallī virōs Rōmānōs īn forō sedentēs vīdērunt.*
3. *puerī equum prope mūrum stantem cēpērunt.*
4. *imperātōrem Rōmānum mīlitēs in pugnam dūcentem spectābāmus.*
5. *poētam in hortō cantantem audīvī.*
6. *Troiānī Graecōs dōna ferentēs nōn satis timēbant.*
7. *servus dominum in agrōs ineuntem vīdit.*
8. *rēx potēns populum terrēbat.*
9. *lēgātus ā fēminīs ē forō festīnantibus vīsus est.*
10. *cūr in hortō stāns cantās clāmāsque?*

Exercise 1. 3
Translate into Latin. Always be sure to make the participle agree with the noun or pronoun to which it refers.

1. We watched the boys running into the field.
2. The son gave a gift to his mother.
3. Sitting under a tree, the farmer watched the slaves.
4. The farmer watched the slaves sitting under a tree.
5. The general praised the fighting soldiers.
6. The school master was reading a book, sitting near the boys and girls.
7. No one knows the name of the sleeping girl.
8. The slaves will not overcome the fighting Romans, will they?
9. Why have the women left the boy crying in the garden?
10. Have you heard the poet singing in the forum?

Using Latin	***Timeō Danaōs et dōna ferentēs***
	"I fear the Greeks, even when bearing gifts."
	(Virgil, *Aeneid* 2, 49).

Present participles and English spelling

It is a well known fact that English spelling is difficult. How, for example, would you explain to a Martian that the words "plough", "enough", and "through" – which sound completely different – are spelt in the same way?

But Latin is often there in the background, easing our way through these little minefields. And, now that you have met present participles, there is a whole range of English words which you stand a pretty good chance of spelling correctly, namely those ending in -ent, -ant, -ence or -ance. Take the following:

- Ambulance
- Audience
- Convenience
- Credence
- Repellent
- Repugnant

The difficulty with words such as these is knowing which vowel to use before the n; is it an *a* or an *e*? The following principle won't always work, I'm afraid, but it's pretty good. Just think about which Latin verb is involved, and then look at that verb's present participle. Thus ambulance, from *ambulāns*; audience from *audiēns*; and so on. Neat, eh?

Of course, there is a problem with this, which we can blame on the French. Some words in –ant have come to us via French, rather than directly from Latin. Thus the word "descendant" has come from the French *descendre*, with its participle *descendant,* not *dēscendō* with its participle *dēscendēns*. And the word "servant", which looks from its spelling as though it comes from the Latin *servō, servāre,* in fact comes from *serviō, servīre* = "I serve" and thus has no business being spelt with an *a*. Again, this is because it comes to us via the participle of the French *servir,* i.e. *servant*. Still, you can't win them all, can you?

Vocabulary 1

Verbs		**Adverbs**	
absum, abesse, āfuī	I am absent	*bene*	well
adsum, adesse, adfuī	I am present	*nūper*	recently
salvē, salvēte	hello, greetings!	*nūsquam*	nowhere
Nouns		*paulum*	a little
aedificium, -ī, n.	building	*quō?*	where to? (whither?)
rēgīna, -ae, f.	queen	*quot?*	how many?
Adjectives		*satis*	enough
plēnus, -a, -um	full	*sīcut*	just as
(+ abl. or gen.)		*unde?*	from where?
quālis, quāle?	of what kind?		(whence?)
Conjunction		**Pronoun**	
priusquam	before	*quīdam*	a certain

So you really want to learn Latin...

Exercise 1. 4

Study the information on the left-hand page about participles and English spelling. Translate and then give an English word derived from the following Latin participles. In all cases the most common mis-spelling involves the *a* or *e* near the end of the word:

1. *cōnstituēns*
2. *agēns*
3. *ambulāns*
4. *ascendēns**
5. *audiēns*

6. *cadēns*
7. *cōgēns*
8. *crēdēns*
9. *repellēns*
10. *exspectāns*

* Note that the English word from this may be spelt either with an –e (if you're following the Latin) or with an –a (if you're following the French). Pity those Martians!

Exercise 1. 5

Translate into English the following story, which is adapted from one of Aesop's fables:

agricola quīnque fīliōs habuit. fīliī saepe <u>disputābant</u> neque bene labōrābant. pater igitur <u>fascem</u> ūnī fīliō dedit et "potesne" inquit "hunc fascem frangere?" puer fascem frangere nōn potuit. tum pater fascem alterī fīliō dedit. "potesne tū" inquit pater "hunc fascem frangere?" nōn potuit. mox omnēs puerī fascem frangere cōnātī sunt sed frūstrā. deinde agricola fascem <u>solvit</u> et <u>virgās</u> <u>singulās</u> fīliīs dedit. puerī virgās facile frēgērunt. inde pater rīdēns "sōlī" inquit "validī nōn estis. <u>ūnā</u> tamen vōs ā nūllō superābiminī!"

disputō, -āre, -āvī, -ātum = I argue; *fascis, fascis,* m. = a bundle of sticks; *solvō, solvere, solvī, solūtum* = I untie; *virga, -ae,* f. = stick; *singulī, -ae, -a* = one at a time; *ūnā* (adv.) = together.

Exercise 1. 6

Translate into Latin:

1. A farmer was working in his fields, preparing the land.
2. "Are you able", he said to his son, "to conquer all your brothers?"
3. The boy ran towards his brothers and, holding a sword, tried to wound them.
4. The father was angry and seized his fighting sons.
5. "You are strong" he said, "but, fighting alone, you cannot overcome your enemies."

Exercise 1. 7

Revision. Translate into English:

1. *omnēs gaudēbant, īn forum festīnantēs.*
2. *Mārcus sorōrem sub mēnsā flentem invēnit.*
3. *nōnne nāvēs in portum nāvigantēs spectāre cupis?*
4. *dux exercitūs mīlitēs castra prope flūmen pōnentēs spectāvit.*
5. *unde veniēbant cīvēs rēgīnam laudantēs?*

Using Latin

Et al.

Et al. is short for *et aliī* = and others. For example, a book may be said to have been written by N. Oulton *et al.*

Future participle

The future participle describes a noun or pronoun as being *about to* do something and is formed from the supine stem.

amāt-ūrus, -a, -um	About to love
monit-ūrus, -a, -um	About to warn
rēct-ūrus, -a, -um	About to rule
audīt-ūrus, -a, -um	About to hear
capt-ūrus, -a, -um	About to take

These participles are always **active** in meaning and decline like *bonus*.
E.g. He saw the girls *about to overcome* the farmer =
    *puellās agricolam **superātūrās** vīdit.*

The future participle of *sum* is *futūrus* = "about to be". *Possum* has no future participle. Almost all other verbs form their future participles regularly from the supine.

Perfect participle passive

As you already know, the perfect participle passive, or PPP as it likes to be called, is formed from the supine stem and declines like *bonus*. So far, you have only used it as part of the perfect passive tense, but it survives perfectly well on its own.

amātus, -a, -um	Having been loved
monitus, -a, um	Having been warned
rēctus, -a, -um	Having been ruled
audītus, -a, um	Having been heard
captus, -a, um	Having been taken

When you are getting used to this little chap, always use the words "having been" and you will not go far wrong.
E.g. *puellam ā mīlitibus captam vīdimus* =
    We saw the girl *having been captured* by the soldiers.

This can then be put into more natural English as follows:
    We saw the girl *captured* by the soldiers; or
    We saw the girl *who had been captured* by the soldiers.

As you can see, the best translation of a PPP will almost never involve the words "having been". But if you translate a PPP with these words to start with, you can always put it into more natural English later, when you are certain that you know what you are doing. Above all, the most important thing to remember about the PPP is that it is **passive**. You would be amazed how many people forget this simple fact.

So you really want to learn Latin...

Exercise 1. 8

Study the information on the left-hand page about future participles. Then translate into English:

1. *Gallōs urbem oppugnātūrōs spectābāmus.*
2. *mīlitēs, prō patriā pugnātūrī, arma parābant.*
3. *Ulixēs, domum reditūrus, dīs grātiās ēgit.*
4. *quālis vir iuvenem interfectūrus rīdet?*
5. *Hannibal hostēs castra positūrōs spectāvit.*

Exercise 1. 9

Study the information on the left-hand page about the perfect participle passive. Before translating the following sentences, bracket the PPP with the noun with which it agrees (as if it were a normal adjective). The first two are done for you. Then translate into English:

1. *puer parvus [agricolam interfectum] vīdit.*
2. *[servus inventus] domum quam celerrimē missus est.*
3. *puella librum lēctum amicō dedit.*
4. *puellam ā mātre relictam invenīre nōn poterāmus.*
5. *nāvis in portū aedificāta tempestāte dēlēta est.*

Exercise 1. 10

We do not often say "having been" in English (e.g. "having been loved"), but this phrase is jolly useful for showing that a PPP is being used. Bearing this in mind, translate the following into Latin:

1. We see the horses walking into the field.
2. They saw the cavalry about to attack the town.
3. He led the (having been) captured slaves into the forum.
4. Soldiers about to fight always obey their leaders.
5. The gods seemed to be angry with the (having been) conquered citizens.
6. The young man found a beautiful gift (having been) left under the table.
7. The consul watched the soldiers talking in the forum with the prisoners.
8. The Romans were able to wage another war against the (having been) defeated enemy.
9. The soldiers saw the girl playing outside the walls of the city.
10. Having been seized by the soldiers, she was killed by their shields.

Using Latin

Prīmā faciē

This expression is used, particularly in law, to mean "at first appearance", i.e. "on the face of it" or "on first consideration".

Using participles

As we have seen, one of the cleverest things you can do with a participle is to cut out the need for a separate clause. Examine the following examples:
- The farmer *was sitting* under a tree and *was reading* a book.

One of the verbs in italics can be changed into a participle as follows:
- The farmer, sitting under a tree, was reading a book =
  agricola sub arbore **sedēns** *librum legēbat.*

This is even more impressive when we use perfect participles:
- The farmer *captured* the slave and *killed* him.

This can be changed by substituting a participle for the first verb:
- The farmer killed the having been captured slave =
  agricola servum **captum** *interfēcit.*

When translating from Latin you obviously do this in reverse:
- *imperātor servōs* **captōs** *Rōmam dūxit* =
  The general led the having been captured slaves to Rome; this then becomes:
  The general captured the slaves and led them to Rome.

Participles of deponent verbs

Deponent verbs have all three participles, but the present and future have an active *form* (which is odd, because deponent verbs normally always look passive) and the perfect participle, of course (being deponent), has the usual passive form with an active *meaning*:

Present: *loquēns* = speaking.
Future: *locūtūrus* = about to speak.
Past: *locūtus* = having spoken.

The present participle of a deponent verb is formed by establishing what conjugation the verb is and then - ignoring the fact that it is deponent - following the pattern for that conjugation. Thus *loquor* in the example above is 3rd conjugation, following *regō*. *Regō* has the present participle *regēns,* thus loquor has *loquēns.* *Cōnor* is 1st conjugation, following *amō.* *Amō* goes *amāns,* thus *cōnor* goes *cōnāns.* Easy, isn't it?

The future participle is formed from the past participle (*locūtus* gives *locūtūrus*). As for the perfect participle itself, it is simply the 3rd principal part without the *sum* (*locūtus sum* gives *locūtus*). Couldn't be simpler. Note that, while one can say "having spoken" using the perfect participle of a deponent verb, there is no way of saying in Latin "having loved", because the PPP of *amō* is, by definition, *passive*.

N.B. The verb *morior, morī, mortuus sum* has the future participle *moritūrus*.

Aliī...aliī

The Latin for "some" when it is followed by "others" is *aliī...aliī*.
E.g. *aliī dormiēbant, aliī legēbant* = some were sleeping, others were reading.

So you really want to learn Latin...

Exercise 1. 11

Study the information on the left-hand page about using participles. Then translate into English:

1. *fortasse dī dē caelō dēscendent et fēminās captās servābunt.*
2. *librum ā tē mihĭ datum nōn legam.*
3. *pecūniam sub mēnsā iūdicis positam invenīre nōn poterāmus.*
4. *noctū ferte aquam ad mīlitēs dormientēs.*
5. *ī Rōmam, Rēgule, et quam celerrimē fer verba pācis ad Rōmānōs.*
6. *puellae fēlīcēs ab urbe captā fūgērunt.*
7. *intereā Poenī bellum in Africā gerēbant nec legiōnēs victās līberāvērunt.*
8. *līberōs cīvium in hortō lūdentēs vidēre poterāmus.*
9. *Gallī audācēs Rōmānōs in colle manentēs superāre nōn poterant.*
10. *cīvēs optimī imperātōrem trāns flūmen festīnantem sequī cupiēbant.*

Exercise 1. 12

Translate into Latin, using one main verb and one participle in each sentence:

1. We attacked the city and captured it.
2. We killed the soldier and dragged him into the wood.
3. The Romans defeated the Gauls and led them to the city.
4. After I have captured the slave I shall kill him.
5. You will read the book which has been given to you, won't you?

Exercise 1. 13

Study the information on the left-hand page about *aliī…aliī.* Then translate into English:

post bellum, mīlitēs Pūnicī domum regressī sunt. pecūnia tamen eīs dēbita nōn trādita est. īrātissimī igitur in urbem prōgressī sunt et ducem, nōmine <u>Hannōnem</u>[1], petīvērunt. hunc invēnērunt īn forō ambulantem. "vestram pecūniam" inquit "vōbīs dare nōn possum. nōs Rōmānī vīcērunt nec praedam ab eīs capere potuimus." aliī mīlitēs īrātī sunt; aliī, tamen, in bellum iterum proficīscī cōnstituērunt. inter hōs erat iuvenis, nōmine Hannibal. hic, fīlius imperātōris fortissimī, patrem in Hispāniam sequī cupiēbat et maximam fāmam <u>parere</u>[2].

1. *Hannō, -ōnis,* m. = Hanno (a Carthaginian general).

2. N.B. Don't muddle the following: *parō, parāre* = I prepare;
   pāreō, pārēre (+ dat.) = I obey;
   pario, parere = I produce, win (a victory), gain.

	Avē imperātor, moritūrī tē salūtant
Using Latin	These words were spoken by gladiators entering the arena to fight: "Hail, emperor, those about to die salute you!"

Adsum / absum

Two important compounds of *sum* are *adsum* = "I am present" and *absum* = "I am absent". They go just like *sum*, but with *ad* or *ab* in front.
E.g. *Caesar aderat* = Caesar was present.
E.g. *Caesar aberit* = Caesar will be absent.

Quīdam = a certain

The Latin for "a certain", as in "a certain farmer was walking down the street", is *quīdam*, which declines as follows:

Nom.	*quīdam*	*quaedam*	*quiddam/quoddam*[1]
Acc.	*quendam*	*quandam*	*quiddam/quoddam*[1]
Gen.	*cuiusdam*	*cuiusdam*	*cuiusdam*
Dat.	*cuidam*	*cuidam*	*cuidam*
Abl.	*quōdam*	*quādam*	*quōdam*
Nom.	*quīdam*	*quaedam*	*quaedam*
Acc.	*quōsdam*	*quāsdam*	*quaedam*
Gen.	*quōrundam*	*quārundam*	*quōrundam*
Dat.	*quibusdam*[2]	*quibusdam*[2]	*quibusdam*[2]
Abl.	*quibusdam*[2]	*quibusdam*[2]	*quibusdam*[2]

1. See N.B. below.   2. or *quīsdam*

Quīdam is used to refer to a noun, not (yet) mentioned by name.
E.g. *rēx quīdam fīlium habuit* = "A certain king had a son".

It is very often used on its own as a pronoun.

E.g. *quīdam fīlium habuit* = "A certain man had a son".

N.B. In the neuter singular there are two different forms, depending on whether it is being used as a pronoun or an adjective: *quiddam* is a pronoun; *quoddam* is an adjective.
E.g. *quiddam timuit* = "he feared something" (lit. "a certain thing").
E.g. *quoddam perīculum timuit* = "he feared some danger" (lit. "a certain danger").

Adjectives for adverbs

In Latin we often find an adjective where in English we would expect an adverb or an adverbial phrase (i.e. a preposition + noun). Thus, instead of writing "they returned safely" or "in safety", Latin prefers "they returned safe".
E.g. *īrātus clāmāvit* = "he shouted angrily/in anger".
E.g. *tacita sedēbat* = "she was sitting quietly/in silence".

This is just one of many ways in which Latin and English express ideas in different ways. One of the key skills when learning a language involves learning about such differences of expression.

So you really want to learn Latin...

Exercise 1. 14
Read the information on the left-hand page about *adsum, absum* and *quīdam*. Note also what it says about adjectives for adverbs. Then translate into English:

1. *imperātor quīdam in Hispāniā aderat.*
2. *nōn sōlum pecūniam cupiēbat sed etiam fāmam maximam.*
3. *profectus in Hispāniam, diū bellum gerēbat.*
4. *multa aedificia cēpit et prō patriā semper bene pugnābat.*
5. *oppidum Saguntum ā Poenīs oppugnātum est.*
6. *"quid putātis?" inquit cīvis quīdam īrātus, "et quid faciēmus?"*
7. *auxilium ā Rōmānīs quam celerrimē petēmus.*
8. *ita locūtus, ille cīvis Rōmam tacitus profectus est.*
9. *lēgātōs Hispānōs īn forō loquentēs cōnsul Rōmānus audiēbat.*
10. *ōrātiō vestra nōs mōvit, nec hostēs mox moritūrōs timēmus.*

Exercise 1. 15
Translate into Latin:

A Carthaginian general called Hannibal lived in Africa. Once upon a time he set out from there and came* into Spain. Here he waged many wars and captured many Roman soldiers. Walking in silence with the other generals one day he adopted this plan. He decided to lead his army into the mountains and from there into Italy. Some praised the plan, others were a little afraid. But Hannibal, who was very brave, did not fear the dangers of the journey.

*Cut out the "and" by translating this as "having set out from there, he came".

Exercise 1. 16
Translate into English:

multīs cum mīlitibus Hannibal ex Hispāniā profectus in Galliam ingressus est. Rōmānōs diū vītāre poterat sed tandem ā duce exercitūs in Hispāniam festīnantis vīsus est. ubī hoc cognōvit "quot mīlitēs adsunt?" inquit Hannibal īrātus, "et quō eunt? quālem imperātōrem habent?" antequam tamen amīcī eius respondēre potuērunt, Hannibal cōnsilium quoddam cēpit. "in montēs ībimus. Rōmānī nōs illūc nōn sequentur. inde Rōmam ipsam ībimus. Rōma enim, urbs cibī et vīnī plēna, maximum praemium nōbīs erit."

cognōscō, -ere, cognōvī, cognitum = I find out, learn.

Adeste fidēlēs
In Latin *adeste fidēlēs* = "Be present, faithful ones!" and is the first line of the carol "O come all ye faithful".

Using Latin

Hannibal and those elephants

At the end of Book II we saw how Hannibal, son of the great Carthaginian general Hamilcar, had the extraordinary idea of marching from Spain, up over the Alps, and down the other side into Italy. Here, in more detail, is how he did it.

Sending a small number of forces to make diversionary raids on the west coast of Sicily and Italy, Hannibal set out from New Carthage at the head of an army of 38,000 foot-soldiers and 8,000 horsemen. He also brought 37 elephants, no doubt to add tone to what would otherwise have been a vulgar rabble. Anyway, at the head of this army, Hannibal marched up through the Pyrenees and along the south coast of Gaul, crossing the River Rhone near Arles. Ferrying his elephants across the river on rafts, Hannibal then took to the mountain passes of the Alps, escaping the clutches of the Roman general, Scipio, who simply could not believe that anyone would be foolhardy enough to risk crossing the Alps.

Guided by local friendly Gauls and greatly impeded by some hostile ones, Hannibal made his way slowly up into the mountains. He fought two pitched battles against a far from friendly Gallic tribe called the Allobroges, and there was a constant stream of boulders, men and animals rolling down the mountain-sides as the army made its perilous way across the snow-covered passes of the Alps. Morale was getting rather low, to put it mildly, when at last Hannibal was able to point out to his lieutenants the plains of northern Italy, spread out below them like a map. The end, at last, was in sight.

At one place on the descent the Cathaginians found their way blocked by a huge boulder. As nobody had yet discovered gunpowder, they dealt with this by lighting a fire next to the rock until it was red hot. They then poured vinegar on it, which caused the rock to crack, and then smashed it all up with pick-axes. Rather a waste of the soldiers' wine, you might say, but it certainly did the job.

The Carthaginians finally arrived on the plains of Italy near the River Po, having lost 18,000 foot-soldiers and 2,000 horsemen on the way. It had been quite a journey.

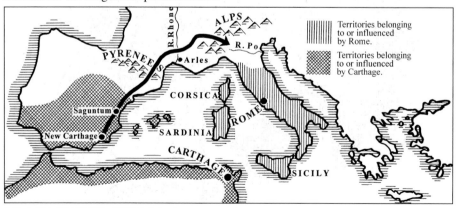

So you really want to learn Latin...

Exercise 1. 17

Read the information on the left-hand page about Hannibal and his elephants. Then answer the following questions in complete sentences:

1. Who was Hannibal's father?

2. Describe the content of Hannibal's army as he set off for Italy.

3. Which mountains did he have to negotiate before tackling the Alps themselves?

4. How did Hannibal get his elephants across the River Rhone?

5. Which Roman general failed to prevent Hannibal from leading his men up into the Alps?

6. Which hostile Gallic tribe gave Hannibal and his men grief once they had begun the climb into the Alps?

7. What was it that restored morale to Hannibal's lieutenants as the journey neared its close?

8. Describe how the Carthaginians dealt with the obstruction of the boulder, without having recourse to gunpowder.

9. Near which river did the Carthaginians finally enter Italy?

10. What casualties had they suffered?

Using Latin

Dēlīrium tremēns
This affliction, generally abbreviated to the "D.T.s",
is the Latin for "trembling frenzy".

CHAPTER 2

The ablative absolute; more adjectives like ūnus; adjectives like vetus

The ablative absolute

An ablative absolute consists of a noun or pronoun in the ablative, together with a participle agreeing with it. Ablative absolutes are often used in Latin to state the circumstances under which an action takes place. They may thus be said to be "setting the scene" for the rest of the sentence.

An ablative absolute may be used with any type of participle, although the use of the future participle is extremely rare and can be disregarded.

1. Present participle

E.g. ***puellā spectante**, pater discessit* = "**With the girl watching**, the father departed." The noun *puellā* is in the ablative (thus "with the girl") and the participle *spectante* agrees with it (thus "watching"). This can be put into more natural English as follows: "While the girl was watching, the father departed".

N.B. A present participle has its ablative singular ending in *–e* (rather than *–ī* when used in an ablative absolute.

2. Perfect participle passive

E.g. ***puellā monitā**, pater discessit* = "**With the girl having been warned**, the father departed"; or:
"After the girl had been warned, the father departed".

3. Perfect participle deponent

With deponent verbs, the perfect participle is, of course, active in meaning, allowing us to say things such as "having followed" or "having set out".
E.g. ***puellā profectā**, pater discessit* = "**With the girl having set out**, the father departed"; or:
"After the girl had set out, the father departed".

A word of advice

The best way to cope with ablative absolutes is to translate them literally first, i.e. using a phrase such as "with the girl having been loved", or whatever it might be. Only then should you try to put it into real English. It is, of course, essential that you identify the *tense* of the participle correctly (i.e. is it "loving", "about to love" or "having been loved"?). You should be particularly careful not to confuse the perfect participle passive of a normal transitive verb with the perfect participle of a *deponent* verb. **Only deponent verbs can have a perfect participle with an active meaning.**

E.g. *secūtus* = "having followed";
 profectus = "having set out"; **but**
 monitus = "having **been** warned".

So you really want to learn Latin...

Exercise 2. 1
Study the information on the left-hand page about ablative absolutes. Then translate the following into English:

1. *hostibus victīs...*
2. *patre spectante...*
3. *agricolā monitō...*
4. *rēgīnā regente...*
5. *librīs lēctīs...*

6. *nūllō discēdente...*
7. *mēnsā parātā...*
8. *tēlīs iactīs...*
9. *lēgātīs missīs...*
10. *exercitū profectō...*

Exercise 2. 2
Translate the following phrases into Latin, using the ablative absolute construction:

1. After the king had been killed...
2. After these things had been done...
3. When the story had been told...
4. While the young man was following...
5. While the girls were fleeing...

Exercise 2. 3
Translate into English:

1. *hostibus vīsīs, imperātor exercitum suum in campum celeriter dūxit.*
2. *castrīs prope flūmen positīs, Rōmānī ad hostēs prōgressī sunt.*
3. *librīs ā puerīs lēctīs, magister hanc fābulam eīs nārrāvit.*
4. *poētā sīc locūtō, cīvēs magnopere timēbant.*
5. *verbīs iūdicis nōn intellēctīs, servus līberātus est.*
6. *leōne ā mīlite occīsō, omnēs cīvēs gaudēbant.*

Exercise 2. 4
Translate into Latin, using ablative absolutes where appropriate:

1. After the slaves had been warned, the master returned to the forum.
2. While the consul was listening, we told our story to the people.
3. When the soldier had been killed, peace was made with the enemy.
4. After the Romans had set out, the barbarians fled towards the mountains.
5. When the ships were destroyed, all the sailors waited for death.
6. After the enemy had attacked the town, the citizens fled.

Using Latin

Vice versā
This common expression is an ablative absolute, meaning "with the change having been turned", i.e. swapped around.

More on ablative absolutes

1.   An ablative absolute is often used to translate an English temporal or causal clause (referring to time and cause respectively). Very often these will have to be "turned" (like a pancake) to allow the passive participle to be used. This is because, unless we are using a deponent verb, there is no way in Latin of saying "having loved", or "having prepared", or whatever it is, so instead we have to turn it round and say "having been loved", "having been prepared", etc.

E.g. "After she had prepared the tables, she returned home" (i.e. with the tables having been prepared, she returned home) = *mēnsīs parātīs, domum rediit.*

2.   An ablative absolute must **not** be used to refer to any noun or pronoun grammatically connected in any way to the verb in the main clause. For example, a noun cannot be put into an ablative absolute if it goes on to be the subject or object of the main clause. E.g. "After the boy had been seen, he (i.e. the boy) went home" =
puer vīsus domum rediit.

An ablative absolute could not have been used for the "boy had been seen", because the boy went on to be the *subject* of the verb in the main clause. Instead, the boy is in the nominative and *vīsus* agrees with him; and thus the whole thing means "the having been seen boy returned home".

E.g. "After the soldiers had been captured, the king killed them (i.e. the soldiers)" =
rēx mīlitēs captōs interfēcit.

An ablative absolute could not have been used for "the soldiers had been captured", because they went on to be the *object* of the verb in the main clause. Instead we write "the king killed the having been captured soldiers".

Vocabulary 2

Nouns			Preposition	
leō, leōnis, m.	lion		*ob* (+ acc.)	on account of
senātor, -ōris, m.	senator		**Adverbs**	
timor, timōris, m.	fear		*umquam*	ever
vīnum, -ī, n.	wine		*undique*	from all sides
ventus, -ī, m.	wind		*vērō*	indeed
Adjectives			**Conjunctions**	
nūllus, -a, -um*	no		*vel*	or
sōlus, -a, -um*	alone		*vel...vel*	either...or
tōtus, -a, -um*	whole		**Verbs**	
ūllus, -a, -um*	any		*pūniō, -īre, -īvī, -ītum*	I punish
vērus, -a, -um	true		*rumpō, -ere, rūpī, ruptum*	I break
vetus, veteris	old		*taceō, -ēre, tacuī, tacitum*	I am silent
* (goes like *ūnus*)			*valē / valēte*	goodbye, farewell

So you really want to learn Latin...

Exercise 2. 5
Study the further information on the left-hand page about ablative absolutes. Then translate into English:

1. *templīs ā cōnsule aedificātīs, cīvēs cibum nōn habēbant.*
2. *templa ab imperātōre aedificāta laudābant.*
3. *omnēs mīlitēs in proeliō captī interfectī sunt.*
4. *gladium celeriter captum in corpus servī pepulit.*
5. *fābulā nārrātā, magister puerum domum redūxit.*
6. *tabernā subitō vīsā, agricolae iterum laetī erant.*
7. *cōpiās trāns montēs ductās Rōmānī spectāvērunt.*
8. *cōpiīs trāns montēs ductīs, Hannibal in Ītaliam festīnāre cupiēbat.*
9. *cōpiae trāns montēs ductae Hannibalem in Ītaliam sequēbantur.*
10. *pāce ab hostibus frūstrā petītā, in campō trēs hōrās pugnātum est.*

Exercise 2. 6
Translate into Latin, being sure not to use an ablative absolute if it involves a noun or pronoun grammatically connected to the verb in the main clause:

1. After the Romans had captured the women, they killed them.
2. While the sailors were looking for an inn, the cavalry advanced.
3. While no one was watching, the whole army set out.
4. After throwing their spears, the soldiers fled.
5. After a great wind had arisen, the sailors decided to remain in the harbour.
6. While the farmer was preparing the wine, we were sitting in the inn.
7. We waited for the ambassadors who were about to set out from Rome.
8. After these things had been done, the messengers returned home.

Exercise 2. 7
Study the vocabulary on the left-hand page. From which Latin words do the following derive. Translate the Latin word and explain the meaning of the English one:

1. Nullify
2. Senatorial
3. Timorous
4. Verily
5. Punitive
6. Veteran
7. Viniculture
8. Total
9. Sole
10. Valedictory

Using Latin	**Sub iūdice** If a legal matter is *sub iūdice*, it is "under the judge", i.e. under consideration by the courts.

Nūllus, ūllus, sōlus, tōtus

These adjectives are declined in the singular like *ūnus* (which we hope you have not forgotten!). Thus *nūllus* in the singular goes as follows:

	M	**F**	**N**
Nom.	*nūllus*	*nūlla*	*nūllum*
Acc.	*nūllum*	*nūllam*	*nūllum*
Gen.	*nūllĭus*	*nūllĭus*	*nūllĭus*
Dat.	*nūllī*	*nūllī*	*nūllī*
Abl.	*nūllō*	*nūllā*	*nūllō*

All of these adjectives decline like this, i.e. they go *-ĭus* in the genitive and *-ī* in the dative. In the plural they are regular and go like *bonus*.

   N.B. *ūllus* = "any" is generally only found after a negative particle or in a question. E.g. Does he have any friends? = *ūllōsne habet amīcōs?*
E.g. He is sad and does not have any friends = *trīstis est neque ūllōs habet amīcōs.*

Vetus

A small number of adjectives decline like *vetus* = "old". Note that in the ablative singular they end in *−e* (not *−ī*), in the genitive plural they end in *−um* (not *−ium*) and in the neuter plural, if it exists at all, they end in *−a* (not *−ia*).

	M	**F**	**N**
Nom.	*vetus*	*vetus*	*vetus*
Acc.	*veterem*	*veterem*	*vetus*
Gen.	*veteris*	*veteris*	*veteris*
Dat.	*veterī*	*veterī*	*veterī*
Abl.	*vetere*	*vetere*	*vetere*
Nom.	*veterēs*	*veterēs*	*vetera*
Acc.	*veterēs*	*veterēs*	*vetera*
Gen.	*veterum*	*veterum*	*veterum*
Dat.	*veteribus*	*veteribus*	*veteribus*
Abl.	*veteribus*	*veteribus*	*veteribus*

Adjectives which decline like vetus include *dīves, dīvitis* = "rich" and *pauper, pauperis* = "poor". The neuter plural of *dīves* does not exist, and is supplied by the form *dītia*.

Roman names

Roman *praenōmina* (first names) were often abbreviated, the following being the most commonly used:

A.	Aulus	D.	Decimus	P.	Publius	Ser.	Servius
C.	Gāius	L.	Lūcius	Q.	Quīntus	Sp.	Spurius
Cn.	Gnaeus	M.	Mārcus	S.	Sextus	T.	Titus

So you really want to learn Latin...

Exercise 2. 8

Study the information on the left-hand page about *nūllus, ūllus, sōlus* and *tōtus.* Then translate into Latin:

1. With no friends.

2. Does she trust any soldier?

3. The girls were sitting alone.

4. They destroyed the whole city.

5. Have you seen any senators?

6. Will he punish the whole tribe?

7. Do you have any lions?

8. She is tired and has no food.

9. Did they kill any citizens?

10. They went to Rome but did not seen any temples.

Exercise 2. 9

Study the information on the left-hand page about adjectives declining like *vetus.* Then translate into English:

1. *cīvēs dīvitēs in colle stantēs deōs laudābant.*

2. *nostrīs ā Gallīs superātīs, cīvēs pauperēs auxilium petīvērunt.*

3. *incolīs dīvitibus ad mare pulsīs, equitēs Rōmānī aedificia vetera incendēbant.*

4. *tempestāte magnā ortā, nautae terram quam celerrimē petīvērunt.*

5. *fēminīs sequentibus, virī pauperēs in agrōs regressī sunt.*

Exercise 2. 10

Translate into English: *Saved by the oxen, 217 B.C.*

hīs victōriīs partīs, Hannibal Rōmam ipsam festīnāre cupiēbat. Poenī tamen, incolīs nūllō modō adiuvantibus, urbem sine plūribus cōpiīs capere nōn poterant. trāns Ītaliam, igitur, Rōmānīs sequentibus, Hannibal exercitum suum dūcēbat.

imperātor Rōmānus, nōmine Q. Fabius Maximus, hostēs semper spectābat sed diū cum eīs nōn pugnābat. hostēs tamen paene cēpit, ubī eōs inter montēs quōsdam pepulit. Rōmānī castra circum Poenōs posuerant neque illī fugere poterant. Poenī, tamen, plūrimōs <u>bovēs</u> cēperant, quōrum cornua multīs <u>virgīs</u> decorāverant. hōs, virgīs incēnsīs, ad Rōmānōs pepulērunt. Rōmānī, aliī mīrātī, aliī territī, aciem relīquērunt et Poenī effūgērunt.

bōs, bovis, c. = ox or cow; *virga, -ae,* f. = twig; *decorō, -āre* = I decorate, adorn.

	Sīc
Using Latin	*Sīc* = "thus" is written in brackets after a word or expression to show that it has been quoted exactly, even though it sounds wrong or absurd.

Hannibal runs amok in Italy

Having successfully negotiated the Alps, Hannibal set about the Romans on their own territory. First he beat them between the Rivers Po and Ticino. Then he beat them at the River Trebia, in conditions so cold that his men had to cover themselves with oil, to protect themselves from the icy temperature. Sadly no one thought of covering the elephants with oil, and all but one of them died. Then he advanced further south into Etruria and beat them again at Lake Trasimene. Here the Carthaginian army crept round, under cover of the mist rising off the lake, and attacked the Romans in the rear. The Romans were caught off guard, and were then further unsettled by a sudden, violent earthquake. 3–0 to Hannibal.

From here Hannibal crossed over to the Adriatic coast of Italy, marching around Campania and generally making a nuisance of himself. It was now the turn of Quintus Fabius Maximus to try to stop him. Fabius was elected as dictator* for a period of six months. He began rather well and actually thought he had Hannibal pinned down when the latter tried to lead his army through a mountain pass across the Apennines. Realising that he was about to be ambushed, Hannibal made use of some recently captured cattle to get out of difficulty. Tying lighted torches to their horns, he drove the poor beasts off into the night, throwing the Romans into confusion and allowing him to lead his men through the pass intact. Quite how silly the Romans felt when they discovered that they had been chasing a bunch of cows with burning horns, history does not relate, but it was certainly another victory to Hannibal. Dido's prophecy about the avenger, rising from her ashes to harass the Romans, was certainly coming true.

Fabius continued to pursue Hannibal around Italy and has gone down in history for his tactics of delaying, now known as Fabian tactics. Unwilling to engage Hannibal in pitched battle, he nonetheless wore the Carthaginians down by continually keeping them on the move. However, these tactics were far from popular with the impatient Roman people, who wanted results, not delays. They were, thus, delighted when Fabius's term of office came to an end and command of the army passed back into the hands of the two consuls, Terentius Varro and Aemilius Paullus.

* Dictators were appointed with supreme power to deal with a specific, always very serious crisis. Once the period of crisis was over, the dictator relinquished his powers and returned to his normal way of life.

So you really want to learn Latin...

Exercise 2. 11

Read the information on the left-hand page about Hannibal in Italy. Then answer the following questions in complete sentences:

1. Where did the Carthaginians first defeat the Romans after arriving in Italy?

2. Where did their second victory occur?

3. How did the Carthaginian soldiers protect themselves from the cold before this battle?

4. What happened to the elephants?

5. How did the water of the lake help the Carthaginians to win the battle of Lake Trasimene?

6. What else caused the Romans to feel somewhat unsettled that day?

7. Which Roman general had to face Hannibal after he had crossed over to the Adriatic coast of Italy?

8. What position of authority did he hold and for how long?

9. Describe how Hannibal managed successfully to negotiate the mountain pass through the Apennines.

10. What is meant by "Fabian tactics" and how did this name come about?

<table>
<tr><td>Using Latin</td><td>Interrēgnum
The English word interregnum is simply a Latin word
meaning "the period between two reigns".</td></tr>
</table>

CHAPTER 3

More irregular verbs and nouns; double questions; the locative

Volō, nōlō, mālō

You have already learnt to cope with a number of irregular verbs, so the following should not give you too much trouble. As you will see, they are all similar, based on the basic verb *volō:*

- *volō, velle, voluī* = "I wish", "am willing" (in perfect, often = "I have determined");
- *nōlō, nōlle, nōluī* = "I do not wish", "am unwilling" (in perfect, often = "I have refused");
- *mālo, mālle, māluī* = "I prefer".

Present		
volō	*nōlō*	*mālō*
vīs	*nōn vīs*	*māvīs*
vult	*nōn vult*	*māvult*
volumus	*nōlumus*	*mālumus*
vultis	*nōn vultis*	*māvultis*
volunt	*nōlunt*	*mālunt*
Future		
volam	*nōlam*	*mālam*
volēs	*nōlēs*	*mālēs*
volet	*nōlet*	*mālet*
volēmus	*nōlēmus*	*mālēmus*
volētis	*nōlētis*	*mālētis*
volent	*nōlent*	*mālent*
Imperfect		
volēbam	*nōlēbam*	*mālēbam*
volēbās	*nōlēbās*	*mālēbās*
volēbat	*nōlēbat*	*mālēbat*
volēbāmus	*nōlēbāmus*	*mālēbāmus*
volēbātis	*nōlēbātis*	*mālēbātis*
volēbant	*nōlēbant*	*mālēbant*

Prohibitions

Prohibitions (negative commands) are expressed using *nōlī / nōlīte* (i.e. the imperative of *nōlō*) + the infinitive. Use *nōlī* if addressing one person, *nōlīte* if addressing more than one.

E.g. *nōlī ambulāre, Mārce* = don't walk, Marcus!

E.g. *nōlīte ambulāre, puerī* = don't walk, boys!

Literally these mean "be unwilling to walk!"

So you really want to learn Latin...

Exercise 3. 1

Study the information on the left-hand page about *volō, nōlō, mālō* and prohibitions. Then translate into Latin:

1. He wishes to speak.

2. They are unwilling to flee.

3. We prefer to remain here.

4. They will not wish to work.

5. Hannibal had wished to enter Rome.

6. They preferred to fight on the plain.

7. Do not flee from the camp, soldiers!

8. You do not wish to follow the leader into the mountains, do you?

9. Don't lead your soldiers into the sea!

10. Do not run towards the deep river, Marcus!

Exercise 3. 2

Translate into English:

1. *proximō diē imperātor suōs in campō īnstrūxit.*

2. *ars mīlitum Pūnicōrum maior erat quam vīs Rōmānōrum.*

3. *"ubĭ" inquit cōnsul "sunt cōpiae hostium?"*

4. *incolae Ītaliae numquam hostibus cēdent.*

5. *Fabius agmen suum trāns patriam dūcere nōlēbat.*

6. *via tandem quae ad urbem ferēbat aperta erat Poenīs.*

7. *plūrimīs mīlitibus in proeliō āmissīs, Rōmānī fugere coāctī sunt.*

8. *vix ūnus iuvenis vīvus inventus est.*

9. *nōlī cibum tangere quem māter tua in mēnsā posuit.*

10. *nōlīte legere librōs quōs poēta mihĭ dedit.*

Exercise 3. 3

Translate into Latin:

For many years the Romans waged war against the Carthaginians, but were unable to defeat them. One year, a very brave general called Hannibal, having led his soldiers across Italy, drew up his battle-line near the mountains. The Romans, having pitched their camp, prepared to attack. But with the help of oxen, the Carthaginians were able to drive the Romans from their column and to escape. When these things were heard by the consuls, they decided to lead the army into war themselves.

Inter alia

Inter alia = among other things. E.g. "He decided, *inter alia*, to ban the teaching of Latin."

Double questions

Double, or alternative, questions are questions which give you two alternatives, e.g. "Are you a boy or a girl?" In Latin, they are introduced by *-ne* or *utrum* and are followed by *an* (= or) or *annōn* (= or not).

E.g. Is he alive or dead? = *utrum vīvus an mortuus est?*

E.g. Is he alive or not? = *utrum vīvus est annōn?*

E.g. Shall I go to Rome or return home? = *Rōmamne ībō, an domum reveniam?*

It makes no difference whether you begin with *–ne* or *utrum*, so take your pick.

The locative case

Remember our wonderful rule about towns and small islands etc. (Book II, page 26)? Well, now we are going to extend it. With the names of towns, small islands, *domus* (= home), *humus* (= the ground) and *rūs* (= the countryside), the **locative case** is used, **without a preposition**, to express location. The locative case ceased to exist as a separate form back in the early years of Latin's existence, so it had to be represented by one of the cases which *were* around. As a general rule, for singular place names of the 1st and 2nd declensions, the genitive was used; for 3rd declension and for all plural place names, the ablative was used.

E.g. *Rōmae* = in Rome; *Corinthī* = in Corinth; *Carthāgine* = in Carthage; *Athēnīs* = in Athens.

The following should also be learnt: *domī* = at home; *humī* = on the ground; *rūrī* = in the countryside.

Vocabulary 3

Verbs

accipiō, -ere, accēpī, acceptum	I receive, accept
āmittō, -ere, āmīsī, āmissum	I lose
cēdō, cēdere, cessī, cessum	I yield, give way
īnstruō, īnstruere, īnstrūxī, īnstrūctum	I draw up
mālō, mālle, māluī (irreg.)	I prefer
nōlō, nōlle, nōluī (irreg.)	I do not wish, am unwilling
rīdeō, -ēre, rīsī, rīsum	I laugh, smile
vīvō, vīvere, vīxī, vīctum	I live, am alive
volō, -āre, -āvī, -ātum	I fly
volō, velle, voluī (irreg.)	I wish, am willing

Nouns

aciēs, aciēī, f.	battle line
agmen, agminis, n.	column (of an army)
ars, artis, f.	skill, art
bōs, bovis, c. (irreg.)	ox, cow
fuga, -ae, f.	flight
humus, humī, f.	ground
vīs, (pl. = *vīrēs*), f. (irreg.)	force (in sing.), strength (in pl.)

Adjectives

apertus, -a, -um	open, uncovered
proximus, -a, -um	next, nearest
quantus, -a, -um?	how great?
vīvus, -a, -um	alive

Adverbs

quidem	indeed
vix	scarcely

So you really want to learn Latin...

Exercise 3. 4
Study the information on the left-hand page about double questions. Then translate into English:

1. *curretne iuvenis an ambulābit?*
2. *utrum Rōmānī Poenōs superāvērunt annōn?*
3. *Rōmamne festīnābō an hīc manēbō?*
4. *utrum fīlium an fīliam vērē amat ille agricola?*
5. *utrum vīvī an mortuī crās erimus?*

Exercise 3. 5
Translate into Latin:

1. Do you wish to come home or to remain in the city?
2. Have the ambassadors announced the victory or not?
3. Does the king prefer war or peace?
4. Can you walk to Rome within five days or not?
5. Did the Gauls attack Rome by day or by night?

Exercise 3. 6
Study the information on the left-hand page about the locative case. Note the locative forms for *domus, rūs* and *humus*. Then, (where appropriate) using the place names given in brackets, translate into Latin:

1. I will remain in Rome (*Rōma, -ae*, f.).
2. They do not wish to live in Corinth (*Corinthus, -ī*, f.).
3. You are willing to live in Athens, aren't you? (*Athēnae, -ārum*, f. pl.)
4. Does he want to rule in Alexandria or not? (*Alexandrēa, -ae*, f.)
5. Hannibal did not wish to stay in Carthage (*Carthāgō, Carthāginis*, f.).
6. All the farmers preferred to work in the countryside.
7. Stay at home, soldiers!
8. The body of the king was lying on the ground.

Exercise 3. 7
Study the vocabulary on the left-hand page. From which Latin words do the following derive? Translate the Latin word and explain the meaning of the English one:

1. Proximity
2. Artistic
3. Concession
4. Instruction
5. Quantity
6. Volition
7. Accept
8. Aperture
9. Bovine
10. Approximate

Using Latin

Cf.
The letters *cf.* stand for *cōnfer* = "bring together", i.e. compare.

Mad cow disease?

The declension of *bōs, bovis*, c. = a bull, ox or cow (mad or otherwise) is irregular:

	Sing.	Pl.
Nom.	*bōs*	*bovēs*
Voc.	*bōs*	*bovēs*
Acc.	*bovem*	*bovēs*
Gen.	*bovis*	*boum*
Dat.	*bovī*	*bōbus or būbus*
Abl.	*bove*	*bōbus or būbus*

Vīs

While we're looking at irregular nouns, here is my own particular favourite, *vīs*, f. = "force" in the singular and "strength" in the plural:

	Sing.	Pl.
Nom.	*vīs*	*vīrēs*
Acc.	*vim*	*vīrēs*
Gen.	-	*vīrium*
Dat.	-	*vīribus*
Abl.	*vī*	*vīribus*

As you can see, this noun has no genitive or dative singular, and has the added advantage of being easily confused with *vir* = a man. Good, eh?

By Jove!

Finally, Jupiter, the king of the gods himself, is a bit odd. The first thing to note is that in Latin he has two 'p's while in English he has only one. Secondly, take a look at his oblique cases, by Jove! By "oblique cases", by the way, we mean all but the nominative and vocative. For pretty obvious reasons, he doesn't have a plural.

Nom.	*Iuppiter*
Voc.	*Iuppiter*
Acc.	*Iovem*
Gen.	*Iovis*
Dat.	*Iovī*
Abl.	*Iove*

Ablative absolutes with sum "understood"

As you know, there is no present participle of the verb *sum*. However, it is quite common to create an ablative absolute in which a participle of *sum* is "understood", i.e. it isn't actually there but we pretend that it is.

E.g. *Mārcō duce* = "with Marcus (being) leader", i.e. with Marcus as leader.

So you really want to learn Latin...

Exercise 3. 8

Study the irregular nouns on the left-hand page. Then translate into Latin:

1. Has the farmer departed with his oxen or not?
2. Having been warned by the messenger of Juppiter, he remained in the country.
3. In Rome the citizens feared the strength of the enemy.
4. How great is the column of footsoldiers which has been drawn up in Carthage?
5. The consul wished to read at home the books which you sent him.
6. Are men who live and work in the country able to fly?
7. The art of peace having been lost, no one will ever find it again.
8. Don't leave your friends at home!
9. Did he prefer to pray to Jupiter or to the other gods?
10. The father of that boy lived alone in Rome for twenty years.

Exercise 3. 9

Translate into English: *The Battle of Cannae, 216 B.C.*

Rōmānī, Fabiō <u>duce</u>[1]*, cum hostibus in proeliō pugnāre diū nōlēbant. sed proximō annō, cōnsilium quoddam pessimum cēpērunt. omnēs enim Poenōs vincere volēbant et tum quidem plūrimās cōpiās habēbant. nōn arte, igitur, sed vīribus, in illō bellō ūtī cōnstituērunt. duŏ autem cōnsulēs, L. Aemilius Paullus et M. Terentius Varrō, quī eō tempore cum Hannibale numquam pugnāverant, exercitum Rōmānum ad Poenōs dūcere cōnstituērunt.*

prope oppidum, nōmine <u>Cannās</u>*, Poenī cōpiās īnstrūxērunt.* <u>in mediā aciē</u>[2] *paucōs peditēs posuērunt. quō vīsō, Rōmānī, plūrimīs cum peditibus, impetum maximum in mediam aciem fēcērunt. hostēs prīmō regredī vidēbantur. equitēs tamen hostium, circum* <u>ālās</u> *Rōmānōrum prōgressī, equitēs Rōmānōs īn fugam pepulērunt. inde ā tergō Rōmānōs aggressī sunt.*

mox Rōmānī superātī sunt et plūrimī sunt interfectī. post proelium, Poenī ā digitīs Rōmānōrum <u>ānulōs</u> *cēpērunt quōs Carthāginem mīsērunt.*

1. See note on left-hand page about ablative absolutes.
2. See note on p. 36 about *ad summum montem*.

Cannae, -ārum, f. pl. = Cannae; āla, -ae, f. = wing (of army); ānulus, -ī, m. = ring.

Exercise 3. 10

Revision. Translate into English:

1. *velle*	6. *īnstruī*
2. *rīdent*	7. *īnstrūxī*
3. *cēdent*	8. *īnstrūctī*
4. *domī*	9. *adesse*
5. *rūrī*	10. *āfuī*

Using Latin

Ultrā vīrēs

Ultrā vīrēs = beyond (one's) power or authority. E.g. "In arresting the man, the police were acting *ultrā vīrēs*."

The Battle of Cannae, 216 B.C.

The consuls for the year 216 were, as we have seen, Terentius Varro and Aemilius Paullus. Terentius Varro was the plebeian candidate and had no military skill whatever. The patrician Aemilius Paullus, by contrast, was a skilful general and a friend of Fabius. So concerned was Fabius about his friend's consular colleague that he warned him as they set off from Rome that he would be contending, not only with Hannibal, but also with his own rash colleague, who would soon be the cause of another Trasimene. How right he was.

Meanwhile Hannibal, running short of supplies, had captured the town of Cannae, where he reinvigorated his troops with good old Italian cooking. He knew that the Romans outnumbered him, but he knew, too, that the two consuls were at loggerheads and commanded the army on alternate days. Aemilius Paullus was keen to continue with Fabius' delaying tactics, but as soon as Terentius Varro was in command he drew up the army for battle and advanced. Hannibal deliberately allowed the Romans to break through his centre and then, encircling the impetuous Romans who had charged through the middle like kittens after a ball of string, he proceeded to annihilate them. It was the classic example of a numerically weaker force encircling and overcoming a superior one.

The Romans, having fallen into this pretty simple trap, resolved to die like Romans. A horse was offered to Aemilius Paullus on which he could have made his escape, but he preferred to die with his men. The other consul, Terentius Varro, did manage to escape but the total number of Roman casualties on that day was numbered at 45,500 foot-soldiers and 2,700 horsemen. Hannibal could easily have pressed home his advantage by advancing on Rome. He would almost certainly have captured the city, whose inhabitants were shocked and demoralised by the news of the disaster at Cannae. As it was, he preferred to weigh up his options, and this delay saved Rome from the ultimate humiliation of falling into Carthaginian hands.

On the day after the battle, a pretty gruesome sight met the Carthaginians as they returned to the battle-field in search of booty. The sheer number of dead was enough to put anyone off his porridge, but it was quite another thing to find that some of the Romans had buried their own heads in the soil rather than face death at the hands of the enemy. Of those who were still alive, some were exposing their throats and begging to be despatched. One sight was particularly strange. One of the Carthaginian allies, a Numidian warrior, was found, still alive, with nose and ears badly lacerated, lying on top of a Roman. The Roman, too weak to make use of his weapon, had died in the very act of biting his attacker.

Cannae was a disaster in the history of Rome which she would never forget. She had lost a huge number of men, including a substantial part of her equestrian class who made up the cavalry. As a mark of his victory, Hannibal took the gold rings from the fingers of these Roman horsemen and sent them back to Carthage, to show the extent of the slaughter.

So you really want to learn Latin...

Exercise 3. 11

Read the information on the left-hand page about Hannibal. Then translate into Latin:

1. Was Hannibal or Fabius the wiser general?

2. Why did the Romans not favour Fabius?

3. After the Romans had been defeated, Hannibal did not attack Rome.

4. This consul wished to fight with the Carthaginians, but that one preferred to remain in the camp.

5. On the next day, Terentius led his forces into the middle of the enemy battle-line.

6. After the army had been overcome, many citizens were killed, the rest were captured.

7. Aemilius Paullus was unwilling to flee and died with his soldiers.

8. The other consul escaped from the slaughter and returned to Rome.

9. After the battle, the Carthaginians found an ally, wounded by the teeth of a Roman foot-soldier.

10. Shall we believe this story or not?

Using Latin	**Cornūcōpia**
	Cornūcōpia, or more correctly *cornū cōpiae*, = "horn of plenty". A *cornucopia* is a traditional symbol of plenty, normally depicted as a horn overflowing with flowers and fruit.

CHAPTER 4

Indirect statement; reflexive pronouns

Indirect statement

After verbs of saying, knowing, believing, perceiving, hearing and other similar verbs, we often have an indirect statement; that is, the words of the speaker are reported *indirectly*. E.g. He says that the Romans are attacking the town.

In Latin, indirect statement follows the *accusative and infinitive* construction, whereby the subject of the indirect statement is put in the accusative and the verb is put in the infinitive. The object, if there is one, remains unchanged in the accusative.

E.g. *dīcō* **servum labōrāre** = "I say that the slave is working" (literally: I say the slave to work, i.e. to be working).

E.g. *dīcit* **Rōmānōs** *oppidum* **oppugnāre** = "he says that the Romans are attacking the town" (literally: he says the Romans to attack the town, i.e. to be attacking the town).

This is one of the most common constructions used in Latin, so make sure you get the hang of it!

Active tenses of the infinitive

So far you have met only the present infinitive, active and passive. But in fact, infinitives in Latin exist in the future and perfect as well. This is jolly lucky, actually, because, apart from the fact that it is nice to have some more grammar to learn, we *need* these different tenses to cope with the different types of indirect statement. Here are the three active infinitives:

1. Present

You already know these:

amāre   monēre   regere   audīre   capere ("To love", "To warn", etc.)

2. Future

These are formed from the supine, by changing *–um* to *-ūrus esse*. In other words, they are the future participle of the verb, with *esse* (= "to be") added on the end to make it an infinitive.

E.g. *amātūrus esse, monitūrus esse*, etc. ("To be about to love", "To be about to warn", etc.)

The *–us* bit of the participle declines like *bonus*, as you would expect.

3. Perfect

These are formed from the perfect stem, by adding *–isse*.

E.g. *amāvisse, monuisse, rēxisse*, etc. ("To have loved", "To have warned", etc.)

Using these three active infinitives, we can write three different types of indirect statement:

Present: He says that the enemy **are coming** = *dīcit hostēs* **venīre**.

Future: He says that the enemy **will come** = *dīcit hostēs* **ventūrōs esse**.

Perfect: He says that the enemy **have come** = *dīcit hostēs* **vēnisse**.

So you really want to learn Latin...

Exercise 4. 1

Study the information on the left-hand page about indirect statements. Note how these use the "accusative and infinitive" construction, with the subject going into the accusative (shock horror) and the verb going into the infinitive. Then translate into English. As a concession to the modern "nanny state", we will begin with simple present infinitives, and the first one is done for you:

1. *dīcit agricolās in agrīs labōrāre* = He says that the farmers are working in the fields.

2. *dīcit fēminam in hortō ambulāre.*   4. *dīcit poētam librum amāre.*

3. *dīcit mīlitēs urbem oppugnāre.*   5. *dīcō bellum esse malum.*

Exercise 4. 2

Once you have mastered the basic structure of an "accusative and infinitive", you should be able to cope with it in your sleep. Here are some examples for you to put into Latin. Remember, the subject goes into the accusative, the verb goes into the infinitive.

1. He says that the girl is singing.   4. He hears that the enemy are coming.

2. They say that the soldiers are fighting. 5. We know that the sailor is tired.

3. We know that the master is reading.   6. They know that the girl is sleeping.

Exercise 4. 3

Study the information on the left-hand page about the active tenses of the infinitive. Then translate into English:

1. *dīcunt nautās tabernās amāre.*

2. *mīles nūntiat Hannibalem trāns montēs vēnisse.*

3. *dīcit Rōmānōs castra prope flūmen posuisse.*

4. *crēdimus barbarōs mox Rōmam oppugnātūrōs esse.*

5. *spērāmus imperātōrem auxilium crās lātūrum esse.*

Exercise 4. 4

Translate into Latin. Remember that when the infinitive contains a participle ending in -*us* this must agree with the noun (in the accusative) to which it refers:

1. He says that the Romans are attacking the town.

2. He says that the soldiers are fighting bravely.

3. He knows that the enemy will attack the town.

4. He knows that the enemy have attacked the town.

5. We believe* that the soldier will kill the general.

*Verbs such as *crēdō*, which govern an indirect object in the dative case, may be used to introduce an indirect statement just like any other verb, with the normal accusative and infinitive construction. Do not try to put "the soldier" in the dative!

	Mēns sāna in corpore sānō
	One of Juvenal's most famous lines: "a healthy mind in a healthy body".

Passive tenses of the infinitive

Just as Latin has active infinitives in a number of tenses, so it has *passive* ones in a number of tenses. You already know the present infinitive passive and the perfect passive is very easy. That just leaves us with the future passive, which needs some explaining (to say the least of it). First, though, here they are:

1. Present

You already know these:

amārī, monērī, regī, audīrī, capī ("To be loved", "To be warned", etc.)

2. Perfect

These are easily formed from the PPP, by adding *esse*.

E.g. *amātus esse, monitus esse, rēctus esse, audītus esse*, etc. ("To have been loved", "To have been warned", etc.)

Literally, these mean "to be (*esse*) having been loved (*amātus*)", etc.

3. "Future"

The honest truth, I'm afraid, is that **Latin does not have a future infinitive passive**. People will *tell* you that it does, but only because they are afraid to put you off by explaining the terrible truth. A sort of hotch-potch future infinitive *appears* to have been created by adding the word *īrī* to the supine of the verb (e.g. *amātum īrī*). But it is not a genuine future infinitive at all. The word *īrī* is the passive infinitive of *eō*, being used **impersonally** (i.e. having a meaning such as "it is gone" or "there is a going"). If to this we add the supine of a verb (which after a verb of motion has the meaning "in order to..."), and use it in an indirect statement, we get sentences such as: *dīcit urbem oppugnātum īrī* = "he says that there is a going in order to attack the city". From this, we get "he says that the city is going to be attacked" and it is this, beautiful translation, which has misled people into thinking that they are dealing with a future infinitive passive. However, if you *do* choose to treat this beast as a normal infinitive, you will be fine.

Passive indirect statements

Using the above, we can now complete our list of indirect statements, adding the passive ones as follows:

Present: He says that the enemy **are being defeated** = *dīcit hostēs **superārī**.*

Future: He says that the enemy **will be defeated** = *dīcit hostēs **superātum īrī**.*

Perfect: He says that the enemy **have been defeated** = *dīcit hostēs **superātōs esse**.*

Note in this last example how the participle *superātōs* is agreeing with the accusative masculine plural, *hostēs*. Never, however, try to make a **supine** agree with anything!

Ad summum montem

Latin sometimes uses an adjective where in English we use a noun followed by "of". Most notably this applies to words expressing *whole, middle, top*, etc. Thus, instead of writing "to the top *of* the mountain", Latin prefers *ad summum montem*, with the adjective *summus* agreeing with the noun *montem*. Other common examples are:

in mediam urbem = "into the middle *of* the city";

tōta Graecia = "the whole *of* Greece".

So you really want to learn Latin...

Exercise 4. 5

Study the information on the left-hand page about passive infinitives. Enjoy the wonders of the "future infinitive passive", as not many people will let you into secrets such as this. Now translate into English:

1. *vulnerārī*
2. *dēfendī*
3. *īnstrūctus esse*
4. *ductus esse*
5. *prōmissus esse*

6. *interficī*
7. *superātus esse*
8. *tangī*
9. *datus esse*
10. *vēnditus esse*

Exercise 4. 6

Translate into Latin. Don't assume that these are all passive, because they're not!

1. To be called
2. To be advised
3. To be about to carry
4. To have told
5. To be about to overwhelm

6. To have been conquered
7. To have feared
8. To have been opened
9. To be about to announce
10. To have prepared

Exercise 4. 7

Study the information on the left-hand page about passive indirect statements. Then translate into English:

1. *dīcit urbem oppugnatam esse.*
2. *nūntiat mīlitēs ab hostibus interfectōs esse.*
3. *sciunt imperātōrem ā cōnsule monitum esse.*
4. *dīcunt Rōmam ā Gallīs mox oppugnātum īrī*.*
5. *scīmus carmina ā poētīs īn forō cantāta esse.*

*N.B. When dealing with the so called "future infinitive passive", note that the supine ending in –*um* does not decline in any way and you must not try to make it agree with anything.

Exercise 4. 8

Translate into Latin:

1. He says that the town is being built.
2. They say that the work has already been completed.
3. We know that the ships will be built as quickly as possible.
4. They announce that many victories have been won by Hannibal.
5. They say that the cows have been driven towards the enemy.

	Rabiēs
Using Latin	The disease *rabies* which afflicts dogs, cats etc. takes its name from the Latin *rabiēs* = madness.

Primary and historic

Now is a good time to learn about the difference between primary and historic tenses. *Primary* tenses are: present, future, perfect, future perfect. *Historic* **tenses** are: imperfect, aorist/simple past and pluperfect. The imperative counts as a primary tense.

In all the examples of indirect statements that you have met so far, the verb introducing the indirect statement has been in a primary tense: "he says", "he knows", "he has said", "he will know", etc.

But if the verb introducing the indirect statement is in a *historic* tense (e.g. "he said" or "we had known"), the English will adapt as follows:

He *said* that the enemy *were fighting.*

He *said* that the enemy *would fight.*

He *said* that the enemy *had fought.*

When translating such a sentence into Latin, it may not appear obvious at first which infinitive to use. After all, there is no such thing as an imperfect infinitive, so how do we do "*were attacking*" as an infinitive? Luckily there is a simple rule to follow: go back to what the words of the original direct statement would have been (e.g. "the enemy are attacking") and use the tense of the verb there.

E.g. He said that the enemy *were coming* (original words: "the enemy *are coming*") = *dīxit hostēs venīre.*

E.g. He *said* that the enemy *would come* (original words: "the enemy *will come*") = *dīxit hostēs ventūrōs esse.*

E.g. He *said* that the enemy *had come* (original words: "the enemy *have come*") = *dīxit hostēs vēnisse.*

Vocabulary 4

Nouns		Verbs	
āra, -ae, f.	altar	*appropinquō, -āre,*	I approach
honor/honōs,	honour	*-āvī, -ātum*	
honōris, m.		*cognōscō, -ere,*	I get to know,
imperium,	command, empire	*cognōvī, cognitum*	learn
imperiī, n.		*faveō, favēre,*	I favour, support
impetus, -ūs, m.	attack, charge	*fāvī, fautum* (+ dat.)	
senātus, -ūs, m.	senate	*negō, -āre, -āvī, -ātum*	I deny
vāllum, -ī, n.	rampart	*quaerō, quaerere,*	I look for, ask
Adjectives		*quaesīvī, quaesītum*	
adversus,	opposite,	*resistō, -ere, restitī* (+ dat.)	I resist
-a, -um	unfavourable	*spērō, -āre, -āvī, -ātum*	I hope
attonitus,	astonished	**Adverbs**	
-a, -um		*anteā*	before,
certus, -a, -um	certain, resolved		previously
ferōx, ferōcis	fierce, spirited	*forte*	by chance

So you really want to learn Latin...

Exercise 4. 9

Study the information on the left-hand page about primary and historic tenses. Translate the following into English, assuming that the initial verb in each case is in a historic tense. The first one is done for you.

1. *dīxit agricolās in agrīs labōrāre* =
   He said that the farmers were working in the fields.

2. *dīxērunt nautās tabernās amāre.*

3. *mīles nūntiāvit Hannibalem trāns montēs vēnisse.*

4. *dīxit castra forte* prope flūmen posita esse.*

5. *crēdēbāmus barbarōs oppidum mox oppugnātūrōs esse.*

* N.B. *forte* (+ a verb) is the best way of translating the English phrase "happens to". E.g. He happens to be working = *forte labōrat.*

Exercise 4. 10

Translate into Latin. Remember to go back to the original words of the direct statement to get the correct tense of the infinitive.

1. He said that the slaves were leading the horses into the field (original words: "the slaves are leading…").

2. They announced that the enemy had been defeated (original words: "the enemy have been defeated").

3. She was saying that her brother had been killed in the war.

4. We happened to learn that the rest had fled.

5. I believed that the inhabitants were fierce.

6. We know that the girls happen to be living at home with their mother.

7. Do not tell your master that the slaves have sold all the cows!

8. We heard that the ambassador was laughing in the forum with the consuls.

Exercise 4. 11

Study the words in Vocabulary 4. From which Latin words do the following derive? Translate the Latin word and explain the meaning of the English one:

1. Resist
2. Certainty
3. Recognition
4. Ferocious
5. Impetuous

6. Honorary
7. Adverse
8. Astonished
9. Imperial
10. Favour

Quid prō quō

A *quid prō quō* is a form of compensation or payment for something, from the Latin meaning "something for something".

Using Latin

Reflexive pronouns

A reflexive pronoun refers back to the subject of the verb.
E.g. I wash *myself*; I sing *to myself*; etc.
Those of you who know some French will be familiar with this idea:
E.g. *Je me lève; tu te lèves; il se lève*; etc.
In Latin, the reflexive pronoun of the 3rd person, singular and plural, all genders, is *sē*, which, by definition, can only be found in the oblique cases (i.e. all but nominative and vocative):

Acc.	*sē*
Gen.	*suī*
Dat.	*sibī̆*
Abl.	*sē*

E.g. The king killed himself = *rēx sē interfēcit*.
E.g. The soldiers killed themselves = *mīlitēs sē interfēcērunt*.

The personal pronouns of the 1st and 2nd persons may be used reflexively, often strengthened by a part of *ipse* = "self".
E.g. I wounded myself = *mē (ipsum) vulnerāvī*.
E.g. We wounded ourselves = *nōs (ipsōs) vulnerāvimus*.
The most common case in which to find a reflexive pronoun is the accusative, but the other oblique cases can easily occur.
E.g. He is singing to himself = *sibī̆ cantat*.
As with the personal pronouns, the preposition *cum* = "with", when used, is *added on* to the reflexive pronoun: thus *sēcum*.

Reflexive pronouns and indirect statements

Where the subject of an indirect statement is the same as the subject of the main verb, a reflexive pronoun must be used. The "participle bit" of the infinitive, if there is one, must agree with this pronoun, which will of course be in the accusative.
E.g. I said that **I** would come = *dīxī mē ventūrum esse*.
E.g. The Romans said that **they** (i.e. they themselves) would come =
    Rōmānī dīxērunt sē ventūrōs esse.
If, however, the Romans said that **they** (i.e. some other people) would come, a demonstrative pronoun is used:
    Rōmānī dīxērunt eōs ventūrōs esse.
Reflexive pronouns can be emphasised, if required, using *ipse*.
E.g. He said that **he himself** would come = *dīxit sē ipsum ventūrum esse*.

Negative indirect statements

Where an indirect statement is negative, *negō* = "I deny" should be used for "say that...not."
Thus, instead of "he said that he would not come", we write "he denied that he would come".
E.g. He said that the enemy were **not** fighting = *negāvit hostēs pugnāre*.
E.g. They said that they would **not** fight = *negāvērunt sē pugnātūrōs esse*.
Do **not** be lured into the dreadful trap of writing *dīxit...nōn*!

So you really want to learn Latin...

Exercise 4. 12

Study the information on the left-hand page about reflexive pronouns. Then translate into Latin:

1. The queen has killed herself.
2. I do not wish to kill myself.
3. We will always defend ourselves.
4. You (sing.) were reading to yourself.
5. She will teach herself.
6. I have taught myself to read.
7. You (sing.) have never loved yourself.
8. We will defend ourselves bravely.
9. The king himself had killed himself.
10. Soldiers, why do you never guard yourselves?

Exercise 4. 13

Study the information on the left-hand page about reflexive pronouns and indirect statements. Then translate into English:

1. *rēx dīcēbat sē hostēs superātūrum esse.*
2. *agricola quīdam clāmābat sē aurum in agrō invēnisse.*
3. *Rōmānī nesciēbant Hannibalem trāns montēs ventūrum esse.*
4. *puella audiēbat sē in Ītaliam mox ductum īrī.*
5. *abhinc duōs diēs dux cognōvit multōs equitēs iam profectōs esse.*
6. *puer negāvit sē mēnsam frēgisse.*
7. *nōnne, ō Rōmānī, vōs ipsōs semper custōdiētis?*
8. *nōnne cīvēs gladiīs hastīsque sē dēfendent?*
9. *num rēgīna gladiō sē interfēcit?*
10. *cōnsulēs ipsī cum hostibus prō patriā pugnābunt et fortiter eam dēfendent.*

Exercise 4. 14

Study the information on the left-hand page about negative indirect statements. Then translate into Latin:

1. He said that he would not come to Rome.
2. We said that we had not prepared the food.
3. You say that you do not like the boy's father.
4. She said that she would not prepare the altar of the goddess.
5. I have already said that I will not give a present to my friend.

	Data
	The word *data* is simply the Latin for "things having been given".

Verbs of hoping, promising and threatening

After a verb of hoping, promising or threatening, when followed by the word "to", we use the **future infinitive** with a reflexive pronoun.

E.g. *spērō mē Poenōs victūrum esse* = "I hope to conquer the Carthaginians" (literally: I hope me to be about to conquer the Carthaginians).

E.g. *prōmīsit sē reventūrum esse* = "He promised to return" (literally: he promised himself to be about to return).

Most people forget this one, so put it on your "amazingly important" list and commit it carefully to memory.

Which accusative, which infinitive?

When translating an accusative and infinitive, it can sometimes be hard to tell *which accusative* to take as part of the accusative and infinitive.

E.g. *iūdex sciēbat servum mīlitem interfēcisse.*

In this example, did the judge know that the slave had killed the soldier, or that the soldier had killed the slave? The normal policy is to take the first accusative first, although you will obviously have to be guided by the context.

Similarly, it can sometimes be hard to tell *which infinitive* to take as part of the accusative and infinitive.

E.g. *lēgātus nūntiāvit hostēs pācem accipere velle.*

Having established that *hostēs* must be the subject of the indirect statement, do we then go to *accipere* or *velle*? Again, you need to rely on the context. However, if you remember that verbs such as *volō, nōlō, possum* etc. generally govern an infinitive, this should help to explain why a sentence like this one has *two* infinitives.

Revision

The list of things you are now supposed to know is getting really quite alarming, so we will go for some recent highlights:

- Deponent verbs.
- *Possum, ferō, eō, volō, nōlō, mālō.*
- Formation and declension of the three participles.
- Formation of the infinitives, active and passive.
- Reflexive pronouns.
- Vocabularies 1–4 in this book.

Don't for a moment think that you can forget about everything else. All I'm saying is that this is the latest little lot to be working on.

So you really want to learn Latin...

Exercise 4. 15
Study the information on the left-hand page about verbs of hoping, promising etc. Then translate into English:

1. *pater spērāvit sē mox reditūrum esse.*
2. *fīlia rēgis prōmīsit sē intrā mūrōs mānsūram esse.*
3. *spērō mē hostēs crās victūrum esse.*
4. *omnēs prōmīsimus nōs prō patriā fortiter pugnātūrōs esse.*
5. *mīles prōmīsit sē dōnum fīliābus datūrum esse.*

Exercise 4. 16
Translate into Latin:

1. The mother of the young man promised to lead him to the king.
2. Aeneas promised to build a new city in Italy.
3. The Trojans hoped to find food on the island.
4. Yesterday you all promised to read your books at home.
5. Why did you promise to return after the war, Marcus?

Exercise 4. 17
Translate into Latin:

1. We hoped to watch the charge of the cavalry.
2. The soldiers fought for (i.e. on behalf of) the honour of the Romans.
3. The senate gave command of the army to the two consuls.
4. They learnt that the rest of the soldiers were looking for me.
5. He informed me* that the Carthaginians had resisted our attack.

*I inform = *certiōrem faciō* (i.e. "I make more certain"), where the adjective *certiōrem* (singular) or *certiōrēs* (plural) agrees with the person or persons being informed.

Exercise 4. 18
Revision. Translate:

1. *potest*
2. *nōlent*
3. *velle*
4. *loquī*
5. *discēdēns*

6. *māluit*
7. *monitus*
8. *advēnisse*
9. *lātus esse*
10. *futūrus esse*

	Per sē
Using Latin	*Per sē* = "through itself", i.e. intrinsically or essentially. For example: "the idea was, *per sē*, a good one."

After Cannae: the Romans re-group

After the disaster at Cannae, the Romans, far from chucking in the towel, re-grouped and resolved to rid themselves of the Carthaginian nuisance once and for all. Hannibal's failure to capitalise on his success at Cannae cost him dear and, as the Italian states united against him, Hannibal, with an army of no more than 20,000 men, was reduced to wandering around Italy more or less aimlessly. For fifteen long years he continued to score minor victories against a succession of Roman generals, but the task of conquering the Roman people was, quite simply, beyond him.

In Spain, things weren't going too well for the Carthaginians either. In 210 B.C. the Romans, under the young general Publius Cornelius Scipio, captured New Carthage and it was clear that the Carthaginians' grip on that country, let alone Italy, was looking decidedly shaky. Realising this, Hannibal sent word to his brother Hasdrubal (who was in Spain), insisting that he needed reinforcements in Italy. Avoiding Scipio by marching round the extreme north of Spain, Hasdrubal crossed over the Pyrenees and Alps and, in 207, reached Italy.

The Romans knew how important it was to prevent the two brothers from joining up and accordingly they divided their army in two. One consul, Marcus Livius Salinator, kept watch over Hasdrubal, while the other, Gaius Claudius Nero, kept tabs on Hannibal. It was then that a piece of luck went the Romans' way.

Four Gallic messengers, sent by Hasdrubal to convey instructions to Hannibal, fell into the hands of Gaius Claudius Nero. Under questioning, they revealed that Hasdrubal's intention was to meet up with his brother in Umbria. Taking off at top speed, Gaius Claudius marched his men, day and night, to join up with his consular colleague and engage Hasdrubal before Hannibal could join him. The two Roman forces united and managed to deceive Hasdrubal as to the fact by not enlarging their camp in any way to accommodate the new troops. This worked until Hasdrubal noticed that the trumpet call, which traditionally was sounded outside the consul's tent at supper time, was being sounded twice, signifying the presence of two consuls! At this stage, poor old Hasdrubal realised that his message must have fallen into enemy hands and that he was about to face a "double-whammy".

The battle which followed was fought near the River Metaurus. The Carthaginians were defeated and Hasdrubal fell in the battle. His head was un-ceremoniously chopped off its body and taken south to where Hannibal was still encamped, having failed to receive the vital message from his brother. The head was then lobbed over the ramparts into his camp. Consequently, the first Hannibal knew of his brother's fate was when a familiar face landed on the ground outside his tent. Not a pretty sight.

So you really want to learn Latin...

Exercise 4. 19

Read the information on the left-hand page about the Romans after Cannae. Then answer the following questions in complete sentences:

1. What did Hannbal fail to do immediately after Cannae which he clearly should have done?

2. How large was Hannibal's army and for how long did he roam around Italy?

3. What was the situation in Spain at this time, and what happened in 210 B.C. to highlight the plight of the Carthaginians.

4. Which Roman general was responsible for this success?

5. Why did Hasdrubal set off from Spain to Italy?

6. How did his intentions come to be revealed to the Romans?

7. What steps did Gaius Claudius Nero take to frustrate the plan of Hasdrubal?

8. How did he keep the fact of his presence concealed from Hasdrubal?

9. What was it that eventually gave away the fact that there were two consuls, not one, camped opposite Hasdrubal's position?

10. How did Hannibal learn of his brother's defeat at the Battle of Metaurus, 207 B.C.?

Using Latin	**Quō vādis?** In St. John's Gospel, Ch. 16, Christ is surprised that his disciples do not ask him this: "Whither goest thou?"

CHAPTER 5

The subjunctive; final clauses; the sequence of tenses

Present subjunctive

The tenses you have learnt so far have all been in the **indicative mood**. The indicative is used to express facts, such as "the farmer loves the girl" or "the soldiers are fighting". You are now going to step up a gear by learning about the **subjunctive mood**, which is used when we are dealing with matters which are *not* expressed as definite facts. For example, we use the subjunctive in Latin to express purpose, wishes, possibilities, etc. There are four subjunctive tenses. The way in which these are translated depends on the nature of the construction, and the first one we are going to meet is the present subjunctive:

		Present subjunctive active		
am-em	mone-am	reg-am	audi-am	capi-am
am-ēs	mone-ās	reg-ās	audi-ās	capi-ās
am-et	mone-at	reg-at	audi-at	capi-at
am-ēmus	mone-āmus	reg-āmus	audi-āmus	capi-āmus
am-ētis	mone-ātis	reg-ātis	audi-ātis	capi-ātis
am-ent	mone-ant	reg-ant	audi-ant	capi-ant
		Present subjunctive passive		
am-er	mone-ar	reg-ar	audi-ar	capi-ar
am-ēris	mone-āris	reg-āris	audi-āris	capi-āris
am-ētur	mone-ātur	reg-ātur	audi-ātur	capi-ātur
am-ēmur	mone-āmur	reg-āmur	audi-āmur	capi-āmur
am-ēminī	mone-āminī	reg-āminī	audi-āminī	capi-āminī
am-entur	mone-antur	reg-antur	audi-antur	capi-antur

It is relatively simple to learn this new tense if you notice that verbs in the present subjunctive use the *wrong vowel*. Thus *amō*, which is very much an '*a*' verb, uses '*e*', whereas the others, which are very much '*e*' (or '*i*') verbs, use '*a*'.

Final clauses

The first construction involving the subjunctive which you are going to meet is called a final (or purpose) clause. A final clause expresses **purpose**. It is introduced by the conjunctions *ut* = "in order that", or *nē* = "in order that...not" (i.e. "lest"), and has its verb in the subjunctive.

E.g. I have come to Rome to see my father (i.e. *in order that I may see my father*) =
    *Rōmam vēnī **ut patrem videam**.*

E.g. I have left Rome lest I see my father (i.e. in order that I may not see my father) =
    *Rōmā discessī **nē patrem videam**.*

Note that in English we use a simple infinitive for this construction, e.g. "to see" or "to kill", etc. **Be careful not to do this in Latin.**

So you really want to learn Latin...

Exercise 5. 1

Study the information on the left-hand page about the present subjunctive and final clauses. Notice how in the present subjunctive the verbs appear to *use the wrong vowel*. Translate into Latin using *ut* (+ subjunctive) for "in order that":

1. He walks
2. In order that he may walk
3. They fall
4. In order that they may fall
5. You (sing.) make

6. In order that you (sing.) may make
7. They are wounded
8. In order that they may be wounded
9. They try
10. In order that they may try

Exercise 5. 2

Study the information on the left-hand page about final clauses. Notice how, if at all possible, the "worm" should be avoided (see Introduction, page 5). Translate into English:

1. *fēmina ut agricolam inveniat in agrōs festīnat.*
2. *imperātor ut cum hostibus pugnent cōpiās īnstruit.*
3. *nē mīlitēs nōs interficiant Rōmā discēdēmus.*
4. *puella ut mēnsam paret domum festīnat.*
5. *ad āram veniunt ut deōs laudent.*
6. *hostēs nē Rōmānī aquam inveniant castra prope flūmen pōnent.*
7. *Hannibal suōs in montēs dūcit ut in Ītaliam iter faciant.*
8. *Poenī, ut ānulōs eōrum domum mittant, corpora Rōmānōrum capient.*
9. *duŏ cōnsulēs, ut castra Hasdrubalis capiant, ad flūmen adeunt .*
10. *num Rōmam veniēs ut templa nova videās?*

Exercise 5. 3

Translate into Latin. Remember that with Final Clauses, where in English we use a simple infinitive (e.g. "to see"), Latin uses *ut* or *nē* plus the subjunctive.

1. We have come to Rome to see your friends.
2. You have departed from Rome in order that you may not see my mother.
3. Have you come to the city to read all my books?
4. The farmer hurried into the forum to attack* his brother.
5. Hannibal will send messengers to Spain to seek help from his brother.

* The Latin verb *oppugnō* is only used of attacking towns and cities. If these are not involved, you need either to use *aggredior*, or else in a military context use a phrase such as *impetum facere* (= make a charge), followed by *in* (+ acc).

Using Latin

Dē factō

Dē factō = "from the accomplished fact" and is used to describe the *actual* situation. E.g. "Although he had not been elected by them, he was their *dē factō* representative."

Imperfect subjunctive

The imperfect subjunctive of a verb is so easy to form that there are dead slugs on Mars capable of doing it. Simply go to the present infinitive of the verb and add *-m, -s, -t*, etc., lengthening the preceding '*e*' where necessary.

Imperfect subjunctive active				
amāre-m	monēre-m	regere-m	audīre-m	capere-m
amārē-s	monērē-s	regerē-s	audīrē-s	caperē-s
amāre-t	monēre-t	regere-t	audīre-t	capere-t
amārē-mus	monērē-mus	regerē-mus	audīrē-mus	caperē-mus
amārē-tis	monērē-tis	regerē-tis	audīrē-tis	caperē-tis
amāre-nt	monēre-nt	regere-nt	audīre-nt	capere-nt
Imperfect subjunctive passive				
amāre-r	monēre-r	regere-r	audīre-r	capere-r
amārē-ris	monērē-ris	regerē-ris	audīrē-ris	caperē-ris
amārē-tur	monērē-tur	regerē-tur	audīrē-tur	caperē-tur
amārē-mur	monērē-mur	regerē-mur	audīrē-mur	caperē-mur
amārē-minī	monērē-minī	regerē-minī	audīrē-minī	caperē-minī
amāre-ntur	monēre-ntur	regere-ntur	audīre-ntur	capere-ntur

When forming the imperfect subjunctive of a *deponent* verb, you need to establish which conjugation the verb is and then follow the pattern of that verb type in the passive.

E.g. *loquor, loquī, locūtus sum* follows *regō*. *Regō* in the imperfect subjunctive passive goes *regerer, regerēris, regerētur*; thus *loquor* goes *loquerer, loquerēris, loquerētur*, *etc.*

The sequence of tenses

The tense of the subjunctive in a Final Clause depends on the **sequence of tenses**. If the main verb is primary (see page 38) the verb in the subjunctive will be present subjunctive; if the main verb is historic, the verb in the subjunctive will be imperfect subjunctive.

E.g. I **have come** to Rome to see my father = *Rōmam vēnī ut patrem* **videam**; but

I **came** to Rome to see my father = *Rōmam vēnī ut patrem* **vidērem**.

Now that you are having to cope with the sequence of tenses, it is immensely important that you really take on board the essential difference between the *primary* (perfect tense) *amāvī* = "I have loved" and the *historic* (aorist or simple past) *amāvī* = "I loved" which, of course, look identical. The perfect tense of a verb, although it refers to the past, is considered to be a *primary* tense because it describes the *present* result of an action occurring in the past. The aorist (or simple past) tense of a verb, by contrast, simply refers to an action which occurred in the past, with no reference to its present result.

E.g. *librum lēgī* = "I have read the book".

E.g. *librum herī lēgī* = "I read the book yesterday".

So you really want to learn Latin...

Exercise 5. 4
Study the information on the left-hand page about the imperfect subjunctive. Note how the imperfect subjunctive often means *might* and is formed from the present infinitive by adding '*m*' etc. Translate into Latin:

1. To walk
2. In order that I might walk
3. To fight
4. In order that I might fight
5. To flee
6. In order that I might flee
7. To learn
8. In order that I might learn
9. To leave
10. In order that I might leave

Exercise 5. 5
Once you can do the imperfect subjunctive in the active, putting it into the passive (or using a deponent verb) is simple, using our old conversion chart which we learnt in Book II (*-ō/m, -s, -t, -mus, -tis, -nt* becomes *-or/r, -ris, -tur, -mur, -minī, -ntur*). Translate into Latin, using the imperfect subjunctive:

1. In order that we might be taught
2. In order that she might not be watched
3. In order that they might be feared
4. In order that I might not be captured
5. In order that they might follow
6. In order that they might try
7. In order that you (pl.) might speak
8. In order that we might set out

Exercise 5. 6
Study the information on the left-hand page about the sequence of tenses. Translate into Latin:

1. He ran into the street in order to watch the animals.
2. I was reading the book in order to learn many things about the Romans.
3. They are guarding the bridge lest it be captured by the enemy.
4. Hannibal set out in order to lead his forces into the mountains.
5. I have sent the slave in order that he might help you.
6. He will come back home to see his father.
7. They have come into the city lest they be captured by the enemy.
8. They came into the city lest they be captured by the enemy.
9. Have you come to Rome to see the consuls?
10. Did you go to Greece to look at the old temples?

Using Latin

Caveat ēmptor
A disclaimer on the part of the vendor, this means "let the buyer beware!"

Irregular verbs in the subjunctive

The present subjunctive of irregular verbs has to be learnt, just as the present indicative had to be learnt. The imperfect subjunctive, however, is easy, being formed in the normal way (by adding '*m*' etc. to the present infinitive).

			Present subjunctive			
sim	possim	feram	eam	velim	nōlim	mālim
sīs	possīs	ferās	eās	velīs	nōlīs	mālīs
sit	possit	ferat	eat	velit	nōlit	mālit
sīmus	possīmus	ferāmus	eāmus	velīmus	nōlīmus	mālīmus
sītis	possītis	ferātis	eātis	velītis	nōlītis	mālītis
sint	possint	ferant	eant	velint	nōlint	mālint
			Imperfect subjunctive			
essem	possem	ferrem	īrem	vellem	nōllem	māllem
essēs	possēs	ferrēs	īrēs	vellēs	nōllēs	māllēs
esset	posset	ferret	īret	vellet	nōllet	māllet
essēmus	possēmus	ferrēmus	īrēmus	vellēmus	nōllēmus	māllēmus
essētis	possētis	ferrētis	īrētis	vellētis	nōllētis	māllētis
essent	possent	ferrent	īrent	vellent	nōllent	māllent

The only one of these verbs to have a passive is *ferō*, which forms its passive in an almost absurdly regular way:

Present: *ferar, ferāris, ferātur, ferāmur, ferāminī, ferantur.*
Imperfect: *ferrer, ferrēris, ferrētur, ferrēmur, ferrēminī, ferrentur.*

Vocabulary 5

Nouns

caedes, -is, f.	slaughter	
causa, -ae, f.	cause	
cīvitas, cīvitātis, f.	state, city	
dēns, dentis, m.	tooth	
fīnis, fīnis, m.	end (in pl. = territory)	
lībertās, lībertātis, f.	freedom	
ŏdium, ŏdiī, n.	hatred	
ōs, ōris, n.	mouth, face	
ŏs, ossis, n.	bone	
poena, -ae, f.	penalty	

Adjectives

nōnnūllī, -ae, -a	some
stultus, -a, -um	stupid
tūtus, -a, -um	safe

Verbs

caedō, -ere, cecīdī, caesum	I cut, kill
colligō, -ere, collēgī, collēctum	I collect
oblīvīscor, oblīvīscī, oblītus sum (+ gen.)	I forget
parcō, -ere, pepercī, parsum (+ dat.)	I spare
poenās dō, dare, dedī, datum	I pay the penalty, am punished
studeō, -ēre, -uī, (+ dat.)	I study, am eager about

Adverbs

libenter	gladly, willingly
quotiēns?	how often?

So you really want to learn Latin...

Exercise 5. 7
Study the information on the left-hand page about irregular verbs in the subjunctive. Then translate into Latin:

1. We came to the city in order to be able to read.
2. We have come in order to carry our spears into the camp!
3. We came to the island in order that we might be happy again.
4. How often have you come here to carry water into the city?
5. We have gone away to fight again for our fatherland!

Exercise 5. 8
Translate into English:

1. *Rōmānī nāvēs parāvērunt ut Poenōs vincere possent.*
2. *senex ā mīlitibus interfectus est nē cibum ad cīvēs ferret.*
3. *mīlitēs captī sunt nē domum redīrent.*
4. *nāvem dēlēvimus nē cōpiās ad hostēs ferret.*
5. *puerum bene docuī ut mihĭ saepe legere possit.*

Exercise 5. 9
Translate into English: *The Romans take Spain, 206 B.C.*

Rōmānī, quī plūrimās nāvēs habēbant, Poenōs in bellō semper superāre poterant. eī igitur, quod auxilium ā Graecīs petēbant, ad rēgem Macedoniae lēgātōs mīsērunt. hic tamen, nōmine Philippus, eōs adiuvāre nōn poterat. deinde Rōmānī, quod crēdēbant sē posse bellum cōnficere, in Hispāniam prōgressī sunt. Publius Scīpiō autem cum frātre Cnaeō exercitum in illam terram dūxit ut Poenōs expelleret. hī autem ducēs in bellō interfectī sunt sed fīlius Publiī exercitum ā senātū accēpit. hic, quī artī Hannibalis diū studuerat, peditibus circum aciem hostium missīs, medium agmen eōrum aggressus est. Poenōs autem quī cōpiās prope oppidum, nōmine Ilipam, īnstrūxerant paene dēlēvit. sīc Hispānia, ā Poenīs āmissa, Rōmānīs trādita est.

Ilipa, -ae, f. = Ilipa (a town in Spain).

Exercise 5. 10
Study the words in Vocabulary 5. From which Latin words do the following derive? Translate the Latin word and explain the meaning of the English one:

1. Odious
2. Liberty
3. Finish
4. Dental
5. Student
6. Stultify
7. Collection
8. Oblivious
9. Oral
10. Cause

Exhortations and the jussive subjunctive

1. Exhortations are phrases which in English usually involve the word "let". For example, "let's get out of here!" is an exhortation. In Latin, they are generally expressed by the present subjunctive:

E.g. *magistrum audiāmus* = "may we listen to the master!" (i.e. let us listen to the master!). This use of the present subjunctive is called a hortative subjunctive.

2. Commands may also be given in this way.

E.g. *prō patriā pugnent* = "may they fight for the fatherland"! (i.e. let them fight for the fatherland!). This use of the present subjunctive is called a jussive subjunctive.

Subordinate clauses in indirect speech

Okay, so here we go with one of the all time great rules, designed to make the old brain cells twiddle around like spinning tops. You already know how to cope with indirect statements, and that the construction used in Latin is the accusative and infinitive. But, where there is a subordinate clause tucked inside the indirect statement (i.e. subordinate to it), the verb in that clause generally goes into the subjunctive.

E.g. He said that the girls, *who were walking in the garden*, were beautiful
= *dīxit puellās, **quae in hortō ambulārent**, pulchrās esse.*

This rule applies if the subordinate clause is essentially part of the indirect speech, i.e. if in the example above the original statement was "the girls who are walking in the garden are beautiful". But if the subordinate clause is independent of the indirect statement, and has been added in by the person reporting the indirect statement, then the verb remains in the indicative.

E.g. He said that the girls (i.e. *the ones who are now walking in the garden*) were beautiful
= *dīxit puellās, **quae in hortō nunc ambulant**, pulchrās esse.*

In this example, the relative clause has been added in to clarify which girls the original speaker was describing as beautiful. His original words would only have been "the girls are beautiful".

Signpost words

Because Latin sentences are naturally long and involved, it is both helpful and extremely stylish to point out your intentions by means of **signpost words**. The most common of these are *idcircō* and *ideō*, both meaning "for that reason". These can be used to signal the imminent arrival of (in particular) a final or causal clause, allowing you to produce your main verb earlier in the sentence without chopping "the worm" in two (see Introduction, p. 5)!

E.g. *Caesar **idcircō** ad urbem iter fēcit ut cibum raperet.*

There is no need to translate the word *idcircō*, but it performs the invaluable duty of preventing a "worm". Without it, the sentence could have been chopped in two after *iter fēcit*, leaving the *ut* clause hanging off the end, looking very sad. Obviously in a long and complicated sentence, full of verbs in the subjunctive, the presence of a signpost word, alerting you to the fact that another clause is coming, is extremely comforting.

So you really want to learn Latin...

Exercise 5. 11
Study the information on the left-hand page about exhortations and the jussive subjunctive.
Translate into English:

1. *mīlitēs prō patriā fortiter pugnent!*
2. *domum festīnēmus ut mātrem videāmus!*
3. *quaerāmus amīcum rūrī!*
4. *magistrum audiāmus nē ille nōs pūniat!*
5. *proficīscāmur statim et festīnēmus Rōmam!*
6. *urbem quīnque hōrās custōdiat!*
7. *oppidum vāllīs mūrīsque mūniant!*
8. *"interficiantur" inquit dux "omnēs mīlitēs captī!"*

Exercise 5. 12
Study the information on the left-hand page about subordinate clauses. Then translate into Latin, in all cases assuming the subordinate clause to be part of the original statement:

1. The boy said that the enemy who were attacking the city would overcome the citizens.
2. We heard that the general who was fighting in Africa wanted to come home.
3. He said that the old man who was standing in the street was the father of the consul.
4. We all know that the poets who live in Rome have read many books.
5. They said that the soldiers who were attacking the camp were very fierce.

Exercise 5. 13
Study the information on the left-hand page about signpost words. Then translate into English:

1. *mīlitēs dīxērunt sē ideō moritūrōs esse ut lībertātem amīcōrum servārent.*
2. *dīcit oppidum parvum, quod Poenī capere cupiant, vāllīs maximīs mūnīrī!*
3. *sē idcircō Athēnās nāvigāre velle dīxit ut templa, quae egŏ iam vīdī, vidēret.*
4. *dux celeriter idcircō domum rediit ut sē victōriam peperisse nūntiāret.*
5. *scīmus senem fābulam, quam omnēs audīverīmus, iterum nārrātūrum esse.*

Exercise 5. 14
Revision. Translate:

1. *caesūrus esse*
2. *poenās dedisse*
3. *studēte causīs lībertātis*
4. *stultissimus*
5. *lībertātis oblīvīscēns*
6. *ossibus libenter collēctīs*
7. *in cīvitātis fīnēs*
8. *oblītūrus*
9. *sine dentibus*
10. *lībertāte āmissā*

Using Latin

Stet
If one has wrongly amended a written document and wishes the original wording to remain, one writes "STET". *Stet* = let it stand.

The Romans triumph at Zama, 204 B.C.

After the death of his brother, Hannibal found life in Italy rather hard and very demoralising. The government back home was unable or unwilling to send further troops, and when Scipio won another victory over the Carthaginians in Spain at the Battle of Ilipa in 206 B.C., their grip on that country was lost for ever.

Buoyed by this success, Scipio resolved to invade Africa. Crossing over in 204 B.C., he managed to persuade the brilliant commander of the Numidian cavalry, Masinissa, to defect and fight for him. Masinissa promptly attacked the King of Numidia, Syphax, and captured his capital city, Cirta. There he found the king's beautiful daughter, Sophonisba, who begged him not to hand her over to the Romans. Masinissa was delighted to grant this request and promptly married her, there and then! Scipio, however, was rather worried about this hasty matrimonial alliance and it soon became apparent to Masinissa that he was not going to be allowed to keep his beautiful bride. True to his word, therefore, he sent her a cup of poison with a message saying that he was keeping his promise; she should not come into the hands of the Romans alive. Accepting her fate with good grace, the beautiful girl drank the poison and that was the end of her.

Scipio then advanced towards Carthage and besieged the city. A truce was made but when Hannibal, returning from Italy with his bedraggled army of 24,000 men, landed in Africa, the Carthaginians broke the truce and resumed hostilities. Scipio and Masinissa moved away from Carthage towards Numidia, meeting Hannibal at Zama. There a meeting was arranged between Scipio and Hannibal but, after a mutual admiration session, terms could not be agreed. The next day, battle was joined.

Hannibal began by drawing up 80 elephants in his front line to frighten off the Romans. However, the poor beasts panicked when the Roman bugles sounded and stampeded into their own men. The few elephants that did set off in the right direction were beaten off by the Romans and these, too, soon turned tail and fled, again causing further mayhem amongst their own forces. The Carthaginians, as in all good battle stories, were surrounded by the Romans and attacked from the front and rear. Hannibal was beaten and terms were agreed under which Carthage was not to be sacked, but hostages and cash were to be handed over to the Romans. Scipio then returned in triumph to Rome.

As for Hannibal, he was left to supervise the payments of cash to the Romans. He did this for a bit until his friendship with the king of Syria, an enemy of Rome, got him into trouble again with the Romans. He was forced to flee from Carthage and went first to Crete and then to Bithynia, where he helped King Prusias beat up King Eumenes of Pergamum, hurling jars full of poisonous snakes on to the latter's ships and scaring his sailors away. However, all good things have to come to an end and, when the Romans caught up with him again, he took poison rather than fall into the hands of the Romans who had been pursuing him for so many years. Dido's curse was finally at an end; or was it...?

So you really want to learn Latin...

Exercise 5. 15

Read the information on the left-hand page about Zama. Then answer the following questions in complete sentences:

1. When was the Battle of Ilipa and what was the result?

2. When did Scipio cross over into Africa?

3. Who was Masinissa?

4. Whom did Masinissa attack and which city did he capture?

5. Who was the girl whom Masinissa took a shine to in the captured city?

6. What was her request to him, and how did he respond?

7. What was Scipio's view of these proceedings?

8. How did Masinissa eventually manage to keep his promise to the girl?

9. Why do you think Carthage broke its truce with Scipio when Hannibal landed in Africa?

10. Was Hannibal's army likely to have been in a fit state to take on the Romans?

11. Where did the battle between Scipio and Hannibal take place?

12. What part did the Carthaginians' elephants play in the battle?

13. What happened in the end to Hannibal?

14. Why should this have marked the end of Dido's curse?

Using Latin	**Exeat**
	An *exeat* is a holiday when pupils may leave school. In Latin, **exeat** = let (the school) go out.

CHAPTER 6

Consecutive clauses; perfect and pluperfect subjunctive; temporal and causal clauses; fīō

Consecutive clauses

1. A consecutive clause expresses *result*. It is introduced by *ut* = "with the result that" or *ut nōn* = "with the result that…not", and has its verb in the subjunctive. The main clause will almost always contain an adverb meaning "so", such as *tam* (used with adjectives and adverbs), or *adeō* (used with verbs); or an adjective such as *tantus* = "so great" or *tālis* = "such".

E.g. He was so angry that he ran as quickly as possible =
   tam īrātus erat ut quam celerrimē curreret.

E.g. The consul was leading so great an army that the Romans were not afraid =
   cōnsul tantum exercitum dūcēbat ut Rōmānī nōn timērent.

As with final clauses, the dreaded **sequence of tenses** applies. Note, however, that the present subjunctive is used to describe the *present* result of an action in the past, even after a historic main verb.

E.g. He *was* so terrified that he *does* not dare go out = *adeō territus est ut exīre nōn audeat.*

2. Note that when consecutive clauses are negative, they use *ut…nōn*. This helps to distinguish them from final clauses (which use *nē* in the negative).

E.g. *Rōmā discessit nē patrem vidēret* (final clause) =
   "He departed from Rome lest he see his father".

E.g. *Rōmā tam celeriter discessit ut patrem nōn vidēret* (consecutive clause) =
   "He departed from Rome so quickly that he did not see his father".

Vocabulary 6

Verbs		Adverbs	
addō, addere, addidī, additum	I add	*adeō*	to such an extent
		eō	(to) there, thither
cōnsistō, -ere, cōnstitī, cōnstitum	I halt	*facile*	easily
		simul	at the same time
dubitō, -āre, -āvī, -ātum	I doubt, hesitate	*tam*	so
edō, ēsse, ēdī, ēsum (irreg.)	I eat	**Conjunction**	
fallō, -ere, fefellī, falsum	I deceive, cheat	*simul ac /*	as soon as
Nouns		*simul atque*	
clādes, clādis, f.	disaster	**Adjectives**	
exsilium, -iī, n.	exile	*falsus, -a, -um*	false
fātum, -ī, n.	fate, destiny	*saevus, -a, -um*	savage
gēns, gentis, f.	people, race, clan	*tālis, -e*	such
victor, victōris, m.	victor	*tantus, -a, -um*	so great
vīlla, -ae, f.	country-house	*tot* (indeclinable)	so many

So you really want to learn Latin…

Exercise 6. 1
Study the information on the left-hand page about consecutive clauses. Then translate into English:

1. *puer tam lentē ambulābat ut ā magistrō caperētur.*
2. *puer tam celeriter currēbat ut prīmus ad vīllam advenīret.*
3. *tantum exercitum habēbat ut hostēs facile superāre posset.*
4. *urbs tam bene dēfendēbātur ut ab hostibus nōn caperētur.*
5. *tālem imperātōrem habent ut nihil timeant.*

Exercise 6. 2
Translate into Latin, remembering to follow the sequence of tenses:

1. They fought so bravely that they were able to conquer the enemy.
2. She sang so well that she was led into the country-house of the consul.
3. He has so many books that he is not able to read them all.
4. We fear the anger of the consul to such an extent that we wish to flee from the city.
5. He built so big a house that everyone now praises him.

Exercise 6. 3
Study the words in Vocabulary 6. From which Latin words do the following derive? Translate the Latin word and explain the meaning of the English one:

1. Facility
2. Addition
3. Villa
4. False
5. Indubitably
6. Simultaneous
7. Victorious
8. Exile
9. Fate
10. Fallacious

Exercise 6. 4
It is quite easy to muddle final and consecutive clauses if you are not careful. One very obvious distinction, however, is that negative final clauses use *nē* whereas negative consecutive clauses use *ut nōn*. Translate the following:

1. *ad vīllam celeriter cucurrit ut patrem vidēret.*
2. *ad vīllam tam celeriter cucurrit ut patrem vidēret.*
3. *ab urbe celeriter discessit nē ā custōdibus caperētur.*
4. *ab urbe tam celeriter discessit ut ā custōdibus nōn caperētur.*
5. *urbem bene dēfendēbant nē ab hostibus oppugnārētur.*
6. *urbem tam bene dēfendēbant ut ab hostibus nōn oppugnārētur.*

Using Latin

Drāmatis persōnae
The cast of a play is often referred to in the programme as the *drāmatis persōnae* = "the characters of the play".

Perfect subjunctive

The perfect subjunctive active looks remarkably similar to the future perfect indicative active, with a few long vowels thrown in (although in verse these vowels are regularly found long *or* short). This makes it easy to learn, but of course it does mean that you have to be careful not to confuse it with the future perfect.

The perfect subjunctive passive is the same as the perfect *indicative* passive except that, instead of adding the present *indicative* of sum, we add the present *subjunctive*.

Active

amāv-erim	*monu-erim*	*rēx-erim*	*audīv-erim*	*cēp-erim*
amāv-erīs	*monu-erīs*	*rēx-erīs*	*audīv-erīs*	*cēp-erīs*
amāv-erit	*monu-erit*	*rēx-erit*	*audīv-erit*	*cēp-erit*
amāv-erīmus	*monu-erīmus*	*rēx-erīmus*	*audīv-erīmus*	*cēp-erīmus*
amāv-erītis	*monu-erītis*	*rēx-erītis*	*audīv-erītis*	*cēp-erītis*
amāv-erint	*monu-erint*	*rēx-erint*	*audīv-erint*	*cēp-erint*

Passive

amātus sim	*monitus* sim	*rēctus* sim	*audītus* sim	*captus* sim
amātus sīs	*monitus* sīs	*rēctus* sīs	*audītus* sīs	*captus* sīs
amātus sit	*monitus* sit	*rēctus* sit	*audītus* sit	*captus* sit
amātī sīmus	*monitī* sīmus	*rēctī* sīmus	*audītī* sīmus	*captī* sīmus
amātī sītis	*monitī* sītis	*rēctī* sītis	*audītī* sītis	*captī* sītis
amātī sint	*monitī* sint	*rēctī* sint	*audītī* sint	*captī* sint

Uses of the perfect subjunctive

1. Consecutive clauses

If we wish to stress the fact that the result in a consecutive clause did actually happen (or, if negative, did actually *not* happen), we use the perfect subjunctive, even after a historic main verb.

E.g. *mīlitēs tam fortiter pugnāvērunt ut hostēs vīcerint* = "the soldiers fought so bravely that they conquered the enemy".

This may at first appear to be breaking the rule for the sequence of tenses. But actually this perfect subjunctive (*vīcerint*) may be regarded to be, not a perfect subjunctive (and thus a primary tense), but rather an *aorist* subjunctive (and thus historic). Just as the perfect indicative can double up as an aorist, so the perfect subjunctive seems to be doing the same here.

2. Prohibition

You already know how to express a prohibition using *nōlī/nōlīte* (+ the infinitive). But there is another way, involving *nē* plus the 2nd person of the perfect subjunctive.

E.g. *nē fēcerīs illud, Mārce* = do not do that, Marcus!

E.g. *nē cēperītis urbem, mīlitēs!* = do not capture the city, soldiers!

I can't pretend this is overwhelmingly common, but it's a nice little trick to have up your sleeve, something to bring out on a rainy day, perhaps.

So you really want to learn Latin...

Exercise 6. 5
Study the information on the left-hand page about the perfect subjunctive. Write out the perfect subjunctive, active and passive, of the following verbs:

1. *videō*
2. *ferō*
3. *dēleō*
4. *spectō*

Exercise 6. 6
Study the information on the left-hand page about the uses of the perfect subjunctive in consecutive clauses. Note how it is used to emphasise the completion of the result, and may come after a primary or historic main verb. Then translate into English, taking all the main verbs as being historic:

1. *urbem tam ferōciter oppugnāvērunt ut eam facile cēperint.*
2. *puer tam fessus erat ut ā magistrō nōn pūnītus sit.*
3. *Gallī adeō territī sunt ut īn silvam fūgerint.*
4. *tanta tempestās noctū orta est ut multae nāvēs dēlētae sint.*
5. *Mārcus tam celeriter cucurrit ut sorōrem suam mox cēperit.*

Exercise 6. 7
Translate into Latin:

1. She was walking so slowly that she was soon captured by the guards.
2. He received so many wounds on that day that he died.
3. The battle was fought so fiercely that very many soldiers were killed.
4. They were so afraid that they were not willing to cross the river.
5. The walls of the city were so high that no one was able to climb them.

Exercise 6. 8
Study the information on the left-hand page about prohibitions using *nē* + the perfect subjunctive. Be careful not to muddle this use of *nē* with the use of *nē* in final clauses. Then translate into English:

1. *nē pugnāverītis cum sociīs, Rōmānī!*
2. *nōlīte cum sociīs pugnāre, Rōmānī!*
3. *nē īn silvam ambulāverīs, mī amīce!*
4. *ē silvā celeriter cucurrit nē ā leōne vidērētur.*
5. *ē silvā tam celeriter cucurrit ut ā leōne nōn vīsus sit.*

Viz.
Viz. is an abbreviation for the Latin *vidēlicet* = namely.
E.g. "You must do your shopping on a particular day, *viz.* Thursday."

Pluperfect subjunctive

The pluperfect subjunctive active is formed from the perfect infinitive (e.g. *amāvisse*) by adding '*m*' etc. or, if you prefer, by adding *–issem* etc. to the perfect stem. The passive is the same as the indicative except that, in place of the imperfect *indicative* of *sum*, it uses the imperfect *subjunctive*.

Active

amāv-*issem*	monu-*issem*	rēx-*issem*	audīv-*issem*	cēp-*issem*
amāv-*issēs*	monu-*issēs*	rēx-*issēs*	audīv-*issēs*	cēp-*issēs*
amāv-*isset*	monu-*isset*	rēx-*isset*	audīv-*isset*	cēp-*isset*
amāv-*issēmus*	monu-*issēmus*	rēx-*issēmus*	audīv-*issēmus*	cēp-*issēmus*
amāv-*issētis*	monu-*issētis*	rēx-*issētis*	audīv-*issētis*	cēp-*issētis*
amāv-*issent*	monu-*issent*	rēx-*issent*	audīv-*issent*	cēp-*issent*

Passive

amātus essem	monitus essem	rēctus essem	audītus essem	captus essem
amātus essēs	monitus essēs	rēctus essēs	audītus essēs	captus essēs
amātus esset	monitus esset	rēctus esset	audītus esset	captus esset
amātī essēmus	monitī essēmus	rēctī essēmus	audītī essēmus	captī essēmus
amātī essētis	monitī essētis	rēctī essētis	audītī essētis	captī essētis
amātī essent	monitī essent	rēctī essent	audītī essent	captī essent

Temporal clauses

Temporal clauses, as we learnt when we met *dum* = "while", refer to time. They generally have their verb in the indicative, and are introduced by the conjunctions *ubĭ* = "when", *postquam* = "after", *antequam* or *priusquam* = "before", *simul atque* (or *simul ac*) = "as soon as", etc.

1. N.B. Where the temporal clause refers to the future, in Latin a future perfect tense is generally used where in English we use what appears to be a present tense.

E.g. **"When you come** to Rome I will lead you into the forum" (i.e. "when you *will have* come to Rome, etc.") = *ubĭ Rōmam vēneris, tē īn forum dūcam.*

2. After the conjunctions listed above, Latin uses a perfect tense where in English we use a pluperfect.

E.g. *ubĭ hoc fēcit* = "when he **had** done this" (or "when he did this").

E.g. *postquam hoc audīvit* = "after he **had** heard this" (or "after he heard this").

But, after *cum* = **"when"**, the pluperfect **subjunctive** is used.

E.g. *cum hoc fēcisset* = "when he had done this".

3. Where some idea other than that of time is introduced (this will normally be *purpose*), the subjunctive is used.

E.g. *priusquam* hostēs castra *pōnerent*, dux impetum in eōs fēcit = "Before the enemy were able to pitch camp, the general made an attack on them."

The idea here is that the leader attacked the enemy *with the purpose of preventing them* from pitching camp. There is thus an idea of purpose as well as of time.

So you really want to learn Latin...

Exercise 6. 9
Study the information on the left-hand page about the pluperfect subjunctive. Write out the pluperfect subjunctive active and passive of the following verbs:

1. *trahō*
2. *ferō*

3. *portō*
4. *vincō*

Exercise 6. 10
Study the information on the left-hand page about temporal clauses. Then translate into English. Where the Latin perfect tense is used, translate this with an English pluperfect where this sounds more natural.

1. *cum Rōmānī cum Hannibale pugnāvissent, eum superāvērunt.*

2. *simul atque Hannibal Rōmānōs vīdit, aciem īnstrūxit.*

3. *priusquam imperātor castra pōneret hostēs exercitum in proelium dūxērunt.*

4. *ubǐ hūc vēnistī, templa tibǐ ostendī.*

5. *antequam domum rediistī, multa loca vīdistī.*

6. *cum templa vīdissēs, domum quam celerrimē rediistī.*

7. *postquam omnia templa vīdistī, tē īn forum dūxī.*

8. *postquam domum rediistī, multa dōna mātrī patrīque dedistī.*

9. *simulac rēx ita locūtus est, nōs fugere cōnstituimus.*

10. *cum hoc cōnsilium cēpissēmus, īn forum festīnāvimus.*

Exercise 6. 11
Translate into Latin, using temporal clauses:

1. When we saw the angry man, we immediately fled towards the woods.

2. After you had prepared the food and wine, you called us into the country house.

3. When you come to our villa, I will show you the gardens.

4. As soon as we found the gold, we carried it into the forum.

5. Before he was able to fight, he used to guard the camp.

Exercise 6. 12
An ablative absolute construction is often used in place of a temporal clause (see page 20). Translate the following, beginning each one with the word "when":

1. *virō vīsō īn silvās fūgimus.*
2. *cibō parātō in vīllam nōs vocāvit.*
3. *castrīs positīs dux rediit.*

4. *mīlite interfectō fūgimus.*
5. *bellō cōnfectō domum rediimus.*
6. *mēnsā parātā cibum ēdimus.*

Using Latin

Hīc iacet
This is often seen on tomb-stones. *Hīc iacet* = here lies.

Causal clauses

A causal clause gives the *cause* of the action of the main verb and is introduced in English by a word such as "because" or "since".

E.g. He went to Rome *because/since* his mother lived there.

In Latin they are introduced by the conjunctions *quod* or *quia* (+ indicative) = "because", *quoniam* (+ indicative) = "since" or *cum* (+ subjunctive) = "since". If, however, only an "alleged reason" is given, the verb *always* goes in the subjunctive.

E.g. *servum interfēcit quod eum timēbat* = He killed the slave because he feared him.

E.g. *servum interfēcit cum eum timēret* = He killed the slave since he feared him.

E.g. *servum interfēcit quia eum timēret* = He killed the slave, *allegedly* because he feared him.

More about cum

The Latin word *cum* can cause all sorts of trouble if you are not careful. As you know, it can be a preposition followed by the ablative, meaning "with" or "together with". But it can also be a conjunction, having a variety of meanings. So, here is a user's guide to *cum*, to help you tackle this little beast:

1. *cum* (+ ablative) = "with", "together with".

E.g. **cum** *amīcō ambulābam* = "I was walking **with** my friend".

2. *cum* (+ indicative) = "when", referring to the present or future.

E.g. *cum hūc veniēs* = "when you come here..."

3. *cum* (+ perfect stem tense of the indicative) = "whenever". The tense used must show that one action precedes the other.

E.g. *cum mē vocāvit, veniō* = "whenever he calls me, I come".

E.g. *cum mē vocāverit, veniam* = "whenever he calls me, I will come".

E.g. *cum mē vocāverat, veniēbam* = "whenever he called me, I came".

4. *cum* (+ imperfect subjunctive) = "when", "since" or "although".

E.g. **cum** *bellum in Ītaliā gereret...* = "**When** he was waging war in Italy..."

E.g. **cum** *esset audāx, in pugnam ruit* = "**Since** he was bold, he rushed into battle."

E.g. *patrem meum,* **cum** *cōnsul nōn esset, laudāvistī* = "You praised my father, **although** he was not a consul."

5. *cum* (+ perfect subjunctive) = "since/because" followed by a true perfect (i.e. with "have/has").

E.g. **cum** *librum lēgerim* = "**Since I have** read the book..."

6. *cum* (+ pluperfect subjunctive) = "when".

E.g. **cum** *domum revēnisset...* = "**When** he had come back home..."

There are other ways in which *cum* may be used but the ones above are by far the most common. If you master these, you should never find yourself stuck.

So you really want to learn Latin...

Exercise 6. 13

Study the information on the left-hand page about causal clauses. Note how, if it is only the "alleged reason" being given, the verb after *quod* or *quia* goes in the subjunctive. Then translate into English:

1. *trīstis sum quod discessistī.*
2. *trīstis eram cum discēderēs.*
3. *Rōmam festīnāvit quia mātrem patremque vidēre cupīvit.*
4. *in vīllam iniit* quod omnēs librōs legere volēbat.*
5. *in montēs iter fēcit cum Ītaliam vincere vellet.*

* N.B. When using compound verbs, note how a preposition is regularly used twice, first with the noun and then as a prefix to the compound verb.

Exercise 6. 14

Study the information on the left-hand page about *cum*. Then translate into Latin:

1. He is playing in the garden with his sister.
2. They attacked the battle-line of the enemy when the general had given the signal.
3. Since he was tired, he returned home before night.
4. Although he was tired, he decided to remain in Rome for seven days.
5. When he was fighting with the enemy, he was wounded in the face.

Exercise 6. 15

Now for some more practice at the various constructions and uses of the subjunctive you have met so far. Translate into English: *The end of Hannibal, 183 B.C.*

1. *Poenī Hannibalem idcircō in exsilium mīsērunt cum hostēs superāre nōn posset.*
2. *hic ad rēgem quendam idcircō ībat nē ā Poenīs caperētur.*
3. *tot bellīs prō patriā gestīs, dux audāx ab amīcīs dēceptus est.*
4. *in vīllā rēgis cuiusdam diū ideō habitābat nē domī poenās daret.*
5. *tandem mortem adeō cupīvit ut sē interfēcerit.*

Exercise 6. 16

Translate into Latin:

1. The Romans feared the Carthaginians to such an extent that they sent another army to Africa.
2. They defended their city so well that the Roman soldiers were not able to capture it.
3. The next year the Roman senate sent a young man called Cornelius to attack Carthage.
4. Since this general had a very big army, he was able to break the walls of the city.
5. For a few days the enemy were able to defend themselves so fiercely that Cornelius was unable to overcome them.

Using Latin	**In extrēmīs** *In extrēmīs* = "in the most extreme ends" and is most dramatically used to refer to the point of imminent death. E.g. "the survivors of the air crash were *in extrēmīs*".

Edō = I eat

Edō, ēsse, ēdī, ēsum = I eat. This is a lovely little verb because it looks very similar to the verb *sum* in some of its forms, but uses a long *ē* instead of a short one. It can also be confused with the verb *ēdō* = "I produce". It has a present tense which goes: *edō, ēs, ēst, edimus, ēstis, edunt*. The imperatives are *ēs* and *ēste*. Most of the other forms are regular. Thus the future goes *edam, edēs, edet*, etc.; the imperfect goes *edēbam, edēbās, edēbat*, etc. The full conjugation is given on page 120.

In the good old days they used to fail anyone taking an exam who was unable to translate correctly the following sentence: *puer mālum ēst*. In those days, of course, they would not have helped by marking the vowel quantities. I'm sure you would have no trouble with this, but just in case, the answer is given on page 67.

Fīō = I become

Our last irregular verb (honestly!) is *fīō, fīĕrī, factus sum* = "I become" *or* "I am made". It has the following forms, rare ones being shown in brackets:

	Indicative	**Subjunctive**
Present	*fīō*	*fīam*
	fīs	*fīās*
	fit	*fīat*
	(fīmus)	*fīāmus*
	(fītis)	*fīātis*
	fīunt	*fīant*
Future	*fīam*	
	fīēs	
	fīet	
	fīēmus	
	fīētis	
	fīent	
Imperfect	*fīēbam*	*fīĕrem*
	fīēbās	*fīĕrēs*
	fīēbat	*fīĕret*
	fīēbāmus	*fīĕrēmus*
	fīēbātis	*fīĕrētis*
	fīēbant	*fīĕrent*

Fīō means "I become" or "I am made". It is used as the passive of the verb *faciō* because, horror of horrors, *faciō* has no present, future or imperfect passive. It should always be pretty obvious from the context which meaning to use, but occasionally either would do. E.g. *rēx fīet* = "he will become king" or "he will be made king". E.g. *cōnsul factus est* = "he has been made consul" or "he has become consul" or "he became consul.

So you really want to learn Latin...

Exercise 6. 17

Study the information on the left-hand page about the verb *fīō*. Translate into Latin:

1. He will be made consul.
2. He came to Rome in order to be made consul.
3. He has been made consul.
4. He will become consul.
5. After he had been made consul he departed from the city.

Exercise 6. 18

Revision. Translate into Latin:

1. After the Roman forces had captured the citadel they put the enemy to flight.
2. So many soldiers had been killed that the rest were forced to accept peace.
3. The Roman general hated the enemy to such an extent that he destroyed all their buildings.
4. After this had been done, the Carthaginian race never again terrified the Romans.
5. After Carthage had been destroyed, Rome ruled so many peoples that it became the greatest city.

Exercise 6. 19

Revision. Translate into English:

1. *Rōmānī tam superbī fīēbant ut omnēs eōs timērent.*
2. *cum Rōmānī Poenōs superāvissent, urbem eōrum idcircō dēlēvērunt nē ab eīs iterum vincerentur.*
3. *dominus quīdam vīllam suam idcircō incendit nē ā Poenīs caperētur.*
4. *tot fēminae et virī Rōmam ductī[1] sunt ut plūrimī servī in urbe adessent.*
5. *cīvis Rōmānus, nōmine Tiberius Gracchus, servōs adeō timēbat ut īn senātum festīnāverit et patrēs[2] monuerit.*
6. *agrōs cīvibus dare idcircō volēbat ut illī rūrī habitāre possent.*
7. *frāter quoque eius, nōmine Gāius, cīvēs adiuvāre cupiēbat.*
8. *hic, tamen, multīs cum amīcīs idcircō mortuus est nē mōrēs Rōmānōrum dēlērentur.*
9. *sapientia Rōmānōrum maxima erat; sapientia nostra, tamen, minima est!*
10. *hostibus victīs, mīles fortis dux factus est.*

1. Where the subject consists of nouns of different genders, the adjective generally agrees with the masculine rather than the feminine. However it also frequently agrees with the *nearest* noun.
2. The senators (or patricians) were often referred to as *patrēs* as a mark of respect.

Usîng Latin

Fīat lūx
Fīat lūx = let there be light!

The 3rd (and final) Punic War

Although they had twice defeated her in war, Rome continued to consider the Carthaginians to be a threat to their domination of the western Mediterranean. In 150 B.C. they took exception to the fact that Carthage was re-arming, considering this to be an infringement of the treaty of 201. In particular, a certain Marcus Cato ranted on and on about how the Carthaginians were not to be trusted and should be destroyed, once and for all. *"Dēlenda est Carthāgō"* he said at the end of every speech. You, of course, may not have the first idea what that means, not yet having reached the chapter on gerundives (a treat in store, if ever there was one), but the Romans did. "Carthage must be destroyed," he said, and in due course Carthage *was* destroyed. Embassies were sent, demanding further payments and insisting that the people of Carthage leave their city and go to live in some remote, inland area in Tunisia! This did not fit in with their plans and, having at first complied with the Roman demands, they suddenly did a "u-turn" and prepared for war. They fortified their city and raised an army.

The Romans pitched up in 149 but were unable to make any head-way. The Carthaginian defences were too strong to break through, and they found their own supply-lines constantly being attacked by Carthaginian guerrillas (soldiers, not monkeys!). The people of Rome, as so often, grew impatient and in 147 they sent Publius Cornelius Scipio Aemilianus, the adopted grandson of the famous Scipio Africanus, to sort things out. He launched a ferocious attack on the Carthaginian city, broke through the outer defences, and then, in a week of hand to hand fighting, eventually cornered the survivors in the citadel. 50,000 Carthaginians were sold into slavery and the city was dismantled, stone by stone, until nothing was left but a heap of rubble. The Carthaginian threat was finally at an end.

So you really want to learn Latin...

Exercise 6. 20

Read the information on the left-hand page about the 3rd Punic War and then answer the following questions in complete sentences:

1. Why did Rome continue to distrust Carthage?

2. In which year did the Romans notice that the Carthaginians were re-arming, contravening the treaty of 201 B.C?

3. Which Roman citizen was particularly insistent that Carthage should be destroyed?

4. Which demand of the Romans seemed particularly silly, and led the Carthaginians to prepare for war?

5. Whom did the Romans send in 147 B.C. to sort out the war in Carthage?

6. How many Carthaginians were captured at the end and what happened to them?

7. What happened to the city itself?

8. What is the meaning of the phrase "*dēlenda est Carthāgō*"?

Revision

You would be amazed at how many people find that, once they have started learning really complicated things, they forget all the easy bits. Don't allow this to happen to you! Just check, for example, that you can say by heart, swinging upside down or otherwise:

- *mēnsa*
- *annus* and *bellum*
- *rēx* and *opus*
- *cīvis* and *cubīle*
- *gradus* and *rēs*
- *trīstis*

- *quī, quae, quod*
- *hic, haec, hoc*
- *is, ea, id*
- *ille, illa, illud*
- *amō* all indicative tenses, active and passive
- *regō* all indicative tenses, active and passive

Answer to puer mālum ēst on p. 64

Clearly this does not mean "the boy is bad". The Latin for that would be *puer malus est*. *Puer mālum ēst* = "the boy eats an apple", with *mālum* being a neuter noun like *bellum* and *ēst* coming from *edō*, not *sum*.

Using Latin

Ex officiō

A position, for example on a committee, is sometimes held *ex officiō*, i.e. by virtue of one's office. E.g. the Archbishop of Canterbury might be an *ex officiō* governor of a school in Canterbury.

CHAPTER 7

Indirect command; indirect question; quī + the subjunctive

Indirect Command

You have already met *direct* commands and prohibitions, using the imperative for commands and *nōlī/nōlīte* + infinitive (or *nē* + the perfect subjunctive) for prohibitions. *Indirect* commands are introduced by verbs of ordering, warning, begging, advising, forbidding and the like, and are generally expressed using *ut* + the subjunctive (for commands) or *nē* + the subjunctive (for prohibitions). As ever, our old friend the sequence of tenses applies.

E.g. He advised him to come = *eum monuit ut venīret.*

E.g. He has advised them not to come = *eōs monuit nē veniant.*

Verbs taking this construction include: *rogō* = I ask; *ōrō* = I beg; *hortor* = I encourage; *moneō* = I advise; *imperō* (+ dat.) = I order; *persuādeō* (+ dat.) = I persuade; *petō* = I seek*.

E.g. *mihĭ persuāsit ut venīrem* = "he persuaded me to come" (lit. = he persuaded me that I might come).

E.g. *cōpiās suās hortātus est ut hostēs aggrederentur* = "he encouraged his forces to attack the enemy" (lit. = he encouraged his forces that they might attack the enemy).

* Note that the verb *petō* = "I seek" may be used to mean "I ask" or "I beg".

E.g. *ā mē petīvit ut venīrem* = "he asked me to come" (lit. = he sought from me that I might come).

Vocabulary 7

Verbs

imperō, -āre, -āvī, -ātum (+ dat.)	I order
mereor, -ērī, meritus sum	I deserve, earn
neglegō, -ere, neglēxī, neglēctum	I neglect
opprimō, -ere, oppressī, oppressum	I overwhelm, oppress
ōrō, -āre, -āvī, -ātum	I pray, beg
pereō, perīre, periī, peritum (goes like *eō*)	I die
rapiō, rapere, rapuī, raptum	I seize
sepeliō, -īre, sepelīvī, sepultum	I bury
supersum, superesse, superfuī (+ dat., goes like *sum*)	I survive, outlive
vēndō, -ere, vēndidī, vēnditum	I sell
vetō, -āre, vetuī, vetitum	I forbid

Nouns

dīvitiae, -ārum, f. pl.	riches, wealth
inimīcus, -ī, m.	personal enemy
quiēs, quiētis, f.	quiet, rest
sanguis, sanguinis, m.	blood
scelus, sceleris, n.	crime
terror, terrōris, m.	terror
turba, -ae, f.	crowd

Adjectives

scelerātus, -a, -um	wicked
scelestus, -a, -um	wicked

Adverb

num	whether, if

So you really want to learn Latin...

Exercise 7. 1
Study the information on the left-hand page about indirect commands. Note that, when using the *ut/nē* (+ subjunctive) construction, you must observe the sequence of tenses. Then translate into Latin:

1. He ordered (using *imperō*) the slave to come home.
2. He ordered (using *imperō*) the soldiers to fight.
3. They advised us not to come home.
4. They ordered us (using *imperō*) to fight.
5. The slave begged (i.e. "sought from", using *petō*) his master to send the boys home.
6. The general has ordered (using *imperō*) his forces to build a camp.
7. The enemy have encouraged us to flee.
8. He advised me to remain.
9. Why have we been asked (using *rogō*) to fight?
10. Who ordered you (using *imperō*) to return to the city, girls?

Exercise 7. 2
Translate into English (remembering to observe the sequence of tenses where appropriate):

1. *Rēgulus Rōmānīs imperāvit ut cum hostibus iterum pugnārent.*
2. *impetū factō, imperātor suīs imperāvit ut regrederentur.*
3. *amīcō meō persuāsī ut apud mātrem suam habitet.*
4. *nōs monuērunt ut cōnsilium capiāmus.*
5. *dux suīs persuāsit nē tot sagittīs ūterentur.*
6. *magister puerōs parvōs monuit ut timōrem cēlārent.*
7. *intereā lēgātus ā senātū petēbat ut captīvī līberārentur.*
8. *nōnnūllī cīvēs rēgem monuērunt ut pugnāret.*
9. *Hannibal suās cōpiās hortātus est ut in Rōmānōs impetum facerent.*
10. *hic mīles, ā Poenīs missus, senātum ōrāvit nē pācem faceret.*

Exercise 7. 3
Study the words in Vocabulary 7. From which Latin words do the following derive? Translate the Latin word and explain the meaning of the English one:

1. Rapt
2. Neglect
3. Sanguine
4. Merit
5. Vendor
6. Perish
7. Adoration
8. Inimical
9. Oppressive
10. Quiet

	Vetō
Using Latin	If one puts a *veto* on something, one forbids or bans it. In Latin, *vetō* = I forbid.

More on indirect command

You have already learnt how to cope with indirect commands using *ut/nē* (+ subjunctive). But *some* verbs of ordering take a simple infinitive (as in English). These are:
  iubeō = I order; *vetō* = I forbid; *volō* = I want; *nōlō* = I do not want; *prohibeō* = I prevent, prohibit; *cōgō* = I compel; *cupiō* = I desire.
E.g. He ordered me to come = *mē iussit venīre.*
E.g. He ordered me not to come = *mē vetuit venīre.*

This construction is obviously very much easier than the other one. However, the complication is that you now have to learn which verb takes which construction.

N.B. It is worth pointing out that, when in English we say "tell", we often mean "order". E.g. "He *told* him to do it" (i.e. "He *ordered* him to do it") = *eum iussit id facere.*

The man in the moon

There is a rather wonderful rule which is *generally* observed, namely that a prepositional phrase in Latin must not be dependent on any part of speech other than a verb. It is thus not possible, in Latin, to talk about "the man in the moon", because the phrase "in the moon" would be dependent on a noun ("the man"), whereas it can only correctly be dependent on a verb. To get around this little problem, we have to introduce a verb for the prepositional phrase to be dependent upon. For example, we could change "the man in the moon" into "the man **who lives** in the moon" (= *homŏ quī in lūnā habitat*).

Consider the following sentence: *oppidum prope flūmen oppugnāvērunt.*
Tempting as it may be to translate this as "they attacked the town near the river", we know that it cannot quite mean that, because of our "man in the moon" rule. The prepositional phrase *prope flūmen* has to be dependent on the **verb *oppugnāvērunt***, and thus it follows that it is not that "the town was near the river", which would have made *prope flūmen* dependent on the *noun*, *oppidum*, but that "they attacked near the river". Subtle stuff but, hey, we're going to the top!

So you really want to learn Latin...

Exercise 7. 4
Study the information on the left-hand page about indirect commands. Notice how some verbs take the *ut/nē* (+ the subjunctive) construction, and some take a simple infinitive. Now translate into Latin:

1. He ordered me to come to Rome (using *iubeō*).
2. He ordered me not to come to Rome (using *vetō*).
3. He wanted me to remain in the countryside (using *volō*).
4. They did not want me to fight with the Carthaginians (using *nōlō*).
5. The king prevented him from escaping (using *prohibeō*).

Exercise 7. 5
Translate into English:

1. *dux imperāvit mīlitibus ut aciēs in eō locō īnstruerētur.*
2. *cōnsul mīlitēs iussit aciem īnstruere.*
3. *cīvēs Rōmānī mē monuērunt nē id facerem.*
4. *hōc audītō, puellam iussimus domum quam celerrimē currere.*
5. *pater vetuit puerōs librōs magistrī legere.*

Exercise 7. 6
Study the information on the left-hand page about the man in the moon. Then translate into Latin, being sure that you do not make any prepositional phrases dependent on a part of speech other than a verb.

1. The girls in the street were very beautiful.
2. He pitched camp near the river.
3. We knew the farmers in the field.
4. The swords on the table terrified the girl.
5. Hannibal defeated the Romans near the town.

Exercise 7. 7
Translate into English, making it very clear that you understand the importance of the "man in the moon" rule. The first one has been done for you.

1. *puellam prope tabernam spectāvit* = "He watched the girl *while he was* near the inn". (This shows that *prope tabernam* is dependent on *spectāvit*, not on *puellam*. In other words it was the "*watching*" that was going on "near the inn", rather than that "the *girl*" was "near the inn".)
2. *Rōmulus urbem prope flūmen vīdit.*
3. *cōpiās in campō Hannibal dēlēvit.*
4. *cōnsul deōs īn forō laudāvit.*
5. *omnēs sonitum in vīllā audiēbant.*

Q.V.
The letters *q.v.*, often found in dictionaries, indexes and foot-notes, stand for *quod vidē* = "which see" (i.e. look this up, too).
E.g. "He was the son of Hamilcar, *q.v.*"

Indirect Question

You already know how to cope with direct questions in Latin. But, just as a statement (e.g. "he is fighting") may be reported indirectly (e.g. "they said that he was fighting"), so questions can be reported indirectly. Thus a direct question such as "why is he fighting?" may be reported indirectly as "they asked why he was fighting".

1. Indirect questions are introduced by an interrogative word and have their verb in the subjunctive (using the same *tense* as in English).

E.g. They asked him why he was fighting = *eum rogāvērunt cūr pugnāret.*
E.g. They asked him why he had fought = *eum rogāvērunt cūr pugnāvisset.*

2. The verb which introduces the indirect question need not necessarily be a verb of "asking".

E.g. He *knew* why he was fighting = *sciēbat cūr pugnāret.*
   N.B. the verb *quaerō* = "I seek" is often used with a preposition such as *ā/ab* to mean "I ask" (literally "I seek from").
E.g. I ask the boy = *ā puerō quaerō.*

3. The English "if" in indirect questions should be translated by *num* = "whether". Try not to muddle this with the *num* you have already met, introducing a question which expects the answer "no".

E.g. He asked him **if** he was fighting = *eum rogāvit **num** pugnāret.*

4. In double or alternative indirect questions, "if...or" is translated by *utrum* followed by *an*. But if the second part of the question is negative, *utrum* is followed, not by *annōn*, as in direct questions, but by *necne*.

E.g. *rogāvit **utrum** laetus esset **an** trīstis* = he asked whether he was happy or sad.
E.g. *rogāvit **utrum** laetus esset **necne*** = he asked whether he was happy or not.

5. In the indirect question construction, there is sometimes a need to ask a question referring to the future. There is no future subjunctive in Latin, but a sort of "made-up" subjunctive may be formed by adding the subjunctive of *sum* to the future participle of the verb you are using. The *present* subjunctive is added where the main verb is *primary*, the *imperfect* subjunctive where the main verb is *historic*. (By the way, this hotch-potch is called a **periphrastic** tense; now *that's* a word to try out on your friends and relations!)

E.g. We ask what he will do = *rogāmus quid factūrus sit.*
   We asked what he would do = *rogāvimus quid factūrus esset.*

Compound verbs: a note on spelling

A compound verb, as you know, consists of a simple verb with a prefix added on, e.g. *adveniō, exeō*, etc. Where the simple verb is spelt with an *a*, however, the compound verb will generally have an *i*. Thus *accipiō* from *capiō, cōnficiō* from *faciō*, etc. Knowing this simple little rule will help you to identify the basic meaning of a whole range of compound verbs which you might not otherwise have recognised.

So you really want to learn Latin...

Exercise 7. 8
Study the information on the left-hand page about indirect questions. Translate into English:

1. *omnēs sciēbant cūr cīvis, nōmine Sulla, Rōmam advēnisset.*
2. *cīvēs <u>inter sē rogābant</u>* quid factūrī essent.*
3. *Rōmānī quaerēbant num Sulla omnēs inimīcos interfectūrus esset.*
4. *Sulla ā cīvibus quaerēbat cūr in bellō pugnāvissent.*
5. *nōnne scīre vīs quandō̆ ille Rōmam reditūrus sit?*
6. *puella frātrem rogāvit utrum timēret necne.*
7. *senem rogāvit utrum domum festīnātūrus esset an rūrī mānsūrus.*
8. *ā puerō quaerimus utrum templa vīderit necne.*
9. *dux suōs rogāvit utrum castra prope flūmen an īn silvā positūrī essent.*
10. *nesciēbat utrum Rōmānī an Poenī victōriam peperissent.*

* *inter sē rogābant* = "They asked between themselves", i.e. "They asked each other".

Exercise 7. 9
Translate into Latin:

1. We asked why he had come.
2. We want to learn who has arrived.
3. They know why he was killed.
4. I will ask him when he is going to depart.
5. I asked the general how many soldiers he had led into the battle.
6. We asked the old men if they had seen the battle or not.
7. You (pl.) will ask your mother whether she wishes to go home or stay in Rome.
8. He did not know whether the Romans or the enemy had pitched their camp near the town.
9. We do not know if you love the man or not.
10. They asked the farmer whether he had led his cows into the field or into the wood.

Exercise 7. 10
Translate into English: *The Italian wars, 91-83 B.C.*
gentēs Ītaliae, Poenīs victīs, senātuī Rōmānō pārēre nōlēbant. Mariō igitur duce, cōpiae Rōmānae cum incolīs Ītaliae bellum gerēbant. Marius, multīs victōriīs partīs, senātum ōrāvit ut ipse exercitum Rōmānum diūtius dūceret. senātus, tamen, quod tantum imperium Mariō dare timēbat, alterī ducī, nōmine L. Porciō Catōnī, imperāvit ut ille sōlus Rōmānōs dūceret.

hic Catō, quī eō tempore cōnsul erat, nōn erat perītus bellī nec hostēs superāre poterat. senātus igitur tandem <u>suffrāgium</u> incolīs dare coāctus est.

* *suffrāgium, -ī*, n. = the vote, franchise.

Cēterīs paribus
Cēterīs paribus is an ablative absolute meaning "with the rest (being) equal". In English, we say "all things being equal".

Quī plus the subjunctive

1.   A *quī* clause may be used to express purpose, with the relative pronoun (followed by the subjunctive) standing in place of *ut*.

E.g. He sent soldiers to attack the town (lit. "who might attack the town") =
   *mīlitēs mīsit **quī** oppidum **oppugnārent**.*

E.g. He drew up his forces to attack the city =
   *cōpiās īnstrūxit **quae** urbem **oppugnārent**.*

2.   If a final clause contains a comparative, *quō* (= "by which") is used in place of *ut*.

E.g. *mīlitēs mīsit **quō** facilius oppidum **caperet*** = "He sent soldiers in order more easily to capture the town" (lit. = by which more easily he might capture the town).

3.   *Quī* (+ the subjunctive) may be used to mean "of such a kind that", normally after the phrases *is quī, dignus quī* and *est/sunt quī* (when these are used *indefinitely*):

E.g. *nōn sum is quī inimīcōs meōs interficiam* = "I am not one to kill my enemies" (lit. = of such a kind that I may kill my enemies).

E.g. *dignus est quī regat* = "he is worthy to rule" (lit. = he is worthy, of such a kind that he may rule).

E.g. *sunt quī perīcula bellī timeant* = "there are some who fear the dangers of war" (lit. = of such a kind that they fear the dangers of war).

N.B. in this last example, the "some" are *indefinite* (i.e. we do not have particular people in mind).   If we were referring to *definite* people, the verb would be in the indicative.

Mounting his horse...

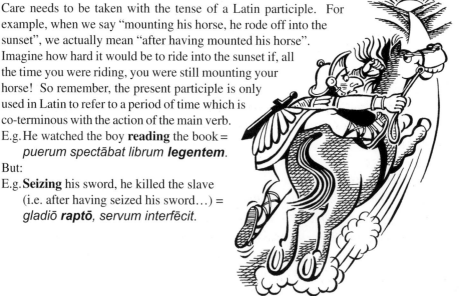

Care needs to be taken with the tense of a Latin participle.   For example, when we say "mounting his horse, he rode off into the sunset", we actually mean "after having mounted his horse". Imagine how hard it would be to ride into the sunset if, all the time you were riding, you were still mounting your horse!   So remember, the present participle is only used in Latin to refer to a period of time which is co-terminous with the action of the main verb.

E.g. He watched the boy **reading** the book =
   *puerum spectābat librum **legentem**.*
But:
E.g. **Seizing** his sword, he killed the slave
   (i.e. after having seized his sword...) =
   *gladiō **raptō**, servum interfēcit.*

So you really want to learn Latin...

Exercise 7. 11
Study the information on the left-hand page about *quī* (+ the subjunctive). Then translate into English:

1. *puerōs in urbem mīsit quī pānem emerent.*
2. *cōnsul mīlitēs in vīllam senis mīsit quī dīvitiās eius raperent.*
3. *fēmina trīstis iuvenēs mīsit quī senem sepelīrent.*
4. *dux impetum in hostēs faciet quō facilius eōs superet.*
5. *sunt quī perīcula urbis semper timeant.*

Exercise 7. 12
Translate into Latin, using *quī* or *quō* (+ the subjunctive) where appropriate:

1. They have sent messengers to announce the victory to the Roman people.
2. He seized the sword so that he might more easily kill the guards.
3. Hannibal is worthy to conquer the Romans.
4. There are those who always oppress their friends.
5. He is not one to neglect the customs of his fatherland.

Exercise 7. 13
Study the information on the left-hand page about "mounting his horse". Then translate into Latin:

1. Seizing the judge's riches, he fled into the woods.
2. Burying his sister near the river, he returned home with his friends.
3. He walked through the streets of the town, singing a beautiful song.
4. Coming down* from the mountains, the Carthaginians attacked the camp of the Romans.
5. Calling his men quickly to arms, the consul ordered them to attack the enemy.

*N.B. If the verb can not be put into the correct tense of the participle, (one cannot say in Latin "having come down"), one has to change the construction completely and say "after they had come down".

Exercise 7. 14
Translate into English:

1. *armīs relictīs, hostēs ā Rōmānīs fūgērunt.*
2. *vīnō raptō, agricola ē tabernā festīnāvit.*
3. *scelere ab omnibus neglēctō, cīvis scelerātus domum rediit.*
4. *dīvitiīs ab hostibus raptīs, senex vīllam suam vēndere coāctus est.*
5. *urbe captā, omnēs cīvēs periērunt.*

Using Latin

Per ardua ad astra
The motto of the Royal Air Force, this means "through lofty places (or difficulties) to the stars".

More about dum

As you know, *dum* = "while". However, it has two other meanings:

(a) *dum* (or *dummodo*) + subjunctive = "provided that".

E.g. *magnō timōre mē līberābis* **dum** *inimīcōs meōs* **interficiās** = "you will free me from a great fear provided that you kill my enemies".

(b) *dum* = "until".

When *dum* = "until", it has its verb in the indicative when it refers to the past, but in the subjunctive when it refers to the future.

E.g. *īn senātū fuit* **dum** *senātus* **dīmissus est** = "he was in the senate until the senate was dismissed".

E.g. *exspectāmus* **dum** *hostēs urbem* **oppugnent** = "we are waiting for the enemy to attack the city".

E.g. *exspectābāmus* **dum** *hostēs urbem* **oppugnārent** = "we were waiting for the enemy to attack the city".

Revision of constructions

You have now met a wide range of constructions and should ensure that you are familiar with them all. Each one has its own little formula (e.g. *ut/nē* + subjunctive), and you need to be able both to recognise them in Latin and use them correctly when writing Latin yourself. A very brief outline is given below:

- **Relative clauses**: the relative pronoun takes its gender and number from the antecedent but its case from its meaning in the relative clause.
- **Ablative absolute**: a noun or pronoun in the ablative with a participle in agreement; it must not be connected in any way to the main verb.
- **Indirect statement**: accusative and infinitive. Negative indirect statements are introduced by *negō* = I deny.
- **Final clauses**: *ut/nē* (+ subjunctive) to express purpose.
- **Consecutive clauses**: a "so" word followed by *ut/ut nōn* (+ subjunctive) to express result.
- **Causal clauses**: these refer to cause and are introduced by *quod* or *quia* (+ the indicative) or *cum* (+ the subjunctive).
- **Temporal clauses**: these refer to time and generally have their verb in the indicative, except when some notion other than time (e.g. purpose) is introduced.
- **Indirect command**: *ut/nē* (+ subjunctive) except after verbs which, like *iubeō* and *vetō*, take an infinitive.
- **Indirect question**: questioning word (+ subjunctive).

Note also:

- **The sequence of tenses**: if the main verb is primary, the subjunctive verb must be primary; if the main verb is historic, the subjunctive verb must be historic.

A thorough knowledge of all of these constructions is essential to accurate translation. If ever you are having trouble with a piece of Latin, ask yourself "which construction is being used?" and very often the Latin will immediately become much more clear.

So you really want to learn Latin...

Exercise 7. 15

Study the information on the left-hand page about *dum*. Then translate into English:

1. *dum ambulat, subitō vōcem audīvit.*
2. *tē hūc venīre volumus dum paucōs diēs maneās.*
3. *Rōmānī fortiter pugnāvērunt dum proelium cōnfectum est.*
4. *Rōmānī prope flūmen exspectāvērunt dum hostēs redīrent.*
5. *dum poēta scrībēbat, servī cantābant.*

Exercise 7. 16

Translate into English: *Sulla retires into private life, 79 B.C.*

hostibus tandem superātīs, Sulla plūrimōs cīvēs interfēcit nē ab eīs opprimerētur. populum Rōmānum adeō terrēbat ut tandem omnēs inimīcī eius domī manēre nōllent. hic enim custōdibus suīs imperāvit ut inimīcōs captōs, dīvitiīs eōrum raptīs, caederent. saepe rogābat quis Marium adiūvisset. tum custōdēs iussī sunt eōs cīvēs petere et interficere.

posteā Sulla dictātor factus est. trēs annōs rēs urbis agēbat dum tandem ex urbe ēgressus in Campāniam ad vīllam suam iit ut quiēte rūrī fruerētur.

fruor, fruī, frūctus sum (+ abl.) = I enjoy

Exercise 7. 17

At this stage you know so many different constructions that half the battle consists of working out which construction you are supposed to be using. Always decide which construction you should be using before trying to translate anything into Latin. Never just translate the sentences word by word, without thinking about the overall sense. You may find the revision of constructions on the left-hand page useful. Now translate into Latin:

1. We asked him why so many citizens had perished at Rome.
2. He said that Sulla had entered the city and captured his enemies.
3. They had begged him not to overwhelm the old men, but in vain.
4. So many men were killed that soon Sulla ruled alone in Rome.
5. He urged the inhabitants of Italy to help the Romans.
6. We all knew why he wished their help.
7. Having captured the city he told his guards to seize the citizens' riches.
8. Those who were unwilling to obey Sulla perished.
9. Sulla's enemies* fled from the city lest they be killed.
10. Who knows if the citizens will overcome this wicked man?

* N.B. Use *inimīcus* for "enemy" when it means a "personal enemy"; hostis should be used to refer to an "enemy of the state".

Passim

Passim = "here and there" is often found in foot-notes, indexes etc., when reference is made to a word or name which occurs over and over again.

Rome at war, home and away

After ridding themselves of the Carthaginian threat, the Romans turned elsewhere for their daily excitement. Between 111 and 105 B.C. they amused themselves with a little war against Jugurtha, the king of Numidia. Jugurtha had driven his brother from the throne and seized it for himself, and the brother was not wildly happy about it. The Romans sent an army under a chap called Marius and he sorted things out, capturing Jugurtha and bringing him back to Rome in chains. After this success, Marius persuaded the senate that the army needed to be expanded and reformed and he accordingly trotted around, making the soldiers carry huge packs around the countryside and dig large ditches. "Marius's mules", as they came to be called, turned into such a fearsome fighting machine that the Romans felt able to take on anyone and everyone.

However, in 91 B.C. the people of Italy started kicking up a fuss about being pushed around by the Romans. Marius marched around a bit, beating them up and so forth, but the senate grew nervous about the extent of his power and so gave the command of the army to a fool called Lucius Porcius Cato. Cato fouled things up pretty spectacularly, losing a succession of battles against various hot and bothered Italians. As a result, large areas of Italy were able successfully to claim the privileges of Roman citizenship which they had been demanding.

Once the rebellious Italians had been brought to order, albeit at the cost of granting them Roman citizenship, civil war broke out among the Romans themselves. The first to march on Rome was Cornelius Sulla, a bitter rival of Marius, and he lost no time in reversing the grants of citizenship and outlawing Marius. In 87 B.C. the consul Cornelius Cinna sought to restore the grants, and when he was driven out of Rome by the mob he raised an army of Italian peasants, joined up with the exiled Marius, and then re-entered Rome at the head of his motley force. There followed a bloody reign of terror, with the aristocratic opponents of Cinna and Marius being executed. Between 86 and 84 B.C. some sort of peace was restored in Rome but this only lasted while Sulla was away in the east, fighting king Mithridates of Pontus. When he returned in 83 B.C. civil war broke out again in earnest and by 80 B.C. he had defeated Marius and was in sole charge of the Roman world. He held the office of dictator for three years, but then, after a bloody purge of his enemies, during which it wasn't safe to show one's face in the street in case one of Sulla's thugs were to rearrange it, Sulla suddenly laid down his office and retired into private life. This decision then became a standard debating topic in the Roman schools of rhetoric, with boys being expected to justify or condemn Sulla's decision to retire to his hammock.

So you really want to learn Latin...

Exercise 7. 18

Read the information on the left-hand page about Italy at war. Then answer the following questions in complete sentences:

1. With whom did the Romans fight between 111 and 105 B.C.?

2. What had this gentleman done to upset his brother?

3. Who led the Roman army in the war that resulted and who won?

4. Who or what were "Marius's mules"?

5. Why did the Roman senate not wish Marius to continue leading the army when the Italians revolted?

6. Who took over the command of the army, and how successful was he?

7. What concession did the Italians manage to win as a result of the war?

8. When Sulla marched into Rome, which two steps did he take?

9. What happened in 87 B.C.?

10. What happened in 83 B.C. when Sulla returned to Rome after fighting with King Mithridates?

11. Which office did Sulla hold for three years, and how pleasant was life for the people of Rome while he held it?

12. Why do you think Sulla eventually decided to retire into private life?

	Nēm. con.
Using Latin	*Nēm. con.* is an abbreviation from *nēmŏ* = "no one" and *contrādīcō* = "I contradict". It means "unanimously".

CHAPTER 8

Conditional sentences; concessive clauses; verbs of fearing; price and value; defective verbs

A conditional sentence is made up of a *protasis*, in which we state the condition, and an *apodosis*, in which we state the result of the condition. There are three main types of conditional sentence: simple, improbable and impossible.

Simple conditions

In a simple (or open) condition nothing is assumed about how likely or unlikely the fulfilment of the condition may be. In these sentences, the **indicative** is used in both the protasis and the apodosis.

E.g. If you are well, I am happy = *sī valēs, laetus sum.*

E.g. If you come you will see him = *sī vēneris, eum vidēbis.*

N.B. When we say "if you come", we are referring to the future. In the protasis of such conditions, the *future perfect* is regularly used. The *future* is generally reserved for threats.

E.g. If you come here, I will kill you = *sī hūc veniēs, tē interficiam.*

Improbable conditions

In an improbable condition, it is assumed that the fulfilment of the condition, while possible, is unlikely. In these sentences the **present subjunctive** is used in both the protasis and the apodosis. In English, the words "would" or "should" will appear.

E.g. If you were to come, he would kill you = *sī veniās, tē interficiat.*

The English doesn't help here, since, instead of "if you were to come", we often say "if you came", even though this refers to an improbable *future*. This is a deadly trap, and proves that Latin isn't the only crazy language.

Impossible conditions

In an impossible condition, it is assumed that the fulfilment of the condition is impossible. These sentences may refer either to the present or to the past. Again, "would" or "should" will appear in the English.

(a) Referring to the present

These use the **imperfect subjunctive** in both protasis and apodosis.

E.g. If you were present (i.e. but you're not) you would be singing = *sī adessēs, cantārēs.*

(b) Referring to the past

These use the **pluperfect subjunctive** in both protasis and apodosis.

E.g. If you had come (i.e. but you didn't) you would have seen me = *sī vēnissēs, mē vīdissēs.*

Negative conditions

In all types of conditional sentence, the Latin for "if...not" is *nisi* (or *nī*).

E.g. If we are not fighting = *nisi pugnāmus...*

E.g. If we had not come to Rome = *nisi Rōmam vēnissēmus...*

The word *nisi* also means "unless", which is of course effectively the same as "if...not".

So you really want to learn Latin...

Exercise 8. 1

Study the information on the left-hand page about conditional sentences. Then, for the sentences below, first identify the type of condition and then translate into Latin.

1. If you are happy, I also am happy.
2. If you were to defeat the enemy, I should praise you.
3. If you had overcome the inhabitants of Italy, you would have captured Rome.
4. If Marius were living in Rome, his enemies would be afraid.
5. If we had not defeated them, we should have fled.
6. If you were to sell your country house, you would receive much wealth.
7. If you walk as quickly as possible, you will arrive tomorrow.
8. If you had not read the letter, you would have learnt nothing about your friend.
9. Unless you come to Rome quickly, you will not see my father.
10. Unless the citizens obey the consul tomorrow, they will be punished.

Exercise 8. 2

Translate into English. Note that "should" is used for the 1st person, "would" for the 2nd and 3rd persons (cf. "shall" and "will").

1. *sī hūc veniās, mātrem meam videās.*
2. *nisi hūc vēneris, mātrem meam nōn vidēbis.*
3. *sī lēgātus pācem petīvisset, eum domum statim mīsissēmus.*
4. *sī meīs mīlitibus imperāveris ut oppidum oppugnent, id oppugnābunt.*
5. *sī iubeās meōs mīlitēs oppidum oppugnāre, tibĭ nōn pāreant.*
6. *Rōmānī hostēs superāvissent, nisi eī castra prope flūmen posuissent.*
7. *sī agricola agrōs bene parāvisset, nōs omnēs cibum habuissēmus.*
8. *nisi labōrābitis, cīvēs pauperēs, frūmentum habēre nōn poteritis.*
9. *diū vīvēs, sī inimīcōs tuōs pessimōs vītāveris.*
10. *sī hūc prīmā lūce vēneris, nautās ē portū nāvigantēs vidēbis.*

Exercise 8. 3

Translate into Latin:

Once upon a time a Roman general called Sulla wished to rule in Rome. If he had been defeated by Marius, he would not have killed so many citizens. However, having entered the city, he commanded everyone to obey him and ordered his guards to put all his personal enemies to death. The rest lived in terror since they did not know whether he would kill them or not[1]. He would perhaps have become a king if he had stayed in Rome any longer[2]. But, having set out for the countryside, he returned to his villa and lived there for many years.

1. See rule for double indirect questions on page 72, note 4. 2. *diūtius*

Ā priōrī

Ā priōrī (an old form of *priōre*) = "from (the thing) before".
If one reasons *ā priōrī*, one does so from first principles.

Mixed conditions

Huge fun can be had from conditional sentences which appear to have got mixed up. For example, an impossible condition may have a protasis which refers to the past but an apodosis which refers to the present.

E.g. If you had come, I would now be happy = *sī vēnissēs, laetus nunc essem.*

This is called a mixed condition. In this example the protasis has its verb in the pluperfect subjunctive (because it refers to what did not happen *in the past*) and the apodosis has its verb in the imperfect subjunctive (because it refers to what is not happening now, *in the present*).

Annōs nātus

When giving someone's age, the normal formula is to give the number of years in the accusative (for "time how long") followed by the participle *nātus* = "having been born".

E.g. He is two years old = *duōs annōs nātus est.*

E.g. She is five years old = *quīnque annōs nāta est.*

Quam = how!

The adverb *quam* may be used to mean "how!", in the sense of "how glad I am", or "how quickly she runs".

E.g. How glad I am to see you = *quam laetus tē videō!*

E.g. How quickly she runs = *quam celeriter currit!*

No doubt the Romans would have used this little word to greet the Red Indians, had they got that far!

Vocabulary 8

Verbs		**Adjectives**	
canō, canere, cecinī, cantum	I sing	*ācer, ācris, ācre*	fierce, keen, spirited
caveō, -ēre, cāvī, cautum	I am cautious (of)	*annōs nātus*	*x* years old
cōnspiciō, -ere, cōnspexī, cōnspectum	I catch sight of	*armātus, -a, -um*	armed
		benignus, -a, -um	kind
custōdiō, -īre, -īvī, -ītum	I guard	*dūrus, -a, -um*	hard
tollō, tollere, sustulī, sublātum	I raise, lift, remove	**Adverbs**	
		adhūc	still
Nouns		*quam* (+ adjective or adverb)	how...!
adventus, -ūs, m.	arrival		
aquila, -ae, f.	eagle	*totiēns*	so often
barba, -ae, f.	beard	*ut* (+ indicative)	as
bona, -ōrum, n. pl.	goods	**Conjunction**	
ferrum, -ī, n.	iron, sword	*nisi* (or *nī*)	if...not, unless
mŏra, -ae, f.	delay		

So you really want to learn Latin...

Exercise 8. 4

Study the information on the left-hand page about mixed conditions. Then translate into Latin the following, being sure to identify the condition type as you go. Some of these, but not all, are mixed conditions.

1. If you had caught sight of the enemy yesterday, we would have driven them out of the country.
2. If he had lived, he would now be an old man.
3. The enemy would still be here now, if you had not warned the general about their arrival.*
4. I would have seized his beard, if he had said that to me!*
5. We will kill you with our swords, if you enter the camp.*
6. If the enemy were to capture our eagles, we would not be able to return home.

* N.B. In conditional sentences, both in Latin and in English, the apodosis is often stated *before* the protasis.

Exercise 8. 5

Study the information on the left-hand page about *annōs nātus* and *quam*. Then translate into English:

1. *fīlia mea septendecim annōs nāta est.*
2. *quot annōs nātus est pater tuus?*
3. *quam laetus sim, sī carmen illud iterum canās!*
4. *bona tua capiet, nisi cavēbis.*
5. *adhūc vīveret, nisi in pugnam sōlus ruisset.*
6. *mīlitem illum num aquilam custōdīre vellet rogāvimus.*
7. *quam ācrēs essent equitēs hostium, sī eīs nostrōs equōs vēndidissēmus!*
8. *sī fāmam cupīvisset, diūtius in Africā bellum gessisset.*
9. *sī pater meus benignior sit, fortasse Rōmam veniam.*
10. *corpus eius sepeliam, sī interfectus erit.*

Exercise 8. 6

Study the words in Vocabulary 8. From which Latin words do the following derive? Translate the Latin word and explain the meaning of the English one:

1. Moratorium	6.	Cautious
2. Advent	7.	Canticle
3. Barber	8.	Durable
4. Conspicuous	9.	Aquiline
5. Benign	10.	Custodian

Using Latin

Mea culpa
If you wish to admit to having made a mistake, this is quite a good way of doing so. *Mea culpa* = my fault.

Concessive clauses

Concessive clauses are introduced by conjunctions meaning "although" or "even if".
E.g. "although it was raining" or "even if it had been raining".
1. If the concession is agreed to be a **fact**, the verb goes in the indicative and the Latin for "although" is *quamquam.*
E.g. *quamquam festīnās, hostēs nōn capiēs* = "although you are hurrying, you will not catch the enemy".
2. If, however, the concession is accepted only as a **hypothesis**, for the sake of argument, the verb goes in the subjunctive and the Latin for "although" is *quamvīs.*
E.g. *mīlitēs fortēs, quamvīs perīcula bellī timeant, prō patriā semper pugnant* = "brave soldiers, although they (i.e. however much they) fear the dangers of war, always fight for their fatherland".
3. The Latin for "even if" is *etsī* or *etiamsī* which may be used either with the indicative or the subjunctive, following the normal rules for conditional clauses.
E.g. *etsī laetus es/sīs* = "even if you are/were to be happy".

Predicative dative

With a limited number of abstract nouns (the most common of which are given below), the verb *sum* is often followed by a complement in the *dative* case (rather than the nominative).

auxiliō esse = to be helpful	*odiō esse* = to be hateful
cūrae esse = to be an anxiety	*onerī esse* = to be a burden
dēdecorī esse = to be disgraceful	*praesidiō esse* = to be a protection
dolōrī esse = to cause grief	*salūtī esse* = to be the salvation
honōrī esse = to be an honour	*ūsuī esse* = to be useful

Verbs of fearing

So far, after verbs of fearing, you have always used a simple infinitive (e.g. "he is afraid to fight" = *pugnāre timet*). But if one is afraid of what **someone else** may be up to, then one uses *nē* or *nē nōn* (+ the subjunctive).
1. If (as is normally the case) the fear relates to the **future**, the subordinate verb goes in the present subjunctive after a primary main verb or the imperfect subjunctive after a historic main verb.
E.g. He is afraid that the enemy may/will come = *timet nē hostēs veniant.*
E.g. He was afraid that the enemy might/would not come = *timēbat nē hostēs nōn venīrent.*
2. If, however, the fear relates to the **present** or the **past**, the subordinate verb, while still subjunctive, will be in the same *tense* as in the English*.
E.g. *timet nē advēnerit* = "He is afraid that they have arrived".
E.g. *timuit nē advēnissent* = "He was afraid that they had arrived".
*N.B. In the case of fears for the present, this has the undesirable effect of producing the occasional ambiguity, but the context will normally make the meaning obvious.
E.g. *timet nē veniant* = "He is afraid that they are coming/will come".

So you really want to learn Latin...

Exercise 8. 7
Study the information on the left-hand page about concessive clauses. Note carefully the difference between those which require a verb in the subjunctive and those which do not. Then translate into Latin:

1. Although we have defeated the enemy, the citizens now fear their own army.
2. We will never fear the enemy, although they may be brave in war.
3. Even if you run home now, you will not see your mother and father.
4. Even if you were to fight with him, you would not be able to overcome him.
5. Even if you had attacked the town during the night, you would not have captured it.

Exercise 8. 8
Translate into English:

1. *quamquam pugnāre volunt, nōs superāre nōn poterunt.*
2. *quamvīs pugnāre velint, nōs superāre nōn poterunt.*
3. *ad castra rediimus, quamquam hostēs nōn vīcerāmus.*
4. *in campum suōs redūxit, quamquam perīcula bellī timēbant.*
5. *etsī cōnsulem dēlēgissēs, nunc eum timērēs.*

Exercise 8. 9
Study the information on the left-hand page about the predicative dative. Then translate into English:

1. *quamquam pugnāre nōlunt, hostēs nōbīs odiō sunt.*
2. *quamvīs pugnāre nōlit, Hannibal cūrae Rōmānīs est.*
3. *etsī Rōmam nōn oppugnāvisset, cīvēs Rōmānī auxiliō eī nōn fuissent.*
4. *cīvibus Rōmānīs rēx semper odiō erat.*
5. *hostibus victīs, mīlitibus dux nōn iam dēdecorī erat.*

Exercise 8. 10
Study the information on the left-hand page about verbs of fearing. Note that sometimes, especially after *vereor* = "I fear", *ut* may be used instead of *nē nōn*. This is a particularly dirty trick, as it makes the sentence *appear* to mean the exact opposite of what it does mean!

E.g. *verēbātur **ut** cōpiae vēnissent* = "he was afraid that the forces might **not** have come". Then translate into Latin:

1. They are afraid to come to Rome.
2. They are afraid that the enemy may come to Rome.
3. We were afraid that the soldiers might not defeat the Carthaginians.
4. She was afraid that her mother might not see her.
5. We were afraid that our brother had not returned (using *vereor + ut*).

Using Latin

Ex tempore
Ex tempore = out of the time. This phrase means "on the spur of the moment", or "without preparation".

Mīlle and mīlia

You already know that the Latin for "one thousand" is *mīlle*. But there are a couple of things which you now need to know about using *mīlle*.

1. *Mīlle* is an indeclinable adjective meaning "one thousand".
   E.g. *mīlle cīvēs* = "one thousand citizens".
   E.g. *cum mīlle mīlitibus* = "with one thousand soldiers".
2. If, however, there is more than one thousand, we use the neuter plural noun *mīlia, mīlium* = "thousands", **followed by the genitive**.
   E.g. *septem mīlia cīvium* = "seven thousand citizens".
   E.g. *cum duōbus mīlibus mīlitum* = "with two thousand soldiers".

Note the common phrase *mīlle passūs* = "one mile" (lit. = one thousand paces).
   E.g. *quattuor mīlia passuum contendit* = "he marched for four miles".

Price and value

The following coins should be noted (the main unit of Roman currency being the *sēstertius*):
The *lībra* = pound (one *as*);
The *sēstertius* = two and a half pounds;
The *dēnārius* = ten pounds, or four *sēstertiī*.
(The *solidus* was introduced by the emperor Constantine and is the "S" in L.S.D.: see *Using Latin*, p.87).

1. **Price is expressed by the ablative case.**
   E.g. He bought the book for seven *dēnāriī = librum septem dēnāriīs ēmit*.

2. **Value is expressed by the genitive case.**
   E.g. He valued his friendship very highly = *amīcitiam plūrimī habuit* (i.e. "he held his friendship of a very high (value)").

Defective verbs

A number of verbs in Latin are defective, i.e. they have only some of the normal forms. Apart from *inquit/inquiunt*, which you already know, the most common examples are:
   coepī = "I began", *meminī* (+ gen. or acc.) = "I remember" and *ōdī* = "I hate".
These verbs are restricted to perfect tense forms and *meminī* and *ōdī*, although perfect in form, are present in meaning:

coepī	I began	*meminī*	I remember	*ōdī*	I hate
coepistī	You began	*meministī*	You remember	*ōdistī*	You hate
coepit	He began	*meminit*	He remembers	*ōdit*	He hates
Etc.					

Future perfect and pluperfect forms also occur:

coeperō	I shall have begun	*meminerō*	I shall remember	*ōderō*	I shall hate
coeperam	I had begun	*memineram*	I remembered	*ōderam*	I hated

So you really want to learn Latin. . .

Exercise 8. 11
Study the information on the left-hand page about *mīlle* and *mīlia*. Then translate into Latin:

1. The general prepared a thousand ships in order that he might sail across the sea with his army.

2. The leader of the enemy drew up five thousand foot-soldiers and two thousand cavalry.

3. The consul marched towards the city with a thousand foot-soldiers and very many cavalry.

4. The slaves, who had only three thousand foot-soldiers, feared the consuls to such an extent that they fled.

5. The soldiers, who had marched for five miles, were tired.

Exercise 8. 12
Study the information on the left-hand page about price and value. Then translate into English:

1. *senex vīllam multīs sēstertiīs ēmit.*

2. *servum amīco suō mīlle dēnāriīs vēndidit.*

3. *carmina poētārum Graecōrum plūrimī habēmus.*

4. *mīlitēs septem mīlia passuum contendērunt.*

5. *cīvēs Rōmānī lībertātem suam maximī habuērunt.*

Exercise 8. 13
Study the information on the left-hand page about defective verbs. Translate into English:

1. *post cēnam, poēta cantāre coepit.*

2. *quis meminit fīliārum pulchrārum senis?*

3. *"hanc fēminam" inquit iuvenis "nōn amō nec tamen ōdī."*

4. *dīxit sē meminisse omnium bellī perīculōrum.*

5. *Rōmānī semper dīcēbant sē Poenōs ōdisse.*

Exercise 8. 14
Translate into Latin (noting the use of *ut* + indicative for "as"):

1. We all hate the Carthaginians as enemies of Rome.

2. The farmer had begun to build a wall around his fields.

3. We know that the citizens hate Sulla as all soldiers hate the enemy.

4. The young man remembered the wise words of his friends.

5. We will always remember the great courage of the general.

|  | **L.S.D.**
L.S.D., referring to money, stands for *lībrae, solidī,*
dēnāriī = pounds, shillings, pence. |

The revolt of Spartacus, 73 B.C.

After Sulla had retired into private life, Rome continued to extend her power to the east. A Roman general called Pompey brought huge wealth to Rome by his conquests in the east, but trouble at home raised its ugly head in 73 B.C. when a slave rebellion, led by Spartacus, threatened to bring chaos to Italy. Spartacus was a Thracian-born gladiator who escaped from his training school with a small band of companions and set themselves up on Mount Vesuvius. He quickly built up a large following as slaves from around the country flocked to join him. When his army numbered some 70,000 the Senate realised the gravity of the situation and sent both consuls to deal with the problem. These were defeated, however, and so Pompey's rival, Crassus, was appointed commander-in-chief of an army of six legions and sent against Spartacus. Keen to finish the job before Pompey could arrive to claim the credit, Crassus managed to overcome Spartacus. The latter was killed and 6,000 of his followers were crucified along the Appian Way leading into Rome.

So you really want to learn Latin...

Exercise 8. 15

Study the information on the left-hand page about Spartacus. Then answer the following questions in complete sentences:

1. Who was Spartacus?
2. When did he lead the slave rebellion which threatened to bring chaos to Italy?
3. How large did his army of slaves become?
4. What happened when the two consuls were sent to deal with Spartacus?
5. Who was then appointed commander-in-chief and how many legions did he command?
6. Why was Crassus so keen to finish Spartacus off quickly?
7. After Spartacus's death, what happened to 6,000 of his followers?
8. Have you seen the film?

Exercise 8. 16

Translate into English: *The revolt of Spartacus.*

ōlim servus, nōmine Spartacus, ā dominō Rōmānō effūgit. paucīs cum amīcīs ad montem Vesuvium idcircō abiit nē ā custōdibus caperētur. mox, tamen, tot servī ad eum festīnāverant ut Spartacus exercitum contrā Rōmānōs dūcere posset. patrēs perīculum diū neglegēbant sed tandem, duōbus cōnsulibus victīs, Crassum, imperātōrem bellī perītissimum, sex cum legiōnibus idcircō ad copiās servōrum mīsērunt, ut bellum cōnficeret. hic, veritus nē servī Rōmam ipsam oppugnārent, Spartacum interficere cōnstituit.

diū Spartacus Rōmānīs resistere poterat. tandem tamen exercitus eius in duās partēs dīvīsus est et ā Crassō omnēs servī mox superātī sunt. Spartacus ipse caesus est et plūrimī servī in crucēs sublātī sunt ut per viam quae Rōmam fert ab omnibus vidērī possent. nisi nōnūllī servī ducem suum audācem neglēxissent, fortasse Crassum vīcissent.

crux, crucis, f. = cross.

Glōria in excelsīs deō
Glōria in excelsīs deō = "Glory to God in the heights (i.e. highest)."

CHAPTER 9
Gerunds and gerundives; impersonal verbs; more pronouns

Gerunds

A gerund is a singular verbal noun. In English it ends in "-ing" and in Latin it declines like *bellum*. It is formed from the present stem as follows:

ama-ndum	*mone-ndum*	*reg-endum*	*audi-endum*	*capi-endum*
Loving	Warning	Ruling	Hearing	Capturing

These verbal *nouns* should not be confused with present participles ("loving", "warning", etc.), participles being verbal *adjectives*.

Gerunds are found in the accusative case (but only after prepositions) and in the other oblique cases. Examples are given below:

Accusative	*parātus ad regendum* = "prepared for ruling"
	(note this use of *ad* = "for the purpose of").
Genitive	*ars regendī* = "the art of ruling".
Dative	*operam dat regendō* = "He pays attention to ruling".
Ablative	*regendō* = "by ruling".

In Latin, the **infinitive** is used in place of the nominative of the gerund, or if the gerund is a direct object.
E.g. *vidēre est crēdere* = "seeing is believing".
E.g. *amat regere* = "he likes ruling".

N.B. *Sum, possum, volō, nōlō* and *mālō* have no gerund. *Eō* has the gerund *eundum.* Deponent verbs form their gerunds in the same way as they form their present participles, i.e. by copying the form of their own particular conjugation. Thus *loquor* is 3rd conjugation (like *regō*); *regō* goes *regendum*, thus *loquor* goes *loquendum*. *Cōnor* is 1st conjugation (like *amō*). *Amō* goes *amandum*, thus *cōnor* goes *cōnandum*, etc.

Causā = for the sake of

The noun *causa* is used in the ablative to mean "for the sake of". When used like this, it is placed **after** the noun it goes with, which will be in the genitive.
E.g. *pācis causā* = for the sake of peace.
E.g. *pugnandī causā* = for the sake of fighting.

This use with a gerund is very common indeed and is another way of expressing purpose.
E.g. He came to Rome to fight (i.e. for the sake of fighting) = *Rōmam vēnit pugnandī causā*.

So you really want to learn Latin...

Exercise 9. 1

Study the information on the left-hand page about gerunds. Translate into Latin. When using *causā* = "for the sake of", note that it comes *after* the gerund or noun, not before. E.g. *regendī causā* = "for the sake of ruling".

1. He is <u>desirous of</u>[1] walking
2. She is prepared <u>for</u>[2] writing
3. They are tired by running
4. He is eager about reading
5. For the sake of learning
6. For the sake of going
7. Love of fighting
8. By trying
9. Fear of sailing
10. He loves speaking

1. *cupidus, -a, -um* (+ gen.) = desirous (of).
2. Note the use of *ad* = "for the purpose of".

Exercise 9. 2

Translate into English:

1. *omnēs sciēbant Iovem perītum fallendī esse.*
2. *cavēte iuvenēs vēndendī perītōs!*
3. *virtūtī mīlitum, quī artibus pugnandī doctī erant, dux semper <u>fidem habēbat</u>*.*
4. *Iuppiter illam puellam, amōris causā, in caelum rapuit.*
5. *dīxērunt paucōs cīvēs aptōs ad regendum esse.*

* *fidem habeō* (+ dat.) = I put (my) trust in.

Exercise 9. 3

Translate into Latin:

1. They pitched camp for the sake of sleeping.
2. The girl was skilled in speaking.
3. The bird's ears were not suitable for hearing!
4. The lions halted for the sake of eating.
5. He said that his soldiers would come for the sake of fighting.

Exercise 9. 4

Translate into English:

1. *imperātor cōpiās in campō pugnandī causā īnstrūxit.*
2. *nāvem ingentem nāvigandī causā aedificāvit.*
3. *in forum iuvenēs cotīdiē loquendī causā festīnābant.*
4. *mīlitēs Rōmānī, fessī pugnandō, ad castra rediērunt.*
5. *quamquam Gallī Rōmānōs timēbant, modum vīvendī eōrum magnopere amābant.*

Modus vīvendī

A *modus vīvendī* sets out the terms on which people live together, often involving a compromise after a dispute. *Modus vīvendī* = way of living.

The gerundive construction

Gerunds do not like being followed by a direct object. If a gerund is in danger of being followed by a direct object, e.g. "he was keen on ruling the people", then a wonderful animal called the gerundive construction is used.

This involves using a **gerundive** instead of a gerund. A gerundive is a verbal adjective, looking like the gerund but ending in *-us* and declining like *bonus*. It is passive and has the meaning "to be loved", "to be warned", etc.

Thus instead of writing:

> *cupidus regendī urbem* = "desirous of ruling the city";

we write:

> *cupidus urbis regendae* = "desirous of the city to be ruled".

Here *regendae* agrees in gender, case and number with *urbis*.

More examples are given below:

- *cīvium capiendōrum causā* = "for the sake of capturing the citizens".
- *nāvibus eōrum dēlendīs hostēs vīcimus* = "we conquered the enemy by destroying their ships".
- *ad cōnsulēs dēligendōs Rōmam vēnimus* = "we came to Rome to choose the consuls".

This construction is used except when the result would be the ugly-sounding jingle *-ōrum -ōrum* or *-ārum -ārum*. To avoid such jingles, the Romans often allowed the gerund to govern a direct object. Thus, instead of *ars oppidōrum oppugnandōrum*, they generally preferred *ars oppugnandī oppida*. And I can't say I blame them.

Gerundive of obligation

The other use of a gerundive is to express obligation. This is done by using the gerundive with a part of *sum*.

E.g. *urbs oppugnanda est* = "the city is to be attacked" (i.e. ought to be attacked).

E.g. *urbs oppugnanda erat* = "the city was to be attacked" (i.e. ought to have been attacked).

The person on whom the obligation falls is put into the **dative** case.

E.g. *urbs oppugnanda est **mihĭ*** = "the city ought to be attacked **by me**".

This applies unless confusion would arise by the presence of another dative in the sentence. In such a case *ā/ab* (+ abl.) is used.

E.g. The book ought to be given back to me by you = *liber mihĭ reddendus est ā tē*.

Notice also that, in the case of intransitive verbs and other verbs used intransitively, the neuter of the gerundive is used in an **impersonal construction**.

E.g. *mihĭ currendum est* = "I must run" (lit. "it ought to be run by me").

E.g. *Rōmānīs cum hostibus pugnandum est* = "the Romans ought to fight with the enemy" (lit. "it ought to be fought by the Romans with the enemy").

So you really want to learn Latin...

Exercise 9. 5
Study the information on the left-hand page about the gerundive construction and the gerundive of obligation. Then translate into Latin:

1.   The ramparts were suitable for hindering the enemy.

2.   We came to Rome for the sake of seeing the temple of Jupiter.

3.   The Gauls were lying down, tired from running through the streets.

4.   The citizens were always prepared for defending the city walls.

5.   Flames were seen by the soldiers running from the building.

6.   He said that the guards had come for the sake of burying the queen.

7.   Many came from the islands for the sake of buying the best corn.

8.   The enemy deceived us by hiding their weapons near the citadel.

9.   The enemy ought to be overcome by our army within seven days.

10. Food ought always to be handed over to the poorest citizens.

Exercise 9. 6
Translate into English:

1.   *duās legiōnes in proelium mīsit ad hostēs superandōs.*

2.   *nūlla spēs cīvibus data est dīvitiās dīvidendī.*

3.   *nōnne iūdex īn forum vocātus est iuvenis pūniendī causā?*

4.   *nāvēs parandae sunt ut īnsulam capiāmus.*

5.   *librī nōbīs ante noctem legendī sunt.*

6.   *aciēs in campō imperātōrī īnstruenda erat.*

7.   *nōs ipsōs parēmus ad domum aedificandam!*

8.   *propter virtūtem tuam, haec perīcula tibī nōn timenda sunt.*

9.   *castra prope flūmen mīlitibus pōnenda erant.*

10. *urbs illīs cōnsulibus ūnum annum regenda est.*

Exercise 9. 7
Translate into English: *The conspiracy of Catiline, 63 B.C.*

cīvis Rōmānus, nōmine Catilīna, amīcōs ōlim collēgit imperiī rapiendī causā. sciēbat autem cōnsulem, nōmine Cicerōnem, sē impedīre maximē velle. amīcīs imperāvit ut, cōnsule illō interfectō, plūrima aedificia incenderent et servōs līberārent. cōnsiliō tamen eius cognitō, Cicerō rem tam bene gerēbat ut urbem servāverit. amīcīs Catilīnae caesīs ipse in proeliō victus mortuus est.

Nunc est bibendum
This famous phrase of the poet Horace means
"Now one must drink!"

Impersonal verbs

Impersonal verbs have only a 3rd person singular in each tense and have as their subject "it", e.g. "it is pleasing" or "it is lawful". Furthermore, some otherwise perfectly normal verbs may be used impersonally in the third person singular, with special meanings. The thing you need to know about all of these verbs is which construction to use after them. For this you just have to learn how each one works. Here are some of the most common, with a summary of how to use each one in brackets:

miseret = it moves to pity	(+ acc. of the person and gen. of the cause)
paenitet = it repents, makes sorry	(+ acc. of the person and gen. of the cause)
pudet = it shames	(+ acc. of the person and gen. of the cause)
oportet = it is right (that)	(+ acc. and infin.)
decet = it is becoming, suitable	(+ acc. of the person + infin.)
dēdecet = it is unbecoming	(+ acc. of the person + infin.)
iuvat = it pleases	(+ acc. of the person + infin.)
libet = it is pleasing	(+ dat. + infin.)
licet = it is lawful, allowed	(+ dat. + infin.)
placet = it pleases	(+ dat.)
accidit = it happens (that)	(+ *ut* + subjunctive)

Examples of these construction types are shown below:

- *mē fēminae miseret* = I pity the woman.
- *oportet puellam domum redīre* = it is right for the girl to go back home.
- *mē decuit pugnāre* = it was suitable for me to fight.
- *mīlitibus licēbit pugnāre* = it will be lawful for the soldiers to fight.
- *accidit ut mīlitēs occīsī sint* = it happened that the soldiers were killed.

Vocabulary 9

Nouns			Adjectives	
amor, amōris, m.	love		*aptus, -a, -um*	suitable
arx, arcis, f.	citadel		*cupidus, -a, -um* (+ gen.)	desirous (of)
auris, auris, f.	ear		*perītus, -a, -um* (+ gen.)	skilled (in)
avis, avis, f.	bird		**Verbs**	
celeritās, -tātis, f.	speed		*dīvidō, -ere, dīvīsī, dīvīsum*	I divide
culpa, -ae, f.	blame		*iaceō, -ēre, iacuī, iacitum*	I lie (down)
faciēs, faciēī, f.	face, appearance		*impediō, -īre, -īvi, -ītum*	I hinder
fidēs, fideī, f.	faith, loyalty		**Pronouns (see p. 96)**	
flamma, -ae, f.	flame		*aliquis, aliquid*	someone
fōrma, -ae, f.	beauty, shape		*quis, qua, quid*	anyone
fūmus, -ī, m.	smoke		*quisquam, quicquam*	anyone at all
praeda, -ae, f.	booty		*quisque, quaeque, quidque*	each

So you really want to learn Latin...

Exercise 9. 8
Study the information on the left-hand page about impersonal verbs. Note that these can be used in any tense, not just the present. Then translate into English:

1. *mē miseret mortis patris meī.*
2. *cīvem scelerātum perfidiae maximae nōn pudet.*
3. *tē decuit mātrem patremque laudāre.*
4. *Rōmae cīvem interficere nōn licēbat.*
5. *nōs iuvat īn forum convenīre et inter nōs loquī.*
6. *mihĭ placet librōs legere vīnumque bibere.*
7. *placetne tibĭ īn forō ambulāre an domī manēre?*
8. *accidit ut cōnsul īnsidiās prohibēre posset.*
9. *iuvenibus libuit in vīllā pugnāre nec tamen licuit.*
10. *senem paenitēbit omnium scelerum suōrum.*

Exercise 9. 9
Study the words in Vocabulary 9. From which Latin words do the following derive? Translate the Latin word and give the meaning of the English one:

1. Amorous
2. Aural
3. Aviary
4. Fidelity
5. Form
6. Facial
7. Aptitude
8. Division
9. Impede
10. Accelerate

Exercise 9. 10
Translate into English: *Caesar is captured by pirates.*

Iūlius Caesar adhūc iuvenis <u>Rhodum</u> *idcircō profectus est ut ā magistrō doctissimō, nōmine Apollōniō, docērētur. dum autem mare trānsit, ā pīrātīs quibusdam captus est quī prōmīsērunt sē, quīnquāgintā* <u>talentīs</u> *acceptīs, captīvum suum līberātūrōs esse. hīs respondit Caesar sē libenter pecūniam iīs datūrum esse sed, magnā manū mīlitum collēctā, omnēs occīsūrum. prīmō autem pīrātae eum iocārī putāvērunt. sed posteā sē errāvisse cognōvērunt; nam paucīs post mēnsibus Caesar regressus* <u>fidem servāvit</u>.

> *Rhodus, -ī,* f. = Rhodes; *talentum, -ī,* n. = a talent (a large sum of money); *fidem servō* = I keep my word.

Using Latin

Agenda
The *agenda* are things that have to be done. In Latin, the gerundive *agenda* = (things) to be done.

Quis, aliquis, quisque and quisquam

Now for a quick blast on these pronouns, which all decline pretty much like the relative pronoun with the addition of a prefix or suffix here and there (see summary of grammar, p. 127), and which tend to look the same after a hard day's work but which are in fact rather different.

1. **Quis? = "who?"**

The interrogative pronoun *quis? =* "who?" may be used as a pronoun (*quis venit? =* "who is coming?") or as an adjective (*quis homŏ venit? =* "What man is coming?"). This distinction between **pronominal** use and **adjectival** use dogs all of the following pronouns, but is not too bad if you grit your teeth and concentrate!

2. **Quis** = "anyone" is used after *sī, nisi, num* and *nē*.

E.g. *sī quis domum redībit, interficiētur =* "If anyone returns home, he will be killed."

3. **Aliquis** = "someone".

E.g. *fortasse aliquis rēgem interficiet =* "Perhaps someone will kill the king."

4. **Quisque** = "each one".

E.g. *mīlitēs domum rediērunt, cum suā quisque praedā =* "The soldiers returned home, each with his own booty."

Quisque is often used with the superlative: e.g. *optimus quisque =* "each best man" (i.e. all the best people).

5. **Quisquam** = "anyone at all" (the pronoun of *ūllus =* "any", which we have already met) is used after a negative particle (e.g. *nec* or *neque*), a verb of denying, forbidding or preventing, in a question, or in a *sī* clause where a negative is implied.

E.g. *omnēs rēgem timent neque quisquam eum amat =* "Everyone fears the king nor does anyone at all love him."

More about indirect statements

1. As you well know, indirect statements in Latin follow the accusative and infinitive construction. But if the indirect statement goes on for more than one sentence, the accusative and infinitive construction continues, without the need for a phrase such as "he said", or "he continued". The fact that the construction is continuing is enough to make clear that the indirect statement is continuing.

E.g. He said that he had come to Rome. He said that his friends were happy and that his enemies had all left the city. The citizens had come together in the forum and had listened to the consul. Etc.

dīxit sē Rōmam vēnisse; amīcōs laetissimōs esse et inimīcōs omnēs ex urbe discessisse; cīvēs īn forum convēnisse et cōnsulem audīvisse. Etc.

2. You have already learnt that the Latin for "I say that...not" = *negō*. Note also the following:

I say that no one = *negō quemquam*;   I say that nothing = *negō quicquam*;
I say that never = *negō umquam*;   I say that no = *negō ūllum*.

So you really want to learn Latin...

Exercise 9. 11
Study the information on the left-hand page about all those similar-looking pronouns and the note on indirect statements. Take a deep breath. Then translate into English:

Rōmā ēgressus, Caesar in Galliam exercitum dūxit. Gallī magnopere eum timēbant lēgātōsque ad eum mīsērunt. diū autem tacēbant hī lēgātī nec Rōmānīs quicquam respondēbant. sextō tamen diē cōnstituērunt loquī, territī ā custōdibus Rōmānīs. dīxērunt sē velle Caesarem certiōrem facere cūr vēnissent: sē missōs esse quī ducem ōrārent ut, legiōnibus trāns montēs reductīs, Galliam līberam relinqueret. Caesar tamen, cum ex eīs cognōvisset plūrimās cīvitātēs suō imperiō resistere, magnopere īrātus lēgātīs imperāvit ut quam celerrimē domum regrederentur, ad suam quisque gentem. dīxit Gallōs mox cognitūrōs esse suam potestātem maximam esse; incolās enim, oppidīs dēlētīs, in servitium reductum īrī.

servitium, -iī, n. = slavery.

Exercise 9. 12
Translate into Latin, remembering to follow the rule about extended indirect statements:

After this*, Caesar remained in his camp for three days. For he wanted to know what the Gauls would do. However, when his messengers returned, they told him that the Gauls had not returned to their own tribes. They said that they had decided to collect an army immediately and were preparing to lead their forces into the woods. Once Caesar himself had returned into Italy, they continued, they would draw up their battle line and attack the Roman camp with five thousand foot-soldiers and a thousand cavalry. Hearing this, Caesar became very angry and ordered his men to prepare themselves for battle. He said that the Romans would never fear the barbarians and that he himself would soon overcome the whole of Gaul.

* N.B. "After this" = *post haec*. When translating the other way, do not be tempted to translate *post haec* as "after these things". It means "after this"!

Exercise 9. 13
Translate into English: *Caesar crosses the Rubicon, 49 B.C.*

nūntiī autem ad Caesarem missī sunt ut eum certiōrem facerent populum Rōmānum iam hostem eum habēre. per multōs diēs Caesar in castrīs manēbat ut quid Rōmae accidisset cognōsceret. mīlitēs autem convocātōs iussit sē parāre. "nōlīte putāre" inquit "hoc proelium facile fore*. multō quidem difficilius erit quam omnia bella quae egŏ ūnā vōbīscum prius gessī. crās enim flūmen Rubicōnem trānsībimus et, dīs iuvantibus, prōmittō mē vōs incolumēs Rōmam reductūrum esse et omnēs inimīcōs meōs, quī propter nostrās victōriās mē nunc timeant, superātūrum esse. iacta ālea est!"

*N.B. *fore* is a commonly used shortened version of *futūrus esse*, the future infinitive of *sum; Rubicō, -ōnis*, m. = R. Rubicon; *ālea, -ae*, f. = a die (used for games).

Iacta ālea est
The famous remark of Julius Caesar on crossing the Rubicon, *iacta ālea est* = the die is cast.

Julius Caesar

And now for one of the all time great Romans, the one everyone has heard of: Julius Caesar. Julius Caesar was born in 100 B.C. He was nephew (by marriage) of Marius and in 84 he married the daughter of Cinna, so he was pretty much in the thick of things before he even began. As a young man he made his mark when, having been kidnapped by pirates in the Mediterranean, he chased after them once his ransom had been paid and executed the lot.

In 59 B.C. he teamed up with Pompey and Crassus to form an alliance known afterwards as the 1st triumvirate. Granted the provinces of Cisalpine Gaul, Illyricum, and later Transalpine Gaul, Caesar set off in 58 B.C. to wage the Gallic Wars which kept him busy for the next nine years. During this time he conquered the whole of Gaul (apart from one small village…) and even made two invasions of Britain in 55 and again in 54 B.C.

In 53 B.C. Crassus was killed and power thus came to be divided between Pompey and Caesar. Not everyone liked Caesar, despite his amazing military successes in Gaul, and in 49 B.C. Pompey joined with Caesar's enemies in demanding that he lay down his command. Caesar marched towards Italy and paused at the River Rubicon. It was illegal for a Roman general to march into Italy at the head of his army, and the river marked the boundary beyond which he could not pass without breaking the law. He pondered for a bit and then decided to cross, muttering the immortal words "*iacta ālea est*", i.e. "the die is cast".

So you really want to learn Latin…

Caesar quickly overran Italy and in 48 B.C. he crossed to Greece, whither Pompey had fled, and defeated him at the Battle of Pharsalus. Pompey then fled to Egypt and Caesar followed, meeting up with the lovely Cleopatra and making her his mistress. He then marched into Asia Minor to beat King Pharnaces of Bosporus at the Battle of Zela, which allowed him to utter the famous words *vēnī, vīdī, vīcī.* Then it was back to Rome before finally defeating the remaining Pompeian forces in Africa in 47 B.C.

After that, the sky was the limit. Caesar was made dictator, first temporarily, then for ten years, and finally, in 44 B.C., for life. Despite refusing the title *rēx,* Caesar became intolerable to even his staunchest supporters, and on the Ides of March, 44 B.C., Julius Caesar was murdered. His wife at the time, Calpurnia, tried to save her husband from his fate on account of a dream. She begged him not to go to the senate-house that day, having been warned in a dream to "beware the Ides of March". However, Caesar ignored her and, as he reached the steps of the senate-house, he was surrounded by the conspirators who covered him in stab wounds and left him to die. Seeing his beloved young friend Brutus among the assassins, he muttered, quoting Shakespeare (only joking!), *et tū, Brūte?* He then covered his head in his toga and died at the foot of the statue of Pompey. Exit Julius Caesar.

Exercise 9. 14

Translate into English: *The death of Caesar, 44 B.C.*:

Caesaris uxor marītum suum multīs cum precibus ōrāvit nē īn senātum eō diē inīret. ille, tamen, cum timēret nē ignāvus habērētur, cōnsilium eius neglegere cōnstituit. domō igitur ēgressus, Cūriam intrāvit ubǐ ā senātōrum multitūdine statim circumventus est. quōrum ūnus, signō datō, imperātōrem fortissimum gladiō cecīdit. conversus ut sē dēfenderet, amīcum suum Brūtum vīdit. "et tū, Brūte?" inquit. capite togā tēctō, tribus et vīgintī vulneribus caesus imperātor cecidit.

precēs, -um, f. pl. = prayers; *ignāvus, -a, -um* = cowardly; *Cūria, -ae,* f. = senate-house.

Īnfrā dig.
The expression *īnfrā dig.* is short for the Latin *īnfrā dignitātem* = beneath (one's) dignity.

CHAPTER 10

Coping with the set texts; scansion; unseen technique

Coping with the set texts: prose authors

You have now met pretty well all the Latin there is to meet and are ready to throw yourself head-first into a proper Latin author. You may be reading a prose author as a set text, or you may be reading one to prove how good at Latin you now are. Either way you really ought to know which authors are out there, waiting to be read, and how you ought to tackle them.

Among the most famous prose authors writing in Latin were:

- **Caesar, 100–44 B.C.**

None other than the Julius Caesar of *"et tū, Brūte"* fame. He wrote two main works of history, the Gallic War (in which he describes his wars in Gaul) and the Civil War (in which he describes his wars with Pompey and his other opponents in the senate).

- **Cicero, 106–43 B.C.**

Rome's most famous orator, he wrote a huge number of speeches and letters which give us invaluable information about life in Rome in the last days of the republic. He was murdered the year after Julius Caesar.

- **Livy, c. 59 B.C.–c. 17 A.D.**

A historian living in the reign of the emperor Augustus, Livy was famous for his History of Rome, only part of which has survived.

- **Tacitus, c. 56–c. 115 A.D.**

A historian living in the time of some of Rome's less pleasant emperors (notably Domitian), Tacitus wrote a number of historical works which bring ancient Rome to life (as can be seen by the *"I Claudius"* series, which relied heavily on Tacitus as a source).

- **Pliny "the younger", c. 61–112 A.D.**

Pliny witnessed from afar the eruption of Mt. Vesuvius in 79 A.D. and is famous for the huge number of letters he wrote which give us invaluable information about social life in Rome in the 1st century A.D.

Of these, probably the easiest is Caesar. Caesar has had a bad press over the past twenty or thirty years because he wrote exclusively about war and how brilliant he was at winning. After the first few bloody battles this *can* become a little tedious and many a pupil has put his or her dislike of Latin down to the miseries of being forced to translate Caesar. In fact this is most unfair. Their dislike of Latin was almost certainly caused not by their translating Caesar, but rather by their *inability* to translate Caesar! For Caesar wrote in pretty much straight-forward classical Latin which, with practice, can be read with relative ease, page after page. Zipping through page after page of Latin, whether it be about *the Gauls being slaughtered by the spears of the Romans* or not, is intensely satisfying to someone studying Latin. Those who claim to have hated translating Caesar are almost certainly the ones who had not got to grips with the language and sought to blame it on poor old Caesar!

So you really want to learn Latin...

Exercise 10. 1
Read the information on the left-hand page about prose authors. Now translate into English the following chunk of almost completely unadapted Caesar: *The Romans land in Britain, 55 B.C.*

hīs cōnstitūtīs rēbus, nactus idōneam ad nāvigandum tempestātem, Caesar equitēs in portum prōgredī et nāvēs cōnscendere iussit. ubī autem cum prīmīs nāvibus Britanniam <u>attigit</u>, in omnibus collibus īnstrūctās hostium cōpiās armātās cōnspexit. lēgātīs convocātīs, Caesar ab eō locō circiter mīlia passuum septem prōgredī cōnstituit. at barbarī, cōnsiliō Rōmānōrum cognitō, equitēs suōs praemīsērunt quī nostrōs ē nāvibus ēgredī prohibērent. nāvēs propter magnitūdinem nisi in altō <u>cōnstituī</u> nōn poterant. mīlitibus autem, impedītīs manibus, magnō et gravī onere armōrum oppressīs, erat summa difficultās. hīs enim dē nāvibus dēsiliendum erat et in flūctibus cōnsistendum et cum hostibus pugnandum. Rōmānīs autem morantibus, maximē propter altitūdinem maris, is quī decimae legiōnis aquilam ferēbat, <u>contestātus</u> deōs, ut ea rēs legiōnī fēlīciter ēvenīret, "dēsilīte" inquit "mīlitēs, nisi vultis aquilam hostibus prōdere: egō certē meum reīpūblicae atque imperātōrī officium <u>praestiterō</u>." hoc cum vōce magnā dīxisset, sē ex nāve prōiēcit atque in hostēs aquilam ferre coepit. tum Rōmānī, nē tantum dēdecus admitterētur, ūniversī ex nāve dēsiluērunt.

attingō, -ere, attigī, attāctum = I touch (land); *cōnstituō* (in military context) = I station, position; *contestor, -ārī, contestātus sum* = I call as witness; *praestō, -āre, praestitī, praestitum* = I discharge.

Exercise 10. 2
Give yourself a huge pat on the back if you managed to translate the passage above. Now translate into English the following chunk, which also comes directly from the pen of "Big J.C.": *Caesar strikes deep into British territory, 54 B.C.*

Caesar, cognitō cōnsiliō eōrum, ad flūmen <u>Tamesim</u> īn fīnēs <u>Cassivellaunī</u> exercitum dūxit; quod flūmen ūnō <u>omnīnō</u> locō pedibus, atque hōc aegrē, trānsīrī potest. eō cum vēnisset, <u>animadvertit</u> ad alteram flūminis rīpam magnās esse cōpiās hostium īnstrūctās. rīpa autem erat acūtīs <u>sudibus praefīxīs</u> mūnita, eiusdemque generis sub aquā dēfīxae <u>sudēs</u> flūmine tegēbantur. eīs rēbus cognitīs ā captīvīs, Caesar praemissō <u>equitātū</u> statim legiōnēs subsequī iussit. sed eā celeritāte atque eō impetū mīlitēs iērunt, cum capite sōlō ex aquā exstārent, ut hostēs impetum legiōnum atque equitum sustinēre nōn possent ac sē fugae <u>mandārent</u>.

Tamesis, -is, m. (acc.: *Tamesim*) = R. Thames; *Cassivellaunus, -ī,* m.: a British chieftain; *omnīnō* (adverb) = altogether, (here =) only; *animadvertō, -ere, -vertī, versum* = I notice; *sudis, -is,* f. = stake; *praefīgō, -ere, praefīxī, praefīxum* = I set up, fix; *equitātus, -ūs,* m. = cavalry; *mandō, -āre, -āvī, -ātum* = I entrust.

	Mūtātīs mūtandīs
	"With the things which need to be changed having been changed"

Coping with the set texts: verse authors

Reading Latin verse is perhaps the most satisfying aspect of having mastered Latin and allows you to impress your friends and relations by dropping in a couple of lines here and there just to keep them on their toes. Probably the most famous verse authors were:

- **Catullus, 85–54 B.C.**

Famous for his love affair with a girl whom he called Lesbia, Catullus wrote lots of rather wonderful love poems, including one about a sparrow.

- **Virgil, 70–19 B.C.**

The most famous Roman poet, Virgil's poem the *Aeneid* tells the story of Aeneas and his mission to establish a new Troy in Italy. In terms of superstar status, Virgil was to the Romans what Homer was to the Greeks and Shakespeare is to us.

- **Horace, 65 B.C. – 8 A.D.**

A friend of Virgil's, Horace was a perfectionist when it came to writing poetry and particularly enjoyed experimenting with Greek metres. He is most famous for his *Odes*.

- **Ovid, 43 B.C. – 18 A.D.**

Ovid wrote some rather racy poems which did not please the emperor Augustus and he was exiled for his pains. He is most famous for his *Metamorphoses*, a huge poem which tells Greek mythological stories, uniting them under the theme of transformation.

Scansion

To read and appreciate Latin verse, one must first learn about **scansion**. Latin verse, like the Greek verse on which it was based, relies not on stress but on **quantity**. As those of you who managed to get through the guide to pronunciation (pages 2–3) will already know, syllables may be either long or short, the length of the syllable being dependent on certain, easily learnable rules. A line of verse is made up of a subtle combination of these long and short syllables, this combination being dictated by the particular **metre** which the poet is using. There are a wide range of metres used by the Romans, but by far the most commonly used was the **hexameter**, and we are going to use this metre to show you how scansion works.

A hexameter line is made up of six units (like musical "bars") called **feet**. Each foot consists of either a **dactyl** (a long syllable followed by two short ones: – ˘ ˘); or a **spondee** (two long syllables: – –). At the end of the line, just to be awkward, something called a **trochee** (a long syllable followed by one short syllable: – ˘) could also be used. The way these different feet could be combined was fixed as follows:

1	2	3	4	5	6
– ˘ ˘	– ˘ ˘	– ˘ ˘	– ˘ ˘	– ˘ ˘	– –
– –	– –	– –	– –		– ˘

You will notice from this that the first four feet can be any combination of dactyls or spondees, that the fifth foot is (very nearly always) a dactyl, and that the final foot is either a spondee or a trochee.

So you really want to learn Latin...

So, how can we tell whether we have dactyls or spondees? Easy. We learn to **scan** Latin verse, i.e. to mark the syllables of each word as long or short, and then see how these syllables fit into the pattern of the line. Here is the opening line of the *Aeneid*, written out and scanned.

1	2	3	4	5	6

$$- \cup \cup \mid - \quad \cup \cup \mid - \quad - \mid - \quad - \mid - \cup \cup \mid - -$$

Arma vi|rumque ca|no Tro|iae qui|primus ab|oris

From this you will see that words often spread from one foot into the next, and that the pronunciation of the words affects the rhythm of the line, long syllables theoretically taking twice as long to pronounce as short ones. All you need to do now, is learn the rules for determining the length of a syllable, and then you too will be able to write out a line of Latin verse and scan it. Here then, ignoring the exceptions which we will deal with later, are the basic rules:

1.   A syllable is long if it contains a diphthong or a long vowel. Learning the quantity of vowels is thus very important. The final *o* of *canō* for example is long, as it is for all verbs in the first person singular, present indicative, and this tells us that the syllable in which that vowel falls must be long. The diphthong *ae* in *Troiae* is long, and thus the syllable in which this falls, too, is long. There are various rules for determining the length of vowels, but by far the most effective way is (a) to learn them as you meet the words, and (b) to learn your grammar with the correct pronunciation, as the endings of the various declensions and conjugations are pronounced in the same way, whatever the particular word. Thus, for example, all regular verbs like *amō* go *-ō, -ās, -at, -āmus, -ātis, -ant*, with the vowels always pronounced in that way.

2.   A syllable is generally long if it contains a vowel followed by two (or more) successive consonants. Thus the first syllable of our line of Virgil is long because the initial *a* of *arma*, although a short *a* *by nature*, is followed by the consonants *r* and *m*. Note that the two following consonants do not need to be in the same word. One can be in one word and the other at the beginning of the next. The other thing to notice is that, while such a vowel *scans long by position*, it should still be *pronounced* as a short *a*.

3.   A syllable is generally short if it contains a vowel which is immediately followed by another vowel or *h*; thus the countless words such as *vǐa, trǎhō, mě̄i*, in which the first of the vowels is short. The *following* vowel may be either long or short (e.g. *vǐă* or *vǐā*, depending on which case the word is in).

4.   A syllable at the end of a word elides if it ends in a vowel or *m* and the next word begins with a vowel or *h*. Thus the opening line of Book II of the *Aeneid* begins: *conticuēre omnēs* (= "they all fell silent"). Here the final letter of *conticuēre elides*, i.e. is chopped off and is barely pronounced at all. When scanning, elision is shown by placing brackets around the elided letter: *cōntǐcǔ|ēr(e) ōm|nēs*. For the purposes of the metre, the elided letter ceases to exist and the syllable should not be marked as being either long or short.

Using Latin	**Arma virumque canō** These are the opening words of Virgil's *Aeneid*: "I sing of arms and the man…"

Scanning a hexameter line

Once you have read a bit of Latin verse, you will soon find yourself reading it in accordance with the metrical rhythm without even thinking about it. But to begin with, you may find it useful to follow the following procedure when settling down to scan a line:

1. Look for and deal with elision.
2. Look for diphthongs and mark them as long.
3. Look for syllables containing vowels which are followed by two or more consonants and mark these syllables as long.
4. Mark as short syllables containing vowels which are followed by another vowel or *h*.
5. Mark the final five syllables of the line. These will be (unless you have hit an exceptional line): – ∪ ∪ | – ∪
6. Mark the quantity of any syllables which, from your knowledge of grammar, you *know* to be either long or short. E.g. the ō of *amō*, the ī of *annī*, etc.
7. Complete any feet which have now become "obvious". E.g. a single syllable sandwiched between two *long* ones has to be long itself, because short syllables always come in pairs (unless it is the very last syllable of the line). Similarly, a short syllable must be either preceded or followed by another short syllable.
8. Finally, go back to the beginning and work your way down the line, completing the feet which you have not yet completed. N.B. The letter *i* is sometimes a consonant, not a vowel, and should not then be marked (E.g. *iăcŭlātŭs*).

The caesura

A **strong caesura** (*caesūra* = "a cutting") regularly occurs in the middle of the third foot of a hexameter line, after the first long syllable. The caesura falls between words (never in the middle of a word and never between two words which go very closely together, for example between a preposition and its noun). The caesura acts as a convenient point to pause for breath and is marked by two vertical lines (||). Sometimes, however, the break comes between the two *short* syllables of a dactyl. This is called a **weak caesura**. Frequently, instead of a strong caesura in the 3rd foot, we find strong caesuras in the 2nd and 4th feet, with either no caesura at all in the 3rd foot or else a weak one. More rarely, the line will have a strong caesura in only the 2nd *or* 4th foot.

1	2	3	4	5	6
Ārmă vĭ	rūmquĕ că	nō || Trō	iāē quī	prīmŭs ăb	ōrīs

Common exceptions

All rules are made to be broken. Here are some of the more common exceptions:

1. The rule that a syllable in which a vowel is followed by two consonants scans long does not necessarily (but may) apply if the second consonant (where it comes *in the same word*) is either *l* or *r*, in which case the syllable can either scan long *or* short (e.g. *pătrem* or *pātrem*). However, where a vowel is followed by either double-*l* or double-*r*, the syllable *must* be long.
2. The rule that a vowel followed by another vowel or *h* will be short does not apply in

So you really want to learn Latin...

the case of some genitives in *–ius* where the vowel may scan long or short. E.g. *illĭus, ūnĭus,* etc.

3. Some syllables containing short vowels scan long, even when the vowel is followed by only a single consonant. This is generally because the consonant in question is behaving as a double consonant. Examples of this are the (short) *o* of *Troia,* which *scans* long because the consonant *i* that follows is pronounced as a double consonant. It is as if the word were spelt *Troiia.* The same applies in *maior* and *peior.* Another famous example is the *i* of *hic,* which regularly scans long, the word being pronounced as if it were spelt *hicc.*

Exercise 10. 3
Study the rules of scansion on pages 102–104. Then copy out and scan the following lines, showing the length of the syllables, the division into feet and the caesuras:

Tempus erat, quo prima quies mortalibus aegris
incipit, et dono divum gratissima serpit.
in somnis, ecce, ante oculos maestissimus Hector
visus adesse mihi, largosque effundere fletus,
raptatus bigis, ut quondam, aterque cruento
pulvere, perque pedes traiectus lora tumentis*.

* N.B. During the golden age of Latin literature, for nouns and adjectives having their genitive plural in *-ium,* the 3rd declension accusative plural ending *-īs* was preferred to *-ēs,* although both are found.

Exercise 10. 4
Copy out and scan the following lines:

ei[1] *mihi, qualis erat! quantum mutatus ab illo*
Hectore, qui redit exuvias indutus Achilli,
vel Danaum Phrygios iaculatus puppibus ignis[2]*!*
squalentem barbam, et concretos sanguine crinis[2]*,*
vulneraque illa gerens, quae circum plurima muros
accepit patrios. ultro flens ipse videbar
compellare virum, et maestas expromere voces:

1. *ei* = alas! This word is a diphthong. 2. See note above about 3rd declension endings.

Exercise 10. 5
Copy out and scan the following lines:

"o lux Dardaniae, spes o fidissima Teucrum,
quae tantae tenuere morae? quibus Hector ab oris
exspectate venis? ut te post multa tuorum
funera, post varios hominumque urbisque labores
defessi aspicimus! quae causa indigna serenos
foedavit vultus? aut cur haec vulnera cerno?"

	Nīl dēspērandum
	Nīl dēspērandum = "it is in no way to be despaired", i.e. we must not despair at all.

Elegiac couplets

After the hexameter line, the next most common metre used by the Romans was the **elegiac couplet**. This consisted of a hexameter line followed by a **pentameter** line. A pentameter line consisted of five feet, made up of four full feet and two half-feet, with the caesura coming after the first half-foot. The pattern was as follows:

or

$$- \cup \cup \mid - \cup \cup \mid - \parallel - \cup \cup \mid - \cup \cup \mid -$$
$$- - \mid - - \mid \quad \parallel$$

This is a very easy line to scan because so much of it is fixed. The first two feet can be either dactyls or spondees, but after that the line has to go: $- \parallel - \cup \cup \mid - \cup \cup \mid -$

Here is an example of a fully scanned elegiac couplet. Note that the pentameter line is normally indented.

> *dīc ăgĕ | frīgŏrĭ|būs || quā|rē nŏvŭs | īncĭpĭt | ānnūs,*
> *quī mĕlĭ|ūs pēr | vēr || īncĭpĭ|ēndŭs ĕ|rāt?*

Elegiac couplets came to be used by poets such as Ovid for a wide range of subjects, including love poetry, and are quite easy to translate because the sense is generally contained within the couplet, rather than spreading over countless lines of hexameters as in Virgil's verse.

Shortened verb forms

Now that you are coping with Latin verse, you need to know that a number of verb forms could be shortened. The most common ones are given below:

1. Perfect tense, 3rd plural

-*ēre*   instead of   -*ērunt*   E.g. *amāvēre* = they have loved.

2. Perfects in -*īvī*

-*iī*	instead of	-*īvī*	E.g. *audiī* = I have heard.
-*īstī*	instead of	-*īvistī*	E.g. *audīstī* = you have heard.
-*īsse*	instead of	-*īvisse*	E.g. *audīsse* = to have heard.

3. Perfects in -*āvī*, -*ēvī* and -*ōvī*

Perfect stem forms in -*āvī*, -*ēvī* and -*ōvī* sometimes appear without the -*vi*- or -*ve*-. Thus:

amāsse	instead of	*amāvisse*	= to have loved.
dēlēstī	instead of	*dēlēvistī*	= you have destroyed.
cognōrant	instead of	*cognōverant*	= they had learnt.

4. 2nd sing., passive

In the 2nd singular of the passive tenses, -*re* often occurs instead of -*ris*. Thus:

amābere	instead of	*amāberis*	= you will be loved.
amābāre	instead of	*amābāris*	= you were being loved.

N.B. While you are learning to cope with these strange forms, don't forget what you learnt on page 105 about the 3rd declension accusative plural ending in -*īs*.

So you really want to learn Latin...

Exercise 10. 6

Study the information on the left-hand page about elegiac couplets. Notice also what is says about shortened verb forms. Then scan the following lines from Ovid: *The capture of Gabii* (Part 1).

ultima Tarquinius Romanae gentis habebat
  regna, vir iniustus, fortis ad arma tamen.
ceperat hic alias, alias everterat urbes,
  et Gabios turpi fecerat arte suos.
namque trium minimus, proles manifesta Superbi,
  in medios hostes nocte silente venit.
nudarant gladios: "occidite" dixit "inermem,
  hoc cupiant fratres Tarquiniusque pater,
qui mea crudeli laceravit verbere terga."
  dicere ut hoc posset, verbera passus erat.

Exercise 10. 7

Scan the following lines from Ovid: *The capture of Gabii* (Part 2)

luna fuit: spectant iuvenem, gladiosque recondunt,
  tergaque, deducta veste, notata vident;
flent quoque, et ut secum tueatur bella, precantur.
  callidus ignaris annuit ille viris.
iamque potens, misso genitorem appellat amico,
  perdendi Gabios quod sibi monstret iter.
hortus odoratis suberat cultissimus herbis,
  sectus humum rivo lene sonantis aquae.
illic Tarquinius mandata latentia nati
  accipit, et virga lilia summa metit.
nuntius ut rediit, decussaque lilia dixit,
  filius "agnosco iussa parentis" ait.
nec mora, principibus caesis ex urbe Gabina,
  traduntur ducibus moenia nuda suis.

Exercise 10. 8

Study the information on the left-hand page about shortened verb forms. Then identify the normal form of the following and translate into English:

1. *vocāsse*
2. *cognōvēre*
3. *oppugnābere*
4. *rogāstī*
5. *nūdārant*

6. *cognōram*
7. *dēlēsse*
8. *monuēre*
9. *dabere*
10. *mūnīstis*

Using Latin

Addenda
If things have been omitted from a written document, they are sometimes listed in the *addenda* = "things to be added".

Unseen translation technique

The best advice I ever received on this came on the day before I was due to take the first paper of my A Level Latin exam. I was told, very simply, to read the passage of Latin through *three times* before picking up my pen. I laughed, and said how absurd this seemed. But my teacher persevered and, thankfully, I followed his advice. The fact is that, as with a very difficult passage of English (a poem, perhaps), the meaning of a passage of Latin does not always immediately leap up off the page as one would wish. We may find certain phrases or even whole sentences which appear easy, but there will usually be other bits which seem to have been written in some odd dialect of Serbo-Croat. The rule is: **don't panic**. Read it all through, slowly. Just look at all the words and think to yourself, oh look, some of these words are Latin words which I sort of recognise. Then read it again. The second time through you will find that some of the Serbo-Croat has miraculously become Latin. How nice, you will think. About half of this is written in Latin; not bad for a Latin exam! Then a third time, this time trying to piece together the various clauses and sentences, dwelling on the trickier bits until you get depressed and then moving on to the next bit. By the end of this process you will have a fair idea of what is contained, not just in the first sentence, but in the whole passage. Then, **and only then**, pick up your pen and go for it. You will be amazed, first at how difficult it is to restrain yourself from picking up your pen as soon as you find you know the first word of the passage; and second, how much better your translation will be if you don't! So there we are, some free advice for you. No extra charge.

Vocabulary 10

Verbs

		Nouns	
accidit ut (+ subjunctive)	it happens that	*ātrium, -ī*, n.	hall
aggredior, aggredī, aggressus sum	I attack	*amīcitia, -ae*, f.	friendship
		lūx, lūcis, f.	light
minor, -ārī, minātus sum	I threaten	*onus, oneris*, n.	burden
moror, -ārī, morātus sum	I delay	*ōra, -ae*, f.	shore
prōdō, -ere, prōdidī, prōditum	I betray	*praemium, -ī*, n.	reward
sūmō, -ere, sūmpsī, sūmptum	I take up, assume	*regiō, -ōnis*, f.	region
tangō, -ere, tetigī, tāctum	I touch	*rēspūblica, reīpūblicae**, f.	republic
tegō, -ere, tēxī, tēctum	I cover	*rīpa, -ae*, f.	river bank
Adjectives		*sōl, sōlis*, m.	sun
aeger, aegra, aegrum	sick	*vulnus, vulneris*, n.	wound
alter...alter	the one...the other	**Adverbs**	
dubius, -a, -um	doubtful	*semel*	once
mortuus, -a, -um	dead	*bis*	twice
summus, -a, -um	topmost, greatest		

* Both parts of the word decline, *rēs* being 5th declension, *pūblicus* being an adjective.

So you really want to learn Latin...

Exercise 10. 9

Study the tips on unseen translation technique on the left-hand page. Then translate into English: *Augustus Caesar.*

nātus est Rōmae Augustus <u>a.d. IX Kal. Oct</u>. in regiōne Palātiī. sūmptā <u>virīlī togā</u>, <u>mīlitāribus dōnīs</u> dōnātus est, quamquam nōn tunc bellī perītus erat. simul atque autem Caesarem occīsum esse cognōvit, proximās legiōnēs īnstruere cōnstituit. id tamen cōnsilium ut audācissimum mox relīquit Rōmamque ut <u>hērēditātem</u> quaereret adiit, nōlente mātre, <u>vitricō</u> vērō Mārciō Philippō multum dissuādente. atque ab eō tempore, exercitibus comparātīs, prīmum cum M. Antōniō Mārcōque Lepidō, deinde tantum cum M. Antōniō, tandem per quattuor et quadrāgintā annōs sōlus rempūblicam tenuit.

Caesaris et deinde Augustī <u>cognōmina</u> eī data sunt, alterum post <u>maioris</u> <u>avunculī</u> mortem, alterum cum Mūnātius Plancus, quibusdam putantibus eum Rōmulum appellārī oportēre, vehementer monuisset ut Augustus nōn tantum novō sed etiam maiōre cognōmine vocārētur.

a.d. IX Kal. Oct.: for date formats, see Book II, p. 53; *virīlis toga*: the toga adopted by a boy on reaching manhood; *mīlitāria dōna*: the badges presented to soldiers in recognition of their service; *hērēditās, -ātis*, f. = inheritance; *vitricus, -ī*, m. = step-father; *cognōmen*: the Roman surname; *maior avunculus, -ī*, m. (here) = great-uncle.

Exercise 10. 10

Translate into English: *Antony and Cleopatra.*

post Pompeī fugam, M. Lepidum, quem ex Africā in auxilium ēvocāverat, exercitū <u>spoliāvit</u> <u>Circeiōsque</u> relēgāvit.

M. Antōniī amīcitiam semper dubiam et incertam tandem abrūpit, nec multō post nāvālī proeliō eum apud Actium vīcit. adeō prōtrācta erat illa pugna ut in nāve victor <u>pernoctāverit</u>. <u>Actiō</u> autem in <u>hīberna</u> sē recēpit. monitus tamen ā nūntiīs dē sēditiōne mīlitum, praemia et <u>missiōnem</u> volentium, in Ītaliam rediit. deinde, septem et vīgintī diēs <u>Brundisiī</u> morātus, Aegyptum petiit quō Antōnius cum Cleopatrā fūgerat, et Alexandrēam mox cēpit.

et Antōnium quidem, condiciōnēs pācis petentem, ad mortem adēgit, vīditque mortuum, et Cleopatrae, quam vīvam capere magnopere cupiēbat, etiam <u>Psyllōs</u> mīsit, quī venēnum <u>exsūgerent</u>, quod <u>morsū</u> <u>aspidis</u> periisse putābātur. utrīque commūnem <u>sepultūrae</u> honōrem dedit ac <u>tumulum</u> ab ipsīs inceptum perficī iussit.

spoliō, -āre, (+ abl.) = I strip (of); *Circeiī, -ōrum*, m. pl. = Circeii, a town on the coast of Latium; *pernoctō, -āre* = I spend the night; *Actium, -iī*, n. = Actium (on the west coast of Greece); *hīberna, -ōrum*, n. pl. = winter quarters; *missiō, -ōnis*, f. = release (from service); *Brundisium, -iī*, n. = Brundisium (in Italy); *Psyllī, -ōrum*, m. pl.: the Psylli were a tribe of snake-charmers; *exsūgō, -ere* = I suck out; *morsus, -ūs*, m. = a bite; *aspis, aspidis*, f. = an asp; *sepultūra, -ae*, f. = burial; *tumulus, -ī*, m. = tomb.

Using Latin

Quasi

The expression *quasi* means "almost" from the Latin *quasi* = "as if". E.g. "They were engaged in a *quasi* war".

The rise of Augustus

So there he was, lying on the ground, covered in knife wounds: Julius Caesar, the most successful Roman general of all time. As you can imagine, Caesar's murder caused something of a stir and those in the know set about trying to capitalise on the situation. Mark Antony, for one, rushed around saying "Friends, Romans, countrymen, lend me your ears..." and generally trying to turn the mob against the conspirators who had murdered Caesar, led by Brutus and Cassius. Caesar's great-nephew Octavian, whom he had adopted, despite being only a very young man, was also pretty keen to make his mark; and a third chap called Lepidus also joined the party. Together, these three men formed an alliance which came to be known as the second triumvirate and in 42 B.C., after Antony had defeated Brutus and Cassius at the Battle of Philippi, the Roman world was divided between them. After a bit of to-ing and fro-ing, Antony received Egypt and the east, Octavian received Italy and Lepidus was given a strip of North Africa! It was not long before Lepidus was out of the running and the power struggle came to be centred on Antony and Octavian.

At this stage, enter once more Cleopatra, Queen of Egypt. Antony wasted little time in falling in love with the beautiful queen and soon forgot all his Roman virtues of manliness and so on. While Octavian raised support in Italy, Antony stayed in bed in Egypt. This was particularly tactless as at the time Antony was married to Octavian's sister. In 31 B.C. Octavian challenged Antony to a fight and at the Battle of Actium the navy of Antony and Cleopatra was routed by Octavian. The next year the two lovers took their own lives, and Octavian was left sole ruler of the Roman world.

So the adopted son of Julius Caesar was now sole ruler of the Roman world. He returned to Rome in triumph and fooled the people into believing that his only wish in life was to restore the republic which had been so battered and corrupted during the long years of civil war which had dragged on for the past hundred years. He accepted the title of *prīnceps* (= "leader") and yet made out that he only wished to see good old-fashioned republican government restored. In 27 B.C. he was given the name *Augustus* and a golden shield was erected in the senate house, celebrating his valour, clemency, justice and piety. He was granted proconsular powers for various extended periods and an oath of allegiance was sworn to him throughout the empire. The Roman *republic* had effectively ceased to exist; the first Roman *emperor* was now firmly in charge.

The principate of Augustus ushered in a great age of artistic achievement. Poets and historians wrote works of literature celebrating his achievements in restoring peace to the Roman world and looking to a new golden age. It was in this age that much of the literature which you will read was written. Virgil, Horace, Livy *et al.* sang Augustus's praises for all to hear. And here we are, two thousand years later, still reading it. Not bad, eh?

So you really want to learn Latin...

Exercise 10. 11

Study the information on the left-hand page about Augustus. Then answer the following questions in complete sentences:

1. After the murder of Julius Caesar in 44 B.C., who tried to stir up the mob against the conspirators who had killed him?

2. What was the relationship between Julius Caesar and Octavian?

3. Which three men joined to form the second triumvirate?

4. Which three men had joined to form the *first* triumvirate (Chapter 9)?

5. When, and at which battle, were Brutus and Cassius defeated?

6. Why do you think the Roman people disapproved of Antony's behaviour in Egypt?

7. When, and at which battle, did Octavian defeat Antony?

8. What happened to Antony and Cleopatra?

9. Which title was Octavian given in 27 B.C.?

10. What had happened to the Roman republic by this stage?

Using Latin

Q.E.D.
These letters stand for *quod erat dēmōnstrandum* = "which was (the thing) to be proved".

Latin checklist

So that's it. You know a huge amount of Latin now, and can leap into Latin authors with gay abandon. Before you do, though, you might like to pat yourself on the back. Laid out below is all the grammar you have covered and should now know; at the back is an index of subjects. Impressive, isn't it? Tick it off if you know it, revise it if you don't. And well done; if you really do know all this, there isn't very much Latin that you don't know. Well, not too much, anyway…

Vocabulary

☐ Book I, Vocab. 1
☐ Book I, Vocab. 2
☐ Book I, Vocab. 3
☐ Book I, Vocab. 4
☐ Book I, Vocab. 5
☐ Book I, Vocab. 6
☐ Book I, Vocab. 7
☐ Book I, Vocab. 8
☐ Book I, Vocab. 9
☐ Book I, Vocab. 10

☐ Book II, Vocab. 1
☐ Book II, Vocab. 2
☐ Book II, Vocab. 3
☐ Book II, Vocab. 4
☐ Book II, Vocab. 5
☐ Book II, Vocab. 6
☐ Book II, Vocab. 7
☐ Book II, Vocab. 8
☐ Book II, Vocab. 9
☐ Book II, Vocab. 10

☐ Book III, Vocab. 1
☐ Book III, Vocab. 2
☐ Book III, Vocab. 3
☐ Book III, Vocab. 4
☐ Book III, Vocab. 5
☐ Book III, Vocab. 6
☐ Book III, Vocab. 7
☐ Book III, Vocab. 8
☐ Book III, Vocab. 9
☐ Book III, Vocab. 10

Grammar

1. Regular verbs

☐ 6 tenses indic. active
☐ 6 tenses indic. passive
☐ 4 tenses subj. active
☐ 4 tenses subj. passive
☐ Infinitives, act. and pass.
☐ Imperatives, act. and pass.
☐ 3 Participles
☐ Gerunds and gerundives
☐ Shortened verb forms

2. Irregular verbs

☐ *Sum*
☐ *Possum*
☐ *Eō*
☐ *Ferō*
☐ *Volō*
☐ *Nōlō*
☐ *Mālō*
☐ *Edō*
☐ *Fīō*

3. Pronouns

☐ *ego, tū, nōs, vōs*
☐ *ipse*
☐ *quīdam*
☐ *hic, haec, hoc*
☐ *īdem*
☐ *is, ea, id*
☐ *quī, quae, quod*
☐ *quis* and *aliquis*
☐ *ille, illa, illud*

4. Nouns

☐ 1st dec.: *mēnsa*
☐ 2nd dec.: *annus, puer, magister, bellum*
☐ 2nd dec., irreg.: *fīlius, deus, vir*
☐ 3rd dec., increasing: *rēx, opus*
☐ 3rd dec., non-increasing: *cīvis, cubīle*
☐ 4th dec.: *gradus, genū*
☐ 4th dec., irreg.: *domus*
☐ 5th dec.: *rēs, diēs*

5. Adjectives and adverbs

☐ 1st/2nd dec.: *bonus, tener, pulcher*
☐ 3rd dec.: *ingēns, trīstis, ācer*
☐ 3rd dec.: *melior, vetus*
☐ Declension of numerals: *ūnus, duo, trēs*
☐ Pronominal: *alius*
☐ Regular comparison of adjectives
☐ Irregular comparison of adjectives
☐ Formation and comparison of adverbs

6. Numerals

☐ Cardinals 1-1000
☐ Ordinals 1st – 20th

Summary of Grammar

Regular verbs
Amō = I love

	Active Indicative	Subjunctive	Passive Indicative	Subjunctive
Present	amō	amem	amor	amer
	amās	amēs	amāris	amēris
	amat	amet	amātur	amētur
	amāmus	amēmus	amāmur	amēmur
	amātis	amētis	amāminī	amēminī
	amant	ament	amantur	amentur
Future	amābō		amābor	
	amābis		amāberis	
	amābit		amābitur	
	amābimus		amābimur	
	amābitis		amābiminī	
	amābunt		amābuntur	
Imperfect	amābam	amārem	amābar	amārer
	amābās	amārēs	amābāris	amārēris
	amābat	amāret	amābātur	amārētur
	amābāmus	amārēmus	amābāmur	amārēmur
	amābātis	amārētis	amābāminī	amārēminī
	amābant	amārent	amābantur	amārentur
Perfect	amāvī	amāverim	amātus sum	amātus sim
	amāvistī	amāverīs	amātus es	amātus sīs
	amāvit	amāverit	amātus est	amātus sit
	amāvimus	amāverīmus	amātī sumus	amātī sīmus
	amāvistis	amāverītis	amātī estis	amātī sītis
	amāvērunt	amāverint	amātī sunt	amātī sint
Future Perfect	amāverō		amātus erō	
	amāveris		amātus eris	
	amāverit		amātus erit	
	amāverimus		amātī erimus	
	amāveritis		amātī eritis	
	amāverint		amātī erunt	
Pluperfect	amāveram	amāvissem	amātus eram	amātus essem
	amāverās	amāvissēs	amātus erās	amātus essēs
	amāverat	amāvisset	amātus erat	amātus esset
	amāverāmus	amāvissēmus	amātī erāmus	amātī essēmus
	amāverātis	amāvissētis	amātī erātis	amātī essētis
	amāverant	amāvissent	amātī erant	amātī essent

Regular verbs (cont.)

Moneō = I warn, advise

	Active Indicative	Subjunctive	Passive Indicative	Subjunctive
Present	moneō	moneam	moneor	monear
	monēs	moneās	monēris	moneāris
	monet	moneat	monētur	moneātur
	monēmus	moneāmus	monēmur	moneāmur
	monētis	moneātis	monēminī	moneāminī
	monent	moneant	monentur	moneantur
Future	monēbō		monēbor	
	monēbis		monēberis	
	monēbit		monēbitur	
	monēbimus		monēbimur	
	monēbitis		monēbiminī	
	monēbunt		monēbuntur	
Imperfect	monēbam	monērem	monēbar	monērer
	monēbās	monērēs	monēbāris	monērēris
	monēbat	monēret	monēbātur	monērētur
	monēbāmus	monērēmus	monēbāmur	monērēmur
	monēbātis	monērētis	monēbāminī	monērēminī
	monēbant	monērent	monēbantur	monērentur
Perfect	monuī	monuerim	monitus sum	monitus sim
	monuistī	monuerīs	monitus es	monitus sīs
	monuit	monuerit	monitus est	monitus sit
	monuimus	monuerīmus	monitī sumus	monitī sīmus
	monuistis	monuerītis	monitī estis	monitī sītis
	monuērunt	monuerint	monitī sunt	monitī sint
Future Perfect	monuerō		monitus erō	
	monueris		monitus eris	
	monuerit		monitus erit	
	monuerimus		monitī erimus	
	monueritis		monitī eritis	
	monuerint		monitī erunt	
Pluperfect	monueram	monuissem	monitus eram	monitus essem
	monuerās	monuissēs	monitus erās	monitus essēs
	monuerat	monuisset	monitus erat	monitus esset
	monuerāmus	monuissēmus	monitī erāmus	monitī essēmus
	monuerātis	monuissētis	monitī erātis	monitī essētis
	monuerant	monuissent	monitī erant	monitī essent

Regular verbs (cont.)

Regō = I rule

	Active Indicative	Subjunctive	Passive Indicative	Subjunctive
Present	regō	regam	regor	regar
	regis	regās	regeris	regāris
	regit	regat	regitur	regātur
	regimus	regāmus	regimur	regāmur
	regitis	regātis	regiminī	regāminī
	regunt	regant	reguntur	regantur
Future	regam		regar	
	regēs		regēris	
	reget		regētur	
	regēmus		regēmur	
	regētis		regēminī	
	regent		regentur	
Imperfect	regēbam	regerem	regēbar	regerer
	regēbās	regerēs	regēbāris	regerēris
	regēbat	regeret	regēbātur	regerētur
	regēbāmus	regerēmus	regēbāmur	regerēmur
	regēbātis	regerētis	regēbāminī	regerēminī
	regēbant	regerent	regēbantur	regerentur
Perfect	rēxī	rēxerim	rēctus sum	rēctus sim
	rēxistī	rēxerīs	rēctus es	rēctus sīs
	rēxit	rēxerit	rēctus est	rēctus sit
	rēximus	rēxerīmus	rēctī sumus	rēctī sīmus
	rēxistis	rēxerītis	rēctī estis	rēctī sītis
	rēxērunt	rēxerint	rēctī sunt	rēctī sint
Future Perfect	rēxerō		rēctus erō	
	rēxeris		rēctus eris	
	rēxerit		rēctus erit	
	rēxerimus		rēctī erimus	
	rēxeritis		rēctī eritis	
	rēxerint		rēctī erunt	
Pluperfect	rēxeram	rēxissem	rēctus eram	rēctus essem
	rēxerās	rēxissēs	rēctus erās	rēctus essēs
	rēxerat	rēxisset	rēctus erat	rēctus esset
	rēxerāmus	rēxissēmus	rēctī erāmus	rēctī essēmus
	rēxerātis	rēxissētis	rēctī erātis	rēctī essētis
	rēxerant	rēxissent	rēctī erant	rēctī essent

Regular verbs (cont.)

Audiō = I hear

	Active		Passive	
	Indicative	Subjunctive	Indicative	Subjunctive
Present	audiō	audiam	audior	audiar
	audīs	audiās	audīris	audiāris
	audit	audiat	audītur	audiātur
	audīmus	audiāmus	audīmur	audiāmur
	audītis	audiātis	audīminī	audiāminī
	audiunt	audiant	audiuntur	audiantur
Future	audiam		audiar	
	audiēs		audiēris	
	audiet		audiētur	
	audiēmus		audiēmur	
	audiētis		audiēminī	
	audient		audientur	
Imperfect	audiēbam	audīrem	audiēbar	audīrer
	audiēbās	audīrēs	audiēbāris	audīrēris
	audiēbat	audīret	audiēbātur	audīrētur
	audiēbāmus	audīrēmus	audiēbāmur	audīrēmur
	audiēbātis	audīrētis	audiēbāminī	audīrēminī
	audiēbant	audīrent	audiēbantur	audīrentur
Perfect	audīvī	audīverim	audītus sum	audītus sim
	audīvistī	audīverīs	audītus es	audītus sīs
	audīvit	audīverit	audītus est	audītus sit
	audīvimus	audīverīmus	audītī sumus	audītī sīmus
	audīvistis	audīverītis	audītī estis	audītī sītis
	audīvērunt	audīverint	audītī sunt	audītī sint
Future Perfect	audīverō		audītus erō	
	audīveris		audītus eris	
	audīverit		audītus erit	
	audīverimus		audītī erimus	
	audīveritis		audītī eritis	
	audīverint		audītī erunt	
Pluperfect	audīveram	audīvissem	audītus eram	audītus essem
	audīverās	audīvissēs	audītus erās	audītus essēs
	audīverat	audīvisset	audītus erat	audītus esset
	audīverāmus	audīvissēmus	audītī erāmus	audītī essēmus
	audīverātis	audīvissētis	audītī erātis	audītī essētis
	audīverant	audīvissent	audītī erant	audītī essent

Regular verbs (cont.)

Capiō = I take, capture

	Active		**Passive**	
	Indicative	**Subjunctive**	**Indicative**	**Subjunctive**
Present	capiō	capiam	capior	capiar
	capis	capiās	caperis	capiāris
	capit	capiat	capitur	capiātur
	capimus	capiāmus	capimur	capiāmur
	capitis	capiātis	capiminī	capiāminī
	capiunt	capiant	capiuntur	capiantur
Future	capiam		capiar	
	capiēs		capiēris	
	capiet		capiētur	
	capiēmus		capiēmur	
	capiētis		capiēminī	
	capient		capientur	
Imperfect	capiēbam	caperem	capiēbar	caperer
	capiēbās	caperēs	capiēbāris	caperēris
	capiēbat	caperet	capiēbātur	caperētur
	capiēbāmus	caperēmus	capiēbāmur	caperēmur
	capiēbātis	caperētis	capiēbāminī	caperēminī
	capiēbant	caperent	capiēbantur	caperentur
Perfect	cēpī	cēperim	captus sum	captus sim
	cēpistī	cēperīs	captus es	captus sīs
	cēpit	cēperit	captus est	captus sit
	cēpimus	cēperīmus	captī sumus	captī sīmus
	cēpistis	cēperītis	captī estis	captī sītis
	cēpērunt	cēperint	captī sunt	captī sint
Future Perfect	cēperō		captus erō	
	cēperis		captus eris	
	cēperit		captus erit	
	cēperimus		captī erimus	
	cēperitis		captī eritis	
	cēperint		captī erunt	
Pluperfect	cēperam	cēpissem	captus eram	captus essem
	cēperās	cēpissēs	captus erās	captus essēs
	cēperat	cēpisset	captus erat	captus esset
	cēperāmus	cēpissēmus	captī erāmus	captī essēmus
	cēperātis	cēpissētis	captī erātis	captī essētis
	cēperant	cēpissent	captī erant	captī essent

Regular verbs (cont.)

Infinitives
Present active

amāre	*monēre*	*regere*	*audīre*	*capere*

Future active

amātūrus esse	*monitūrus esse*	*rēctūrus esse*	*audītūrus esse*	*captūrus esse*

Perfect active

amāvisse	*monuisse*	*rēxisse*	*audīvisse*	*cēpisse*

Present passive

amārī	*monērī*	*regī*	*audīrī*	*capī*

"Future passive"

(amātum īrī)	*(monitum īrī)*	*(rēctum īrī)*	*(audītum īrī)*	*(captum īrī)*

Perfect passive

amātus esse	*monitus esse*	*rēctus esse*	*audītus esse*	*captus esse*

Imperatives
Active

amā/	*monē/*	*rege/*	*audī/*	*cape/*
amāte	*monēte*	*regite*	*audīte*	*capite*

Passive

amāre/	*monēre/*	*regere/*	*audīre/*	*capere/*
amāminī	*monēminī*	*regiminī*	*audīminī*	*capiminī*

Participles
Present

amāns	*monēns*	*regēns*	*audiēns*	*capiēns*

Future

amātūrus	*monitūrus*	*rēctūrus*	*audītūrus*	*captūrus*

Perfect (PPP)

amātus	*monitus*	*rēctus*	*audītus*	*captus*

Gerunds and gerundives
Gerund

amandum	*monendum*	*regendum*	*audiendum*	*capiendum*

Gerundive

amandus	*monendus*	*regendus*	*audiendus*	*capiendus*

Irregular verbs

Indicative				Active	Passive
Present	sum	possum	eō	ferō	feror
	es	potes	īs	fers	ferris
	est	potest	it	fert	fertur
	sumus	possumus	īmus	ferimus	ferimur
	estis	potestis	ītis	fertis	feriminī
	sunt	possunt	eunt	ferunt	feruntur
Future	erō	poterō	ībō	feram	ferar
	eris	poteris	ībis	ferēs	ferēris
	erit	poterit	ībit	feret	ferētur
	erimus	poterimus	ībimus	ferēmus	ferēmur
	eritis	poteritis	ībitis	ferētis	ferēminī
	erunt	poterunt	ībunt	ferent	ferentur
Imperfect	eram	poteram	ībam	ferēbam	ferēbar
	erās	poterās	ībās	ferēbās	ferēbāris
	erat	poterat	ībat	ferēbat	ferēbātur
	erāmus	poterāmus	ībāmus	ferēbāmus	ferēbāmur
	erātis	poterātis	ībātis	ferēbātis	ferēbāminī
	erant	poterant	ībant	ferēbant	ferēbantur

Subjunctive				Active	Passive
Present	sim	possim	eam	feram	ferar
	sīs	possīs	eās	ferās	ferāris
	sit	possit	eat	ferat	ferātur
	sīmus	possīmus	eāmus	ferāmus	ferāmur
	sītis	possītis	eātis	ferātis	ferāminī
	sint	possint	eant	ferant	ferāntur
Imperfect	essem	possem	īrem	ferrem	ferrer
	essēs	possēs	īrēs	ferrēs	ferrēris
	esset	posset	īret	ferret	ferrētur
	essēmus	possēmus	īrēmus	ferrēmus	ferrēmur
	essētis	possētis	īrētis	ferrētis	ferrēminī
	essent	possent	īrent	ferrent	ferrentur

Infinitives				Active	Passive
Present	esse	posse	īre	ferre	ferrī
Future	futūrus esse/ fore	-	itūrus esse	lātūrus esse	(lātum īrī)
Perfect	fuisse	potuisse	īsse/īvisse	tulisse	lātus esse
Imperatives	es/este	-	ī/īte	fer/ferte	ferre/feriminī
Participles					
Present	-	-	iēns (euntis)	ferēns	
Future	futūrus	-	itūrus	lātūrus	
Perfect (PPP)	-	-	-		lātus
Gerund	-	-	eundum	ferendum	
Gerundive	-	-	-		ferendus

Irregular verbs (cont.)

Indicative

Present

volō	*nōlō*	*mālō*	*edō*	*fīō*
vīs	*nōn vīs*	*māvīs*	*ēs*	*fīs*
vult	*nōn vult*	*māvult*	*ēst*	*fit*
volumus	*nōlumus*	*mālumus*	*edimus*	*(fīmus)*
vultis	*nōn vultis*	*māvultis*	*ēstis*	*(fītis)*
volunt	*nōlunt*	*mālunt*	*edunt*	*fīunt*

Future

volam	*nōlam*	*mālam*	*edam*	*fīam*
volēs	*nōlēs*	*mālēs*	*edēs*	*fīēs*
volet	*nōlet*	*mālet*	*edet*	*fīēt*
volēmus	*nōlēmus*	*mālēmus*	*edēmus*	*fīēmus*
volētis	*nōlētis*	*mālētis*	*edētis*	*fīētis*
volent	*nōlent*	*mālent*	*edent*	*fīent*

Imperfect

volēbam	*nōlēbam*	*mālēbam*	*edēbam*	*fīēbam*
volēbās	*nōlēbās*	*mālēbās*	*edēbās*	*fīēbās*
volēbat	*nōlēbat*	*mālēbat*	*edēbat*	*fīēbat*
volēbāmus	*nōlēbāmus*	*mālēbāmus*	*edēbāmus*	*fīēbāmus*
volēbātis	*nōlēbātis*	*mālēbātis*	*edēbātis*	*fīēbātis*
volēbant	*nōlēbant*	*mālēbant*	*edēbant*	*fīebant*

Subjunctive

Present

velim	*nōlim*	*mālim*	*edam/edim*	*fīam*
velīs	*nōlīs*	*mālīs*	*edās/edīs*	*fīās*
velit	*nōlit*	*mālit*	*edat/edit*	*fīat*
velīmus	*nōlīmus*	*mālīmus*	*edāmus*	*fīāmus*
velītis	*nōlītis*	*mālītis*	*edātis*	*fīātis*
velint	*nōlint*	*mālint*	*edant/edint*	*fīant*

Imperfect

vellem	*nōllem*	*māllem*	*ēssem*	*fierem*
vellēs	*nōllēs*	*māllēs*	*ēssēs*	*fierēs*
vellet	*nōllet*	*māllet*	*ēsset*	*fieret*
vellēmus	*nōllēmus*	*māllēmus*	*ēssēmus*	*fierēmus*
vellētis	*nōllētis*	*māllētis*	*ēssētis*	*fierētis*
vellent	*nōllent*	*māllent*	*ēssent*	*fierent*

Infinitives

Present	*velle*	*nōlle*	*mālle*	*esse*	*fīĕrī*
Future	-	-	-	*ēsūrus esse*	*futūrus esse*
Perfect	*voluisse*	*nōluisse*	*māluisse*	*ēdisse*	-
Imperatives	-	*nōlī/nōlīte*	-	*ēs/ēste*	*fī/fīte*

Participles

Present	*volēns*	*nōlēns*	-	*edēns*	-
Future	-	-	-	*ēsūrus*	*futūrus*
Perfect (PPP)	-	-	-	*ēsus*	*factus*
Gerund	*(volendum)*	*(nōlendum)*	-	*edendum*	-
Gerundive	-	-	-	*edendus*	*faciendus*

Nouns

1st declension

Nominative	*mēnsa*	Table (subject)
Vocative	*mēnsa*	O table
Accusative	*mēnsam*	Table (object)
Genitive	*mēnsae*	Of the table
Dative	*mēnsae*	To or for the table
Ablative	*mēnsā*	With, by or from the table

Nominative	*mēnsae*	Tables (subject)
Vocative	*mēnsae*	O tables
Accusative	*mēnsās*	Tables (object)
Genitive	*mēnsārum*	Of the tables
Dative	*mēnsīs*	To or for the tables
Ablative	*mēnsīs*	With, by or from the tables

2nd declension

Nominative	*annus*	*puer*	*magister*	*bellum*
Vocative	*anne*	*puer*	*magister*	*bellum*
Accusative	*annum*	*puerum*	*magistrum*	*bellum*
Genitive	*annī*	*puerī*	*magistrī*	*bellī*
Dative	*annō*	*puerō*	*magistrō*	*bellō*
Ablative	*annō*	*puerō*	*magistrō*	*bellō*

Nominative	*annī*	*puerī*	*magistrī*	*bella*
Vocative	*annī*	*puerī*	*magistrī*	*bella*
Accusative	*annōs*	*puerōs*	*magistrōs*	*bella*
Genitive	*annōrum*	*puerōrum*	*magistrōrum*	*bellōrum*
Dative	*annīs*	*puerīs*	*magistrīs*	*bellīs*
Ablative	*annīs*	*puerīs*	*magistrīs*	*bellīs*

2nd declension: irregular

Nominative	*fīlius*	*deus*	*vir*
Vocative	*fīlī*	*deus*	*vir*
Accusative	*fīlium*	*deum*	*virum*
Genitive	*fīlī (fīliī)*	*deī*	*virī*
Dative	*fīliō*	*deō*	*virō*
Ablative	*fīliō*	*deō*	*virō*

Nominative	*fīliī*	*dī*	*virī*
Vocative	*fīliī*	*dī*	*virī*
Accusative	*fīliōs*	*deōs*	*virōs*
Genitive	*fīliōrum*	*deōrum (deum)*	*virōrum (virum)*
Dative	*fīliīs*	*dīs (deīs)*	*virīs*
Ablative	*fīliīs*	*dīs (deīs)*	*virīs*

Nouns (cont.)

3rd declension

Nominative	*rēx*	*opus*	*cīvis*	*cubīle*
Vocative	*rēx*	*opus*	*cīvis*	*cubīle*
Accusative	*rēgem*	*opus*	*cīvem*	*cubīle*
Genitive	*rēgis*	*operis*	*cīvis*	*cubīlis*
Dative	*rēgī*	*operī*	*cīvī*	*cubīlī*
Ablative	*rēge*	*opere*	*cīve/cīvī**	*cubīlī*

Nominative	*rēgēs*	*opera*	*cīvēs*	*cubīlia*
Vocative	*rēgēs*	*opera*	*cīvēs*	*cubīlia*
Accusative	*rēgēs*	*opera*	*cīvēs/cīvīs**	*cubīlia*
Genitive	*rēgum*	*operum*	*cīvium*	*cubīlium*
Dative	*rēgibus*	*operibus*	*cīvibus*	*cubīlibus*
Ablative	*rēgibus*	*operibus*	*cīvibus*	*cubīlibus*

* N.B. During the golden age of Latin literature, the accusative plural ending in -*īs* was preferred for nouns (and adjectives) having genitive plural in -*ium*. However both -*īs* and -*ēs* were used. Likewise, the ablative singular for such nouns often ended in -*ī* rather than -*e*.

3rd declension: irregular

Nominative	*bōs*	*vīs*	*Iuppiter*
Vocative	*bōs*	*vīs*	*Iuppiter*
Accusative	*bovem*	*vim*	*Iovem*
Genitive	*bovis*	-	*Iovis*
Dative	*bovī*	-	*Iovī*
Ablative	*bove*	*vī*	*Iove*

Nominative	*bovēs*	*vīrēs*	
Vocative	*bovēs*	*vīrēs*	
Accusative	*bovēs*	*vīrēs*	
Genitive	*boum*	*vīrium*	
Dative	*bōbus/būbus*	*vīribus*	
Ablative	*bōbus/būbus*	*vīribus*	

4th declension

Nominative	*gradus*	*genū*	*domus*
Vocative	*gradus*	*genū*	*domus*
Accusative	*gradum*	*genū*	*domum*
Genitive	*gradūs*	*genūs*	*domūs*
Dative	*graduī*	*genū*	*domuī (domō)*
Ablative	*gradū*	*genū*	*domō*

Nominative	*gradūs*	*genua*	*domūs*
Vocative	*gradūs*	*genua*	*domūs*
Accusative	*gradūs*	*genua*	*domōs (domūs)*
Genitive	*graduum*	*genuum*	*domuum (domōrum)*
Dative	*gradibus*	*genibus*	*domibus*
Ablative	*gradibus*	*genibus*	*domibus*

Nouns (cont.)

5th declension

Nominative	*rēs*	*diēs*
Vocative	*rēs*	*diēs*
Accusative	*rem*	*diem*
Genitive	*reī*	*diēī*
Dative	*reī*	*diēī*
Ablative	*rē*	*diē*

Nominative	*rēs*	*diēs*
Vocative	*rēs*	*diēs*
Accusative	*rēs*	*diēs*
Genitive	*rērum*	*diērum*
Dative	*rēbus*	*diēbus*
Ablative	*rēbus*	*diēbus*

Adjectives

1st / 2nd declension

	M	F	N
Nominative	*bonus*	*bona*	*bonum*
Vocative	*bone*	*bona*	*bonum*
Accusative	*bonum*	*bonam*	*bonum*
Genitive	*bonī*	*bonae*	*bonī*
Dative	*bonō*	*bonae*	*bonō*
Ablative	*bonō*	*bonā*	*bonō*

	M	F	N
Nominative	*bonī*	*bonae*	*bona*
Vocative	*bonī*	*bonae*	*bona*
Accusative	*bonōs*	*bonās*	*bona*
Genitive	*bonōrum*	*bonārum*	*bonōrum*
Dative	*bonīs*	*bonīs*	*bonīs*
Ablative	*bonīs*	*bonīs*	*bonīs*

	M	F	N	M	F	N
Nominative	*tener*	*tenera*	*tenerum*	*pulcher*	*pulchra*	*pulchrum*
Vocative	*tener*	*tenera*	*tenerum*	*pulcher*	*pulchra*	*pulchrum*
Accusative	*tenerum*	*teneram*	*tenerum*	*pulchrum*	*pulchram*	*pulchrum*
Genitive	*tenerī*	*tenerae*	*tenerī*	*pulchrī*	*pulchrae*	*pulchrī*
Dative	*tenerō*	*tenerae*	*tenerō*	*pulchrō*	*pulchrae*	*pulchrō*
Ablative	*tenerō*	*tenerā*	*tenerō*	*pulchrō*	*pulchrā*	*pulchrō*

	M	F	N	M	F	N
Nominative	*tenerī*	*tenerae*	*tenera*	*pulchrī*	*pulchrae*	*pulchra*
Vocative	*tenerī*	*tenerae*	*tenera*	*pulchrī*	*pulchrae*	*pulchra*
Accusative	*tenerōs*	*tenerās*	*tenera*	*pulchrōs*	*pulchrās*	*pulchra*
Genitive	*tenerōrum*	*tenerārum*	*tenerōrum*	*pulchrōrum*	*pulchrārum*	*pulchrōrum*
Dative	*tenerīs*	*tenerīs*	*tenerīs*	*pulchrīs*	*pulchrīs*	*pulchrīs*
Ablative	*tenerīs*	*tenerīs*	*tenerīs*	*pulchrīs*	*pulchrīs*	*pulchrīs*

Adjectives (cont.)

3rd declension

	M	F	N	M	F	N
Nominative	ingēns	ingēns	ingēns	trīstis	trīstis	trīste
Vocative	ingēns	ingēns	ingēns	trīstis	trīstis	trīste
Accusative	ingentem	ingentem	ingēns	trīstem	trīstem	trīste
Genitive	ingentis	ingentis	ingentis	trīstis	trīstis	trīstis
Dative	ingentī	ingentī	ingentī	trīstī	trīstī	trīstī
Ablative	ingentī	ingentī	ingentī	trīstī	trīstī	trīstī
Nominative	ingentēs	ingentēs	ingentia	trīstēs	trīstēs	trīstia
Vocative	ingentēs	ingentēs	ingentia	trīstēs	trīstēs	trīstia
Accusative	ingentēs/īs*	ingentēs/īs*	ingentia	trīstēs/īs*	trīstēs/īs*	trīstia
Genitive	ingentium	ingentium	ingentium	trīstium	trīstium	trīstium
Dative	ingentibus	ingentibus	ingentibus	trīstibus	trīstibus	trīstibus
Ablative	ingentibus	ingentibus	ingentibus	trīstibus	trīstibus	trīstibus

	M	F	N	M	F	N
Nominative	ācer	ācris	ācre	melior	melior	melius
Vocative	ācer	ācris	ācre	melior	melior	melius
Accusative	ācrem	ācrem	ācre	meliōrem	meliōrem	melius
Genitive	ācris	ācris	ācris	meliōris	meliōris	meliōris
Dative	ācrī	ācrī	ācrī	meliōrī	meliōrī	meliōrī
Ablative	ācrī	ācrī	ācrī	meliōre	meliōre	meliōre
Nominative	ācrēs	ācrēs	ācria	meliōrēs	meliōrēs	meliōra
Vocative	ācrēs	ācrēs	ācria	meliōrēs	meliōrēs	meliōra
Accusative	ācrēs/īs*	ācrēs/īs*	ācria	meliōrēs	meliōrēs	meliōra
Genitive	ācrium	ācrium	ācrium	meliōrum	meliōrum	meliōrum
Dative	ācribus	ācribus	ācribus	meliōribus	meliōribus	meliōribus
Ablative	ācribus	ācribus	ācribus	meliōribus	meliōribus	meliōribus

* N.B. During the golden age of Latin literature, the accusative plural ending in -*īs* was preferred for adjectives (and nouns) having genitive plural in -*ium*. However both -*īs* and -*ēs* were used.

	M	F	N
Nominative	vetus	vetus	vetus
Vocative	vetus	vetus	vetus
Accusative	veterem	veterem	vetus
Genitive	veteris	veteris	veteris
Dative	veterī	veterī	veterī
Ablative	vetere	vetere	vetere
Nominative	veterēs	veterēs	vetera
Vocative	veterēs	veterēs	vetera
Accusative	veterēs	veterēs	vetera
Genitive	veterum	veterum	veterum
Dative	veteribus	veteribus	veteribus
Ablative	veteribus	veteribus	veteribus

Adjectives (cont.)

Pronominal adjectives

Alius = other

	M	F	N
Nominative	alius	alia	aliud
Accusative	alium	aliam	aliud
Genitive	alĭus*	alĭus*	alĭus*
Dative	aliī**	aliī**	aliī**
Ablative	aliō	aliā	aliō
Nominative	aliī	aliae	alia
Accusative	aliōs	aliās	alia
Genitive	aliōrum	aliārum	aliōrum
Dative	aliīs	aliīs	aliīs
Ablative	aliīs	aliīs	aliīs

Alter = other (of two)

	M	F	N
Nominative	alter	altera	alterum
Accusative	alterum	alteram	alterum
Genitive	alterĭus	alterĭus	alterĭus
Dative	alterī	alterī	alterī
Ablative	alterō	alterā	alterō
Nominative	alterī	alterae	altera
Accusative	alterōs	alterās	altera
Genitive	alterōrum	alterārum	alterōrum
Dative	alterīs	alterīs	alterīs
Ablative	alterīs	alterīs	alterīs

* *alterĭus*, the genitive singular of *alter*, is normally used in place of *alĭus*.
**alterī, the dative singular of *alter*, is normally used in place of *aliī*.

Pronouns

Personal

					Reflexive
Nominative	egŏ	tū	nōs	vōs	-
Vocative	-	tū	-	vōs	-
Accusative	mē	tē	nōs	vōs	sē
Genitive	meī	tuī	nostrum/ nostrī*	vestrum/ vestrī*	suī
Dative	mihĭ	tibĭ	nōbīs	vōbīs	sibĭ
Ablative	mē	tē	nōbīs	vōbīs	sē

* *Nostrum* and *vestrum* are said to be **partitive genitives** because they are used after words which express a part (e.g. *ūnus nostrum* = one of us). *Nostrī* and *vestrī* are **objective genitives**, used after nouns and adjectives in which a verbal notion is prominent (e.g. your love of us = *amor tuus nostrī*).

Demonstrative

Is = that (near me); he, she, it

	M	F	N
Nominative	is	ea	id
Accusative	eum	eam	id
Genitive	eius	eius	eius
Dative	eī	eī	eī
Ablative	eō	eā	eō
Nominative	eī/iī	eae	ea
Accusative	eōs	eās	ea
Genitive	eōrum	eārum	eōrum
Dative	eīs/iīs	eīs/iīs	eīs/iīs
Ablative	eīs/iīs	eīs/iīs	eīs/iīs

Ille = that (yonder); he, she, it

	M	F	N
Nominative	ille	illa	illud
Accusative	illum	illam	illud
Genitive	illĭus	illĭus	illĭus
Dative	illī	illī	illī
Ablative	illō	illā	illō
Nominative	illī	illae	illa
Accusative	illōs	illās	illa
Genitive	illōrum	illārum	illōrum
Dative	illīs	illīs	illīs
Ablative	illīs	illīs	illīs

Pronouns (cont.)

Demonstrative

Hic = this

	M	F	N
Nominative	hic	haec	hoc
Accusative	hunc	hanc	hoc
Genitive	huius	huius	huius
Dative	huic	huic	huic
Ablative	hōc	hāc	hōc
Nominative	hī	hae	haec
Accusative	hōs	hās	haec
Genitive	hōrum	hārum	hōrum
Dative	hīs	hīs	hīs
Ablative	hīs	hīs	hīs

Relative

Quī = who

	M	F	N
Nominative	quī	quae	quod
Accusative	quem	quam	quod
Genitive	cuius	cuius	cuius
Dative	cui	cui	cui
Ablative	quō	quā	quō
Nominative	quī	quae	quae
Accusative	quōs	quās	quae
Genitive	quōrum	quārum	quōrum
Dative	quibus*	quibus*	quibus*
Ablative	quibus*	quibus*	quibus*

* or *quīs*

N.B. In the dative singular, *huic* and *cui* are diphthongs, pronounced as one syllable.

Intensive

Ipse = self

	M	F	N
Nominative	ipse	ipsa	ipsum
Accusative	ipsum	ipsam	ipsum
Genitive	ipsĭus	ipsĭus	ipsĭus
Dative	ipsī	ipsī	ipsī
Ablative	ipsō	ipsā	ipsō
Nominative	ipsī	ipsae	ipsa
Accusative	ipsōs	ipsās	ipsa
Genitive	ipsōrum	ipsārum	ipsōrum
Dative	ipsīs	ipsīs	ipsīs
Ablative	ipsīs	ipsīs	ipsīs

Definitive

Īdem = the same

	M	F	N
Nominative	īdem	eadem	ĭdem
Accusative	eundem	eandem	ĭdem
Genitive	eiusdem	eiusdem	eiusdem
Dative	eīdem	eīdem	eīdem
Ablative	eōdem	eādem	eōdem
Nominative	eīdem/īdem	eaedem	eadem
Accusative	eōsdem	eāsdem	eadem
Genitive	eōrundem	eārundem	eōrundem
Dative	eīsdem*	eīsdem*	eīsdem*
Ablative	eīsdem*	eīsdem*	eīsdem*

* or *īsdem*

Pronouns (cont.)

Interrogative pronoun
Quis? = who?

	M	F	N	
Nominative	{ *quis*	*quis*	*quid*	(Pronoun)
	{ *qui*	*quae*	*quod*	(Adjective)
Accusative	{ *quem*	*quam*	*quid*	(Pronoun)
	{ *quem*	*quam*	*quod*	(Adjective)

In all other cases, singular and plural, this is exactly like the relative pronoun.

Indefinite pronouns
Quis = anyone

	M	F	N	
Nominative	{ *quis*	*quis*	*quid*	(Pronoun)
	{ *qui*	*qua*	*quod*	(Adjective)
Accusative	{ *quem*	*quam*	*quid*	(Pronoun)
	{ *quem*	*quam*	*quod*	(Adjective)

In all other cases, singular and plural, this is exactly like the relative pronoun.

Aliquis = someone

	M	F	N	
Nominative	{ *aliquis*	*aliquis*	*aliquid*	(Pronoun)
	{ *aliqui*	*aliqua*	*aliquod*	(Adjective)
Accusative	{ *aliquem*	*aliquam*	*aliquid*	(Pronoun)
	{ *aliquem*	*aliquam*	*aliquod*	(Adjective)

In all other cases, singular and plural, this is exactly like the relative pronoun, with the prefix *ali-*, except that the neuter nom. and acc. plural can be *aliquae* or *aliqua*.

Quīdam = a certain

	M	F	N	
Nominative	{ *quīdam*	*quaedam*	*quiddam*	(Pronoun)
	{ *quīdam*	*quaedam*	*quoddam*	(Adjective)
Accusative	{ *quendam*	*quandam*	*quiddam*	(Pronoun)
	{ *quendam*	*quandam*	*quoddam*	(Adjective)

In all other cases, singular and plural, this is exactly like the relative pronoun, with the suffix *-dam* except that *m* becomes *n* in front of *-dam*. E.g. *quorundam* etc.

Quisque = each one

	M	F	N	
Nominative	{ *quisque*	*quaeque*	*quidque*	
	{ *quisque*	*quaeque*	*quodque*	
Accusative	{ *quemque*	*quamque*	*quidque*	
	{ *quemque*	*quamque*	*quodque*	
Genitive	*cuiusque*	*cuiusque*	*cuiusque*	Etc.

Quisquam = anyone at all

	M	F	N	
Nominative	*quisquam*	-	*quicquam/quidquam*	
Accusative	*quemquam*	-	*quicquam/quidquam*	
Genitive	*cuiusquam*	-	*cuiusquam*	Etc.

N.B. When using these interrogative and indefinite pronouns, the distinction should be noted (although it only affects the nominative and accusative singular) between, on the one hand, *quis* and *quid* and their compounds (e.g. *aliquis, aliquid*), which are used as **pronouns**; and, on the other hand, *quī* and *quod* and their compounds, which are used as **adjectives**.

Cardinal numerals

1	I	*ūnus*	11	XI	*ūndecim*	30	XXX	*trīgintā*
2	II	*duŏ*	12	XII	*duodecim*	40	XL	*quadrāgintā*
3	III	*trēs*	13	XIII	*tredecim*	50	L	*quīnquāgintā*
4	IV/IIII	*quattuor*	14	XIV	*quattuordecim*	60	LX	*sexāgintā*
5	V	*quīnque*	15	XV	*quīndecim*	70	LXX	*septuāgintā*
6	VI	*sex*	16	XVI	*sēdecim*	80	LXXX	*octōgintā*
7	VII	*septem*	17	XVII	*septendecim*	90	XC	*nōnāgintā*
8	VIII	*octŏ*	18	XVIII	*duodēvīgintī*	100	C	*centum*
9	IX	*novem*	19	XIX	*ūndēvīgintī*	500	D	*quīngentī*
10	X	*decem*	20	XX	*vīgintī*	1000	M	*mīlle*

Ordinals

1st	*prīmus*	11th	*ūndecimus*
2nd	*secundus*	12th	*duodecimus*
3rd	*tertius*	13th	*tertius decimus*
4th	*quārtus*	14th	*quārtus decimus*
5th	*quīntus*	15th	*quīntus decimus*
6th	*sextus*	16th	*sextus decimus*
7th	*septimus*	17th	*septimus decimus*
8th	*octāvus*	18th	*duodēvīcē(n)simus*
9th	*nōnus*	19th	*ūndēvīcē(n)simus*
10th	*decimus*	20th	*vīcē(n)simus*

Declension of numerals

	M	F	N
Nominative	*ūnus*	*ūna*	*ūnum*
Accusative	*ūnum*	*ūnam*	*ūnum*
Genitive	*ūnĭus*	*ūnĭus*	*ūnĭus*
Dative	*ūnī*	*ūnī*	*ūnī*
Ablative	*ūnō*	*ūnā*	*ūnō*

	M	F	N
Nominative	*ūnī*	*ūnae*	*ūna*
Accusative	*ūnōs*	*ūnās*	*ūna*
Genitive	*ūnōrum*	*ūnārum*	*ūnōrum*
Dative	*ūnīs*	*ūnīs*	*ūnīs*
Ablative	*ūnīs*	*ūnīs*	*ūnīs*

	M	F	N
Nominative	*duŏ*	*duae*	*duŏ*
Accusative	*duōs/duŏ*	*duās*	*duŏ*
Genitive	*duōrum*	*duārum*	*duōrum*
Dative	*duōbus*	*duābus*	*duōbus*
Ablative	*duōbus*	*duābus*	*duōbus*

	M	F	N
Nominative	*trēs*	*trēs*	*tria*
Accusative	*trēs*	*trēs*	*tria*
Genitive	*trium*	*trium*	*trium*
Dative	*tribus*	*tribus*	*tribus*
Ablative	*tribus*	*tribus*	*tribus*

APPENDIX

More on vowel quantity

1. Vowels are marked as long where they are known to be long.
2. Vowels are sometimes marked as short where the tendency to get them wrong is so distressing as to require correction (thus *egŏ)*.
3. Vowels are marked as *anceps* (= ambiguous) where the vowel could be pronounced either long or short as, for example, in: *octŏ, homŏ, quandŏ, ibĭ* and *ubĭ.*
4. Consonant *i*: Both Allen (Vox Latina, p. 38–9) and Kennedy (Revised Latin Primer, p. 42, note 3) agree that consonant *i* between two vowels in words such as *huius* and *eius* was pronounced as a doubled consonant and thus that, while the preceding vowel was short, the **syllable** always *scans* long. Books which thus *mark* words such as *maior, peior, Troia, aiō*, etc. as having a long first syllable are presumably doing so for the benefit of pupils writing or scanning verse. But if macrons are there principally to aid pronunciation, as in a book of this sort, they are clearly most misleading if inserted over what are in fact agreed to be short **vowels**. In this context, note that, in the name *Gāĭus*, the *ĭ* is a vowel, not a consonant, and the *ā* really is long!
5. No attempt has been made to indicate whether the letters *i* and *u* are vowels or consonants. It seems sad that the practice of writing consonant *i* as a *j* has been abandoned but it has, so there we go. As for *u*, how one was ever supposed to know that, in a word such as *persuādeō*, there was a "*w* "sound rather than a "*u*" sound, goodness only knows.
6. Vowels before *ns* and *nf* are always long, even (as Allen tells us, p. 65, note 2) at word junction (in the case of a word such as *in*, which goes closely together with the following word). Thus the need to mark the *i* of *īn sitū*, for example, as long.
7. Latin words which have become, by adoption, English ones have caused me some difficulty in the *Using Latin* boxes. I have had to decide whether to write a word such as *veto* as a Latin word, with macrons where appropriate, or as an English one (and thus with no macrons). My policy here, such as it is, has been always to give the Latin word at the top, correctly marked, but to show the word unmarked in the explanation where it has become so much a part of the English language as to have lost its Latin quality altogether.
8. In the words *cui* and *huic*, the *ui* is a diphthong and is thus not marked with a macron. When pronouncing these words, remember that they are one-syllable words, not two.
9. Vowels before *x* and *z*, whether long or short by nature, always scan long, these two letters counting as double consonants. *X* (*c+s*) was derived from the Greek letter *xi*, and *z* was derived from the Greek letter *zeta* (which itself consisted of the sounds z + d). Latin *z* should always be pronounced as a double consonant (e.g. *Mezentius*, pronounced *Mezzentius*).

Latin – English Vocabulary

(Including all words used in Books I, II and III, together with some additional, commonly-used words)

ā, ab (+ abl.) = by, from

abrumpō, -ere, abrūpī, abruptum = I break, sever

absum, abesse, āfuī (goes like *sum*) = I am absent

ac = and (not before vowels or *h*)

accidit, -ere, accidit (ut) = it happens (that)

accipiō, -ere, accēpī, acceptum = I receive

accūsō, -āre, -āvī, -ātum = I accuse

ācer, ācris, ācre = fierce, keen, spirited

Achillēs, -is, m. = Achilles

aciēs, aciēī, f. = battle line

acūtus, -a, -um = sharp

ad (+ acc.) = to, towards

ad (+ gerund or gerundive) = for the purpose of

addō, addere, addidī, additum = I add

adeō = to such an extent

adeō, adīre, adiī, aditum (goes like *eō*) = I approach

adfuī: see *adsum*

āfuī: see *absum*

adēgī: see *adigō*

adhūc = still

adigō, -ere, adēgī, adāctum = I drive to, force to

adiuvō, -āre, adiūvī, adiūtum = I help

admittō, -ere, admīsī, admissum = I allow (to happen), commit

admoveō, -ēre, admōvī, admōtum = I move to, move near to (trans.)

adnuō, adnuere, adnuī, adnūtum = I nod assent

adsum, adesse, adfuī (irreg.) = I am present

adulēscēns, adulēscentis, c. = young person, young man

adveniō, -īre, advēnī, adventum = I arrive

adventus, -ūs, m. = arrival

adversus, -a, -um = facing, opposite, unfavourable

advertō, -ere, advertī, adversum = I turn towards (trans.)

aedificium, -ī, n. = building

aedificō, -āre, -āvī, -ātum = I build

aeger, aegra, aegrum = sick

aegrē (adverb) = with difficulty

Aegyptus, -ī, f. = Egypt

Aenēās, -ae, m. (voc. *Aenēā*, acc. *Aenēān*) = Aeneas

āēr, āěris, (acc.: *āěra*) m. = air

aes, aeris, n. = bronze

aestās, aestātis, f. = summer

aetās, aetātis, f. = age

ager, agrī, m. = field

aggredior, aggredī, aggressus sum = I attack

agmen, agminis, n. = column (of army)

agnōscō, -ere, agnōvī, agnitum = I recognise

agō, agere, ēgī, āctum = I do, drive

agricola, -ae, m. = farmer

aiō (defective; pres.: *aiō, ais, ait, aiunt*; imperf.: *aiēbam*, etc.) = I say

ālea, -ae, f. = die, gaming cube

aliēnus, -a, -um = belonging to another

aliī...aliī = some...others

aliquī, aliqua, aliquod (adjective) = some

aliquis, aliquid (pronoun) = someone, something

alius, alia, aliud = other

alter, altera, alterum = the other (of two)

alter...alter = the one...the other

altitūdō, altitūdīnis, f. = height, depth
altus, -a, -um = deep, high
ambulō, -āre, -āvī, -ātum = I walk
amīcitia, -ae, f. = friendship
amīcus, -ī, m. = friend
āmittō, -ere, āmīsī, āmissum = I
   lose, let go
amō, amāre, amāvī, amātum = I
   love, like
amor, amōris, m. = love
an = or
animadvertō, -ere, animadvertī,
   animadversum = I notice
animal, animālis, n. = animal
animus, -ī, m. = mind, spirit
annōs nātus, -a, -um = years old
annuō: see *adnuō*
annus, -ī, m. = year
ante = before (adverb)
ante (+ acc.) = before (preposition)
anteā = beforehand, previously
antequam = before (conjunction)
aperiō, -īre, aperuī, apertum = I open
apertus, -a, -um = open
appellō, -āre, -āvī, -ātum = I call
appropinquō, -āre, -āvī, -ātum
   (+ dat. or *ad* + acc.) = I approach
aptus, -a, -um = suitable
apud (+ acc.) = at the house of,
   among, at, near
aqua, -ae, f. = water
aquila, -ae, f. = eagle
āra, -ae, f. = altar
arbor, -ŏris, f. = tree
argentum, -ī, n. = silver
arma, -ōrum, n. pl. = weapons
armātus, -a, -um = armed
ars, artis, f. = skill, art
arx, arcis, f. = citadel
ascendō, -ere, ascendī, ascēnsum =
   I climb
aspiciō, -ere, aspexī, aspectum = I
   look on
aspis, aspidis, f. = asp, viper
assūmō, -ere, assūmpsī,
   assūmptum = I take up

at = but
āter, ātra, ātrum = black
Athēnae, -ārum, f. pl. = Athens
atque = and
ātrium, ātriī, n. = hall
attonitus, -a, -um = amazed
audāx, audācis = bold
audācter (adverb) = boldly
audeō, audēre, ausus sum = I dare
audiō, -īre, -īvī, -ītum = I hear, listen
   to
auferō, auferre, abstulī, ablātum = I
   carry away, steal
auris, auris, f. = ear
aurum, -ī, n. = gold
aut = or
aut...aut = either...or
autem = however, moreover (not
   written 1st word in clause)
avis, avis, f. = bird
āvium, -iī, n. = by-way, trackless
   place, lonely place
avunculus, -ī, m. = uncle
avunculus maior = great-great-uncle;
   (occasionally = great-uncle)
auxilium, -iī, n. = help
barba, -ae, f. = beard
barbarus, -a, -um = barbarian
   (adjective)
barbarus, -ī, m. = a barbarian (noun)
bellum, -ī, n. = war
bene = well
benignus, -a, -um = kind
bibō, -ere, bibī = I drink
bīgae, -ārum, f. pl. = two-horse
   chariot
bis (adverb) = twice
bona, -ōrum, n. pl = goods
bonus, -a, -um = good
bōs, bovis, c. (irreg.) = ox, cow
brevis, breve = short, brief; (*brevī* =
   soon)
Britannus, -a, -um = British
cadō, -ere, cecidī, cāsum = I fall
caedēs, -is, f. = slaughter

caedō, -ere, cecīdī, caesum = I cut, kill

caesus: see **caedō**

caelum, -ī, n. = sky

callidus, -a, -um = skilful, crafty

campus, -ī, m. = plain

canis, canis, c. = dog

canō, -ere, cecinī, cantum = I sing

cantō, -āre, -āvī, -ātum = I sing

capiō, -ere, cēpī, captum = I take, capture

captīvus, -ī, m. = prisoner

caput, capitis, n. = head

carmen, carminis, n. = poem, song

cārus, -a, -um = dear

castra pōnō = I pitch a camp

castra, -ōrum, n. pl. = camp

causa, -ae, f. = cause, reason

causā (follows a genitive case) = for the sake of

caveō, -ēre, cāvī, cautum (+ acc.) = I am cautious (of)

cecidī: see **cadō**

cecīdī: see **caedō**

cēdō, -ere, cessī, cessum = I yield, withdraw

celer, celeris, celere = swift, quick

celeritās, celeritātis, f. = speed

celeriter = quickly

cēlō, -āre, -āvī, -ātum = I hide (trans.)

celsus, -a, -um = lofty

cēna, -ae, f. = dinner

cēnō, -āre, -āvī, -ātum = I dine

centum = one hundred

cēpī: see **capiō**

certiōrem faciō = I inform (lit. make more certain)

certus, -a, -um = certain

cessī: see **cēdō**

cēterī, -ae, -a = other, remaining

cēterum (adverb) = in other respects, otherwise, but

cibus, -ī, m. = food

circiter (adverb) = around

circum (+ acc.) = around

cīvis, cīvis, c. = citizen

cīvitās, cīvitātis, f. = state, city-state, city

clādēs, clādis, f. = disaster

clāmō, -āre, -āvī, -ātum = I shout

clāmor, -ōris, m. = shout

clārus, -a, -um = famous

classis, classis, f. (abl. sing.: **classī** or **classe**) = fleet

claudō, claudere, clausī, clausum = I close

coēgī: see **cōgō**

coepī, coepisse, coeptum (defective) = I began

cognōmen, cognōminis, n. = surname

cognōscō, -ere, cognōvī, cognitum = I learn, find out

cōgō, cōgere, coēgī, coāctum = I compel, force

cohors, cohortis, f. = cohort

collēga, -ae, m. = colleague

colligō, -ere, collēgī, collēctum = I collect

collis, collis, m. = hill

colō, colere, coluī, cultum = I cultivate, worship

comes, comitis, c. = companion

commendō, -āre, -āvī, -ātum = I entrust

commoror, -ārī, -ātus sum = I stay (for some time)

commoveō, -ēre, commōvī, commōtum = I upset, move, disturb (trans.)

commūnis, -e = shared

comparō, -āre, -āvī, -ātum = I get ready, prepare (trans.)

compellō, -āre, -āvī, -ātum = I address

compleō, -ēre, complēvī, complētum = I fill

complūrēs, complūrium = several, many

concidō, -ere, concidī = I fall (in death)

condemnō, -āre, -āvī, -ātum = I condemn

condiciō, -ōnis, f. = agreement, terms

cōnficiō, -ere, cōnfēcī, cōnfectum = I complete

cōnfīdō, -ere, cōnfīsus sum (+ dat. of persons or + dat. or abl. of things) = I trust

cōnfundō, -ere, cōnfūdī, cōnfūsum = I throw into confusion

coniūnx, coniugis, c. = husband/wife

cōnor, cōnārī, cōnātus sum = I try

cōnscendō, -ere, cōnscendī, cōnscēnsum = I climb up, embark

cōnsentiō, -īre, cōnsēnsī, cōnsēnsum = I agree

cōnsilium, -iī, n. = plan

cōnsilium capiō = I adopt a plan

cōnsistō, -ere, cōnstitī, cōnstitum = I halt

cōnspiciō, -ere, cōnspexī, cōnspectum = I catch sight of

cōnstitī: see *cōnsistō*

cōnstituō, -ere, cōnstituī, cōnstitūtum = I decide, settle, station

cōnsul, cōnsulis, m. = consul

contemnō, -ere, contempsī, contemptum = I despise

contendō, contendere, contendī, contentum = I hurry, march

contrā (+ acc.) = against

conveniō, -īre, convēnī, conventum = I come together

convertō, -ere, convertī, conversum = I turn around (trans.)

cōpia, -ae, f. = supply, large amount

cōpiae, -ārum, f. pl. = forces

corōna, -ae, f. = crown, garland

corpus, -ŏris, n. = body

cotīdiē (or *cottīdiē*) = every day

crās = tomorrow

crēdō, -ere, crēdidī, crēditum (+ dat.) = I trust, believe

Crĕūsa, -ae, f. = Creusa, wife of Aeneas

crūdēlis, -e = cruel

cruentus, -a, -um = blood-stained

crux, crucis, f. = cross

cubīle, cubīlis, n. = bed

cucurrī: see *currō*

culpa, -ae, f. = blame, fault, guilt

cultus, -a, -um = cultivated

cultus, -ūs, m. = cultivation

cum (+ abl.) = with, together with

cum (conjunction) = when, since, although, while

cupidus, -a, -um (+ gen.) = desirous (of)

cupiō, -ere, -īvī, -ītum = I want, desire

cūr? = why?

cūra, -ae, f. = care

cūrō, -āre, -āvī, -ātum = I care for

cūrō (*ut* + subj.) = I see to it (that)

currō, -ere, cucurrī, cursum = I run

cursus, -ūs, m. = course, running, direction

custōdiō, -īre, -īvī, -ītum = I guard

custōs, custōdis, c. = guard

Danaī, -ōrum, m. pl. = the Greeks

Dardanius, -a, -um = Trojan

dē (+ abl.) = down from, concerning

dea, -ae, f. = goddess (dat. and abl. pl. = *deābus*)

dēbeō, -ēre, -uī, -itum = I ought, owe

decem = ten

decet, decēre, decuit (impersonal: + acc. of the person + infin.) = it is suitable, becoming

dēcutiō, -ere, dēcussī, dēcussum = I shake, beat, cast down

dēdecet, dēdecēre, dēdecuit (impersonal: + acc. of the person + infin.) = it is unsuitable, unbecoming

dēdecus, dēdecoris, n. = disgrace

dedī: see *dō*

dēdūcō, -ere, dēdūxī, dēductum = I draw down

dēfendō, -ere, dēfendī, dēfēnsum = I
    defend
dēfessus, -a, -um = weary
dēfīgō, -ere, dēfīxī, dēfīxum = I fix
    firmly
dēfīxus: see *dēfīgō*
deinde = then
dēlectō, -āre, -āvī, -ātum = I delight,
    please
dēleō, dēlēre, dēlēvī, dēlētum = I
    destroy
dēligō, -ere, dēlēgī, dēlēctum = I
    choose
dēnārius, -iī, m. (gen. pl. regularly
    dēnārium) = denarius (a coin)
dēnique (adverb) = then, at length
dēns, dentis, m. = tooth
dēscendō, -ere, dēscendī,
    dēscēnsum = I go down
dēsiliō, -īre, dēsiluī = I leap down
dēspērō, -āre, -āvī, -ātum = I despair
deus, deī, m. (irreg.) = god
dexter, dextra, dextrum (or *dexter,*
    dextera, dexterum) = right (as
    opposed to left)
dīcō, dīcere, dīxī, dictum = I say
didicī: see *discō*
diēs, diēī, m. = day (f. if an appointed
    day)
difficilis, -e = difficult
difficultās, -ātis, f. = difficulty
dignitās, dignitātis, f. = distinction,
    importance
dignus, -a, -um (+ abl.) = worthy (of)
dīligēns, -entis = careful
discēdō, -ere, discessī, discessum
    = I depart
discipulus, -ī, m. / *discipula, -ae*, f. =
    pupil
discō, -ere, didicī = I learn
dissuādeō, -ēre, dissuāsī,
    dissuāsum = I advise against
diū (adverb) = for a long time
diūtius (adverb) = for a longer time
dīves, dīvitis (like *vetus*) = rich
dīvidō, -ere, dīvīsī, dīvīsum = I divide

dīvitiae, -ārum, f. pl. = riches, wealth
dīvus, -ī, m. (gen. pl.: *dīvum*) = a god
dīxī: see *dīcō*
dō, dăre, dedī, dătum = I give
doceō, -ēre, docuī, doctum = I teach
doleō, -ēre, doluī, dolitum = I feel
    pain, am sad
dolor, dolōris, m. = pain, grief
dominus, -ī, m. = master, lord
domus, -ūs, f. (irreg.) = house, home
dōnō, -āre, -āvī, -ātum = I bestow,
    present (as a gift)
dōnum, -ī, n. = gift
dormiō, -īre, -īvī, -ītum = I sleep
dubitō, -āre, -āvī, -ātum = I doubt,
    hesitate
dubius, -a, -um = doubtful, doubting
dūcō, -ere, dūxī, ductum = I lead
dulcis, -e = sweet, charming, pleasant
dum = while, until
duŏ, duae, duŏ = two
duodecim = twelve
duodēvīgintī = eighteen
dūrus, -a, -um = hard
dux, ducis, c. = leader
dūxī: see *dūcō*
ē, ex (+ abl.) = out of
eadem: see *īdem*
ecce = look!
ēdō, -ere, ēdidī, ēditum = I produce
edō, ēsse (or *edere*), *ēdī, ēsum*
    (irreg.) = I eat
efficiō, -ere, effēcī, effectum = I
    cause, bring about
effugiō, -ere, effūgī = I escape
effundō, -ere, effūdī, effūsum = I
    pour forth
ēgī: see *agō*
egŏ = I
ēgredior, ēgredī, ēgressus sum = I
    go out
ei = alas!
emō, emere, ēmī, ēmptum = I buy
enim = for (not written 1st word in
    clause)
eō = to that place (thither)

eō, īre, iī (or *īvī*), *itum* (irreg.) = I go

epistola (or *epistula*), *-ae*, f. = letter

eques, equitis, m. = horseman
(pl. = cavalry)

equus, equī, m. = horse

ēripiō, -ere, ēripuī, ēreptum = I
snatch away

errō, -āre, -āvī, -ātum = I wander,
make a mistake

ēsse: see *edō*

esse: see *sum*

et = and

et...et = both...and

etiam = even, also

etiamsī = even if

etsī = even if

ēveniō, -īre, ēvēnī, ēventum = I
come out, turn out, result (of
things)

ēvertō, -ere, ēvertī, ēversum = I
overturn, overthrow

ēvocō, -āre, -āvī, -ātum = I call out

ex (+ abl.) = out of

excēdō, -ere, excessī, excessum (+
abl.) = I depart (from)

excitō, -āre, -āvī, -ātum = I wake,
rouse (transitive)

exclāmō, -āre, -āvī, -ātum = I shout
out

exeō, exīre, exiī, exitum (goes like
eō) = I go out

exercitus, -ūs, m. = army

exilium: see *exsilium*

exitus, -ūs, m. = way out, outcome

exorior, exorīrī, exortus sum = I rise
up

expers, expertis (+ gen.) = not
sharing in

explōrō, -āre, -āvī, -ātum = I explore,
investigate

*exprōmō, -ere, exprōmpsī,
exprōmptum* = I declare, display

exsilium, -iī, n. = exile

exspectō, -āre, -āvī, -ātum = I wait
for

exstō, -āre, exstitī = I stand out

exsūgo, -ere, exsūxī, exsūctum = I
suck out

extrā (+ acc.) = outside

extrēmus, -a, -um = furthest,
outermost

exuviae, -ārum, f. pl. = spoils

fābula, -ae, f. = story

faciēs, faciēī, f. = face, appearance

facile (adverb) = easily

facilis, -e = easy

faciō, -ere, fēci, factum = I do, make

fallō, -ere, fefellī, falsum = I deceive

falsus, -a, -um = untrue, false

fāma, -ae, f. = fame, glory

fātum, -ī, n. = fate, destiny

faveō, -ēre, fāvī, fautum (+ dat.) = I
favour

fēcī: see *faciō*

fefellī: see *fallō*

fēlīciter (adverb) = fortunately, happily

fēlīx, fēlīcis = fortunate, happy

fēmina, -ae, f. = woman

ferō, ferre, tulī, lātum (irreg.) = I
carry, bear; (of roads = I lead)

ferōx, ferōcis = fierce, spirited

ferrum, -ī, n. = iron, sword

fessus, -a, -um = tired

festīnō, -āre, -āvī, -ātum = I hurry

fidēlis, -e = faithful

fidem habeō, -ēre, habuī, habitum
(+ dat.) = I put my trust in

fidem servō, -āre, -āvī, -ātum = I
keep my word

fidēs, fideī, f. = faith, trust

fīdus, -a, -um = trustworthy, safe

fīgō, -ere, fīxī, fīxum = I fasten, fix

fīlia, -ae, f. = daughter (dat. and abl.
pl.: *fīliābus*)

fīlius, fīliī (or *fīlī*), m. (irreg.) = son

fīnis, -is, m. = end (pl. = territory)

fīō, fiěrī, factus sum = I become, am
made, happen

flamma, -ae, f. = flame

fleō, flēre, flēvī, flētum = I weep

flētus, -ūs, m. = weeping (noun)

flōs, flōris, m. = flower

flūctus, -ūs, m. = a wave
flūmen, flūminis, n. = river
foedō, -āre, -āvī, -ātum = I defile
fōns, fontis, m. = fountain, spring
fore: short for *futūrus esse* (fut. infin. of *sum*)
fōrma, -ae, f. = shape, beauty, form
fortasse = perhaps
forte = by chance
fortis, -e = brave, strong
fortiter = bravely
fōrtūna, -ae, f. = fortune
forum, -ī, n. = forum
frangō, -ere, frēgī, frāctum = I break
frāter, frātris, m. = brother
frēgī: see *frangō*
frīgus, frīgoris, n. = cold (noun)
frūmentum, -ī, n. = corn
frūstrā = in vain
fūdī: see *fundō*
fuga, -ae, f. = flight, escape
fugiō, -ere, fūgī, fugitum = I flee (from)
fuī: see *sum*
fūmus, -ī, m. = smoke
fundō, -ere, fūdī, fūsum = I pour, rout, put to flight
fūnus, -eris, n. = death
futūrus esse: fut. infin. of *sum*
Gabiī, -ōrum, m. pl. = Gabii (a city in Italy)
Gallia, -ae, f. = Gaul (the country)
Gallus, -ī, m. = a Gaul (the person)
gaudeō, gaudēre, gāvīsus sum = I rejoice
gaudium, gaudiī, n. = joy
genitor, -ōris, m. = father
gēns, gentis, f. = people, race, tribe
genū, genūs, n. = knee
genus, generis, n. = sort, type, birth
gerō, -ere, gessī, gestum = I manage, wage (a war), wear
gessī: see *gerō*
gladius, gladiī, m. = sword
gradus, gradūs, m. = step
Graecia, -ae, f. = Greece

Graecus, -a, -um = Greek
grātiās agō = I give thanks
grātus, -a, -um = welcome, pleasing
gravis, -e = heavy, serious
habeō, -ēre, -uī, -itum = I have, I consider
habitō, -āre, -āvī, -ātum = I live, inhabit
hasta, -ae, f. = spear
Hector, Hectoris, m. = Hector (son of Priam)
herba, -ae, f. = grass
hērēditās, hērēditātis, f. = inheritance
herī = yesterday
hīberna, -ōrum, n. pl. = winter-quarters
hīc = here
hic, haec, hoc = this; he, she, it
hiems, hiemis, f. = winter, stormy weather
hinc = from here, hence
Hispānia, -ae, f. = Spain
Hispānus, -a, -um = Spanish
hodiē = today
homŏ, hominis, c. = person, man
honōs (or *honor*), *honōris*, m. = honour, office, post
hōra, -ae, f. = hour
hortor, -ārī, hortātus sum = I encourage, urge
hortus, -ī, m. = garden
hospes, hospitis, m. = host, guest
hostis, hostis, c. = enemy (of the state; usually used in plural)
hūc = to here, hither
humus, humī, f. = ground
iaceō, -ēre, iacuī, iacitum = I lie (down)
iaciō, -ere, iēcī, iactum = I throw
iaculor, -ārī, -ātus sum = I hurl
iam = now, already
ibĭ = there
idcircō (adverb) = for this reason
īdem, eadem, ĭdem = the same
ideō (adverb) = for that reason

iēcī: see *iaciō*
idōneus, -a, -um = suitable
igitur = therefore (not generally written 1st word in clause)
ignārus, -a, -um = ignorant, unaware
ignis, ignis, m. (abl. sing.: *ignī* or *igne*) = fire
ignōtus, -a, -um = unknown
ille, illa, illud = that, he, she, it
illīc = there
illinc = from there, thence
illūc = to there, thither
immortālis, -e = immortal
impediō, -īre, -īvī, -ītum = I hinder
impedītus, -a, -um = hampered
imperātor, -ōris, m. = general
imperium, -iī, n. = command, empire
imperō, -āre, -āvī, -ātum (+ dat.) = I order
impetus, -ūs, m. = attack, charge
in (+ abl.) = in, on
in (+ acc.) = into, on to
incendium, -iī, n. = fire
incendō, -ere, incendī, incēnsum = I burn (transitive)
incertus, -a, -um = uncertain
incipiō, -ere, incēpī, inceptum = I begin
incola, -ae, c. = inhabitant
incolō, -ere, incoluī = I inhabit
inde = then, thence
indignus, -a, -um (+ abl.) = unworthy
induō, -ere, induī, indūtum = I put on
ineō, -īre, iniī, initum (goes like *eō*) = I go in
inermis, -e = defenceless, unarmed
īnferior, -ōris = lower
ingenium, -iī, n. = ability (of intellect)
ingēns, ingentis = huge
ingredior, ingredī, ingressus sum = I go in
inimīcus, -ī, m. = private enemy
inīquus, -a, -um = unequal, unfair
initium, -iī, n. = beginning
iniūria, -ae, f. = injustice, wrong, harm
iniustus, -a, -um = unjust

inopia, -ae, f. = shortage, lack
inquit / inquiunt = he/they say(s) (quoting direct speech)
īnsequor, īnsequī, īnsecūtus sum = I pursue
īnsidiae, -ārum, f. pl. = ambush, plot, trap
īnstruō, -ere, īnstrūxī, īnstrūctum = I draw up (for battle)
īnsula, -ae, f. = island
intellegō, -ere, intellēxī, intellēctum = I understand
inter (+ acc.) = between, among
intereā = meanwhile
interficiō, -ere, interfēcī, interfectum = I kill
intrā (+ acc.) = within
intrō, -āre, -āvī, -ātum = I enter
inveniō, -īre, invēnī, inventum = I find
invītus, -a, -um = unwilling, reluctant
iocor, iocārī, iocātus sum = I joke
iocus, -ī, m. (in pl. also *ioca, -ōrum*, n. pl.) = joke
Iovem: see *Iuppiter*
ipse, ipsa, ipsum = self
īra, -ae, f. = anger
īrāscor, īrāscī, īrātus sum (+ dat. of thing or person) = I am angry with
īrātus, -a, -um = angry
is, ea, id = that, he, she, it
ita = thus
Ītalia, -ae, f. = Italy
itaque = therefore
iter, itineris, n. = journey
iterum = again
iubeō, -ēre, iussī, iussum = I order
iūdex, iūdicis, c. = judge
iungō, iungere, iūnxī, iūnctum = I join
Iuppiter, Iovis, m. = Jupiter
iūrō, -āre, -āvī, -ātum = I swear
iūs, iūris, n. = law, right
iussī: see *iubeō*
iussum, -ī, n. = an order
iussus: see *iubeō*

iūstus, -a, -um = just, righteous
iuvenis, iuvenis, c. = young person, young man
iuvat, -āre, iūvit (impersonal: + acc. of the person + infin.) = it pleases
iuvō, iuvāre, iūvī, iūtum = I help
labor, labōris, m. = work, task
labōrō, -āre, -āvī, -ātum = I work
lacerō, -āre, -āvī, -ātum = I tear to pieces
lacrima, -ae, f. = tear
lacus, -ūs, m. = lake
laedō, laedere, laesī, laesum = I harm, hurt
laetus, -a, -um = happy
largus, -a, -um = plentiful
latēns, latentis = secret, hidden
lateō, -ēre, latuī = I lie hidden
lātus: see *ferō*
lātus, -a, -um = wide
latus, lateris, n. = side, flank
laudō, -āre, -āvī, -ātum = I praise
laus, laudis, f. = praise
lectus, -ī, m. = bed, couch
lēgātus, -ī, m. = ambassador
legiō, -ōnis, f. = legion
legō, -ere, lēgī, lēctum = I read, choose
lentē = slowly
leō, leōnis, m. = lion
lēnis, -e = smooth, gentle
levis, -e = light, unimportant
lēvis, -e = smooth
lēx, lēgis, f. = law
libenter = gladly, willingly
līber, -era, -erum = free
liber, librī, m. = book
līberī, -ōrum, m. pl. = offspring, sons and daughters, children (i.e. in relation to their parents)
līberō, -āre, -āvī, -ātum = I free
lībertās, -ātis, f. = freedom
libet, -ēre, libuit (impersonal: + dat.) = it is pleasing (to)
licet, -ēre, licuit (impersonal: + dat.) = it is lawful, allowed

līlium, -iī, n. = lily
lingua, -ae, f. = tongue, language
lītus, lītoris, n. = shore
locus, -ī, m. = place (pl. = *loca, -ōrum*, n. pl. when this refers to a region; *locī* refers to individual places)
longus, -a, -um = long
loquor, loquī, locūtus sum = I speak
lōrum, -ī, n. = rein, thong
lūdō, -ere, lūsī, lūsum = I play
lūdus, -ī, m. = school
lūna, -ae, f. = moon
lūsī: see *lūdō*
lūx, lūcis, f. = light
maestus, -a, um = sad
magister, magistrī, m. = master, schoolmaster
magistrātus, -ūs, m. = magistrate
magnitūdō, magnitūdinis, f. = greatness, large size
magnopere = greatly
magnus, -a, -um = big, great
maior, -us = bigger, greater
male (adverb) = badly
mālō, mālle, māluī (irreg.) = I prefer
mālum, -ī, n. = apple
malus, -a, -um = bad
maneō, -ēre, mānsī, mānsum = I remain
mandātum, -ī, n. = an order
mandō, -āre, -āvī, -ātum = I entrust
manifestus, -a, -um = plain, clear
manus, -ūs, f. = hand, (or band of men)
mare, maris, n. = sea
marītus, -ī, m. = husband
māter, mātris, f. = mother
mātrimōnium, -iī, n. = marriage
maximus, -a, -um = biggest, greatest
mē: see *egŏ*
medicus, -ī, m. = doctor
medius, -a, -um = middle
melior, -us = better
meminī, meminisse (+ gen. or acc.; defective) = I remember

mēns, mentis, f. = mind
mēnsa, mēnsae, f. = table
mēnsis, mēnsis, m. = month
mercātor, mercātōris, m. = merchant
mereō, -ēre, -uī, -itum / mereor,
  merērī, meritus sum = I deserve,
  earn
metō, -ere, messuī, messum = I
  mow, cut down
meus, -a, -um = my
mihĭ: see *egŏ*
mīles, mīlitis, c. = soldier
mīlia, mīlium, n. pl. (+ gen.) =
  thousands
mīlle = one thousand
minimus, -a, -um = smallest
minae, -ārum, f. pl. = threats
minor, minus = smaller
minor, -ārī, minātus sum (+ acc. of
  thing and dat. of person) = I
  threaten
mīrābilis, -e = marvellous, amazing
mīror, mīrārī, mīrātus sum = I
  wonder at, am amazed at
misceō, -ēre, miscuī, mixtum = I
  mix, confuse
miser, -era, -erum = wretched
miseret, -ēre, miseruit (impersonal: +
  acc. of person and gen. of cause)
  = it moves to pity
mīsī: see *mittō*
missiō, -ōnis, f. = release from
  captivity, discharge from service
mittō, -ere, mīsī, missum = I send
mixtus: see *misceō*
modŏ = only
modus, -ī, m. = way, manner
moenia, moenium, n. pl. = fortified
  walls, ramparts
moneō, -ēre, -uī, -itum = I warn,
  advise
mōns, montis, m. = mountain
mōnstrō, -āre, -āvī, -ātum = I show,
  point out
mora, -ae, f. = delay
morior, morī, mortuus sum = I die

moror, morārī, morātus sum = I
  delay
mors, mortis, f. = death
mōrsus, -ūs, m. = a bite
mortālis, -e = mortal
mortuus, -a, -um = dead
mōs, mōris, m. = custom
moveō, -ēre, mōvī, mōtum = I move
  (transitive)
mox = soon
mulceō, -ēre, mulsī, mulsum = I
  stroke
mulier, mulieris, f. = woman
multitūdō, multitūdinis, f. = crowd,
  multitude
multum (adverb) = much
multus, -a, -um = much, many
mūniō, -īre, -īvī, -ītum = I fortify
mūrus, -ī, m. = wall
mūtō, -āre, -āvī, -ātum = I change
nactus: see *nancīscor*
nam = for
nancīscor, nancīscī, nactus (or
  nanctus) *sum* = I obtain
nārrō, -āre, -āvī, -ātum = I tell
nāscor, nāscī, nātus sum = I am
  born
nātus, -a, -um = born, (x years) old
nātus, ī, m. (noun) = son
nauta, -ae, m. = sailor
nāvālis, -e = naval
nāvigō, -āre, -āvī, -ātum = I sail
nāvis, nāvis, f. (abl. sing.: *nāvī* or
  navē) = ship
nē (+ subjunctive) = lest, that...not
-ne?: introduces a question
nec = and not, nor
nec tamen = but...not
nec...nec = neither...nor
necō, necāre, necāvī, necātum = I
  kill
neglegō, -ere, neglēxī, neglēctum =
  I neglect
negō, -āre, -āvī, -ātum = I deny, say
  that...not
negōtium, -iī, n. = business, work

nēmō, (nēminem, nūllĭus, nēminī, nūllō), c. = no one
neque = and not, nor
neque tamen = but...not
neque...neque = neither...nor
nē...quidem = not even
nesciŏ, -īre, -īvī, -ītum = I do not know
niger, nigra, nigrum = black
nihil (or *nīl*) = nothing, in no way
nisi (or *nī*) = unless, if...not, except
nōbilis, -e = noble, famous
nōbīs: see *nōs*
noceō, -ēre, nocuī, nocitum (+ dat.) = I harm
noctū (adverb) = by night, at night
nōlī / nōlīte (+ infin.) = do not!
nōlō, nōlle, nōluī (irreg.) = I do not wish, am unwilling
nōmen, nōminis, n. = name
nōn = not
nōn diūtius = not for a longer time
nōn iam = no longer
nōn sōlum...sed etiam = not only...but also
nōnne?: introduces a question (expecting the answer "yes")
nōnnūllī, -ae, -a = some
nōs = we
noster, nostra, nostrum = our
notō, -āre, -āvī, -ātum = I mark
nōtus, -a, -um = well-known
novem = nine
novus, -a, -um = new
nox, noctis, f. = night
nūdō, -āre, -āvī, -ātum = I uncover
nūdus, -a, -um = naked
nūllus, -a, -um (like *ūnus*) = no (adjective)
num = whether, if
num?: introduces a question (expecting the answer "no")
nūmen, nūminis, n. = divine will, deity
numerus, ī, m. = number
numerō, -āre, -āvī, -ātum = I count
numquam = never

nunc = now
nūntiō, -āre, -āvī, -ātum = I report, announce
nūntius, nuntiī, m. = messenger, message
nūper = recently
nūsquam = nowhere
ob (+ acc.) = on account of, because of
oblātus: see *offerō*
oblīvīscor, oblīvīscī, oblītus sum (+ gen. of person or + gen. or acc. of thing) = I forget
obsideō, -ēre, obsēdī, obsessum = I blockade
obtulī: see *offerō*
occāsiō, -ōnis, f. = opportunity
occīdō, -ere, occīdī, occīsum = I kill
occupō, -āre, -āvī, -ātum = I seize
octŏ = eight
oculus, -ī, m. = eye
ōdī (defective) = I hate
odium, -iī, n. = hatred
odōrātus, -a, -um = sweet-smelling
offerō, offerre, obtulī, oblātum (goes like *ferō*) = I offer
officium, -iī, n. = duty
ōlim = once upon a time
omnīnō (adverb) = altogether
omnis, -e = every, all
onus, oneris, n. = burden
operam dō, dăre, dedī, dătum (+ dat.) = I pay attention (to)
oportet, -ēre, oportuit (impersonal: + acc. and infin.) = it is right (that)
oppidum, -ī, n. = town
opprimō, -ere, oppressī, oppressum = I overwhelm, oppress
oppugnō, -āre, -āvī, -ātum = I attack (a town or city)
optimus, -a, -um = best
opus, operis, n. = work
ōra, -ae, f. = shore
ōrātiō, -ōnis, f. = speech
ōrātor, -ōris, m. = orator

orior, orīrī, ortus sum (mixed
conjugation, despite infinitive in
-īrī) = I arise
ōrō, -āre, -āvī, -ātum = I beg, pray
ōs, ōris, n. = mouth, face
os, ossis, n. = bone
ōsculum, -ī, n. = kiss
*ostendō, -ere, ostendī, ostēnsum /
ostentum* = I show
ōtium, -iī, n. = leisure
paene = almost
paenitet, -ēre, paenituit (impersonal:
+ acc. of person and gen. of
cause) = it repents, makes sorry
Palātium, -iī, m. = the Palatine Hill
pānis, pānis, m. = bread
parcō, -ere, pepercī, parsum
(+ dat.) = I spare
parēns, parentis, c. = parent
pāreō, -ēre, -uī, -itum (+ dat.) = I
obey
pariō, -ere, peperī, partum (or
paritum) = I give birth to, produce,
(of victories =) I win
parō, -āre, -āvī, -ātum = I prepare
pars, partis, f. = part
partus: see *pariō*
parvus, -a, -um = small
passus: see *patior*
passus, -ūs, m. = a pace;
mīlle passūs = one mile
pāstor, -ōris, m. = shepherd
pater, patris, m. = father; in plural (as
mark of respect) = the senators
patior, patī, passus sum = I suffer,
allow
patria, -ae, f. = country, fatherland
paucī, -ae, -a = few
paulum (adverb) = a little
pauper, pauperis (like *vetus*) = poor
pāx, pācis, f. = peace
pectus, pectoris, n. = chest, breast
pecus, pecoris, n. = herd
pecūnia, -ae, f. = money
pedes, peditis, m. = foot soldier
peior, -us = worse

pellō, -ere, pepulī, pulsum = I drive
Penātēs, -ium, m. pl. = the Penates
(household gods)
pepercī: see *parcō*
peperī: see *pariō*
per (+ acc.) = through, along
pereō, -īre, periī, peritum (goes like
eō) = I die
perdō, -ere, perdidī, perditum = I
destroy, ruin, lose utterly
perficiō, -ere, perfēcī, perfectum = I
complete
perfidia, -ae, f. = treachery
perfidus, -a, -um = treacherous
perīculōsus, -a, -um = dangerous
perīculum, -ī, n. = danger
perītus (+ gen.) = skilled (in)
permittō, -ere, permīsī, permissum
(+ dat.) = I allow
pernoctō, -āre, -āvī, -ātum = I pass
the night
*persuādeō, -ēre, persuāsī,
persuāsum* (+ dat.) = I persuade
pēs, pedis, m. = foot
pessimus, -a, -um = worst
petō, -ere, petīvī, petītum = I seek,
make for (+ *ā/ab* + abl. = I ask)
philosophus, -ī, m. = philosopher
Phrygius, -a, -um = Trojan
pīrāta, -ae, m. = pirate
placeō, placēre, placuī, placitum
(+ dat.) = I please
placet, -ēre, placuit (impersonal:
+ dat.) = it is pleasing
plēbs, plēbis, f. = common people,
plebeians
plēnus, -a, -um (+ abl. or gen.) = full
plūrimus, -a, -um = most
plūs, plūris = more (neuter noun in
singular; adjective in plural)
poena, -ae, f. = penalty
poenās dō = I pay the penalty, am
punished
Poenus, -ī, m. = a Carthaginian
(noun)
poēta, -ae, m. = poet

Polītēs, -ae, m. = Polites (a son of Priam)
pōnō, -ere, posuī, positum = I place
pōns, pontis, m. = bridge
pontus, -ī, m. = the sea
populus, -ī, m. = a people, population
porta, -ae, f. = gate
portō, -āre, -āvī, -ātum = I carry
portus, -ūs, m. = harbour
poscō, -ere, poposcī = I demand
possum, posse, potuī (irreg.) = I am able
post (+ acc.) = after (preposition)
post = after (adverb)
posteā = afterwards
postquam = after (conjunction)
postrīdiē = on the next day
posuī: see *pōnō*
potēns, potentis = powerful
potestās, potestātis, f. = power
potior, -īrī, potītus sum (+ acc., gen., or abl.) = I take possession of
potuī: see *possum*
praebeō, -ēre, praebuī, praebitum = I offer
praeda, -ae, f. = booty, plunder
praefectus, -ī, m. = commander
praemittō, -ere, praemīsī, praemissum = I send ahead
praemium, -iī, n. = reward
praestō, -āre, praestitī, praestitum = I offer, discharge
prātum, -ī, n. = meadow
precēs, -um, f. pl. = prayers
precor, -ārī, precātus sum = I pray, beseech
pretium, -iī, n. = price
Priamus, -ī, m. = Priam (King of Troy)
prīmō / prīmum = at first
prīnceps, prīncipis, m. = chief, emperor
priusquam (conjunction) = before
prō (+ abl.) = on behalf of, in place of, in front of, instead of
prōcēdō, -ere, prōcessī, prōcessum = I go forward

procul = far away
prōdeō, -īre, prōdiī, prōditum (goes like *eō*) = I come forth
prōdō, -ere, prōdidī, prōditum = I betray
proelium, -iī, n. = battle
prōiciō, -ere, prōiēcī, prōiectum = I throw forwards
proficīscor, proficīscī, profectus sum = I set out
prōgredior, prōgredī, prōgressus sum = I go forward
prohibeō, -ēre, -uī, -itum = I prevent
prōlēs, prōlis, f. = offspring
prōmittō, -ere, prōmīsī, prōmissum = I promise
prope (+ acc.) = near
propter (+ acc.) = on account of
prōspiciō, -ere, prōspexī, prōspectum = I look forward
prōtrahō, -ere, prōtrāxī, prōtractum = I drag out, drag forth
prōvincia, -ae, f. = province
proximus, -a, -um = next, nearest
prūdēns, prūdentis = sensible
prūdentia, -ae, f. = good sense, judgement
puella, -ae, f. = girl
puer, puerī, m. = boy
pudet (impersonal: + acc. of person and gen. of cause) = it shames
pugna, -ae, f. = battle, fight
pugnō, -āre, -āvī, -ātum = I fight
pulcher, pulchra, pulchrum = beautiful
pulsus: see *pellō*
pulvis, -eris, m. = dust
Pūnicus, -a, um = Carthaginian (adjective)
pūniō, -īre, -īvī, -ītum = I punish
puppis, -is, f. = stern (of a ship), ship
putǒ, -āre, -āvī, -ātum = I think
Pyrrhus, -ī, m. = Pyrrhus (son of Achilles)
quaerō, -ere, quaesīvī, quaesītum = I ask, seek

quālis, -e? = of what kind?

quam = than; (+ adjective or adverb =) how…!

quamquam = although

quamvīs (+ subjunctive) = although, however much

quandŏ? = when?

quantus, -a, -um? = how great?

quārē = why?

quasi (adverb) = as if, just as

quattuor = four

quattuordecim = fourteen

-que = and

queror, querī, questus sum = I complain

quī, qua, quod (indefinite pronoun, used as an adjective) = any

quī, quae, quod (relative pronoun) = who, which

quid? = what?, why?

quīdam, quaedam, quiddam (pronoun) = a certain (man, woman, thing)

quīdam, quaedam, quoddam (adjective) = a certain

quidem = indeed

quiēs, quiētis, f. = quiet, rest

quīndecim = fifteen

quīnque = five

quis? = who?

quis, quid (indefinite pronoun, after *sī* and *nē*) = anyone, anything

quisquam, quicquam (or *quidquam*) = anyone at all

quisque, quaeque, quidque (pronoun) = each, every

quisque, quaeque, quodque (adjective) = each, every

quō? = where to? (whither?)

quod = because

quōmodŏ? = how?

quondam (adverb) = once, formerly

quoniam (+ indic.) = since

quoque = also (comes *after* the word it is emphasising)

quot? = how many?

quotiēns? (or *quotiēs?*) = how often?

rapiō, -ere, rapuī, raptum = I seize

raptō, -āre, -āvī, -ātum = I drag violently

recēns, recentis = recent

recipiō, -ere, recēpī, receptum = I withdraw

recondō, -ere, recondidī, reconditum = I put back again (into storage)

rēctus, -a, -um = right

reddō, reddere, reddidī, redditum = I give back, return

redeō, redīre, rediī, reditum (goes like *eō*) = I go back, return

reditus, -ūs, m. = return

redūcō, -ere, redūxi, reductum = I lead back

rēgīna, -ae, f. = queen

regiō, -ōnis, f. = area, region

rēgnum, -ī, n. = kingdom

regō, -ere, rēxī, rēctum = I rule

regredior, regredī, regressus sum = I go back

relēgō, -āre, -āvī, -ātum = I send into retirement

religiō (or *relligiō*), *-ōnis*, f. = religion, superstition

relinquō, -ere, relīquī, relictum = I leave, abandon

reliquus, -a, -um = remaining

renovō, -āre, -āvī, -ātum = I renew

repetō, -ere, repetīvī, repetītum = I seek again, return to

reportō, -āre, -āvī, -ātum = I carry back

rēs, reī, f. = thing, affair, property

resistō, -ere, restitī (+ dat.) = I resist

respondeō, -ēre, respondī, respōnsum = I reply, answer

rēspūblica, reīpūblicae, f. = state, city, republic (both *rēs* and *pūblica* decline; may be written as two words)

restitī: see *resistō*

reveniō, -īre, revēnī, reventum = I
 return
revertor, revertī, reversus sum = I
 turn back, return
rēx, rēgis, m. = king
rēxī: see *regō*
rīdeō, -ēre, rīsī, rīsum = I laugh,
 smile
rīpa, -ae, f. = riverbank
rīvus, -ī, m. = small stream, brook
rogō, -āre, -āvī, -ātum = I ask
Rōma, -ae, f. = Rome
Rōmānus, -a, -um = Roman
 (adjective)
Rōmānus, -ī, m. = a Roman (noun)
rumpō, -ere, rūpī, ruptum = I break,
 burst (transitive)
ruō, ruere, ruī, rutum (future
 participle: *ruitūrus*) = I rush,
 collapse
rūs, rūris, n. = the countryside
sacer, sacra, sacrum = sacred
sacerdōs, sacerdōtis, c. = priest,
 priestess
sacrificium, -iī, n. = sacrifice
saepe = often
saevus, -a, -um = savage
sagitta, -ae, f. = arrow
salūs, salūtis, f. = safety
salūtō, -āre, -āvī, -ātum = I greet
salvē, salvēte = hello, greetings
sanguis, sanguinis, m. = blood
sānō, -āre, -āvī, -ātum = I cure, heal
sapiēns, sapientis = wise
sapientia, -ae, f. = wisdom
sat: abbreviated form of *satis*
satis = enough
saxum, -ī, n. = rock
scelerātus, -a, -um = wicked
scelestus, -a, -um = wicked
scelus, sceleris, n. = crime
sciǒ, scīre, scīvī, scītum = I know
scrībō, -ere, scrīpsī, scrīptum = I
 write
scūtum, -ī, n. = shield

sē = himself, herself, itself,
 themselves
secō, -āre, secuī, sectum = I cut,
 divide
sed = but
sēdecim = sixteen
sedeō, sedēre, sēdī, sessum = I sit
sēditiō, -ōnis, f. = mutiny
semel (adverb) = once
semper = always
senātor, -ōris, m. = senator
senātus, -ūs, m. = senate
senex, senis, m. = old man
sentiō, -īre, sēnsī, sēnsum = I feel,
 notice, realise
sepeliō, -īre, sepelīvī, sepultum = I
 bury
septem = seven
septendecim = seventeen
sepultūra, -ae, f. = burial
sequor, sequī, secūtus sum = I
 follow
serēnus, -a, -um = calm
sermō, -ōnis, m. = conversation, talk
serpō, -ere, serpsī, serptum = I
 creep
sērus, -a, -um = late
serviō, -īre, -īvī, -ītum (+ dat.) = I
 serve
servō, -āre, -āvī, -ātum = I save
servus, -ī, m. = slave
sēstertius, -iī, m. (gen. pl.:
 sēstertium) = sestertius
 (Roman coin)
sex = six
sī = if
sīc = thus
sīcut = just as
signum, -ī, n. = signal, sign
silēns, silentis = silent, still
silentium, -iī, n. = silence
silva, -ae, f. = wood, forest
similis, -e (+ dat. or gen.) = similar
 (to), like
simul = at the same time

simul ac/atque (*ac* not used before vowels or *h*) = as soon as
simulō, -āre, -āvī, -ātum = I pretend
sine (+ abl.) = without
sinister, -tra, -trum = left, on the left
societās, -ātis, f. = alliance
socius, -iī, m. = ally
sōl, sōlis, m. = sun
soleō, -ēre, solitus sum = I am accustomed
sōlum (adverb) = only
sŏlum, -ī, n. = soil
sōlus, -a, -um (like *ūnus*) = alone
solvō, -ere, solvī, solūtum = I release, let loose
somnium, -iī, n. = dream
somnus, -ī, m. = sleep
sonitus, -ūs, m. = sound, noise
soror, -ōris, f. = sister
spectō, -āre, -āvī, -ātum = I watch
spērō, -āre, -āvī, -ātum = I hope
spoliō, -āre, -āvī, -ātum = I strip (trans.)
sponte = of one's own accord
statim = immediately
statuō, -ere, statuī, statūtum = I set up
stetī: see *stō*
stō, stāre, stetī, stătum = I stand
studeō, -ēre, -uī (+ dat.) = I study, apply myself (to), am eager about
stultus, -a, -um = stupid
sub (+ abl.) = under
subitō = suddenly
sublātus: see *tollō*
subsequor, subsequī, subsecūtus sum = I follow closely, support
subsum, subesse, subfuī (goes like *sum*) = I am near, under
sudis, sudis, f. = stake
sum, esse, fuī (irreg.) = I am
summus, -a, -um = topmost, top of
sūmō, -ere, sūmpsī, sūmptum = I take up, assume
super (+ acc.) = over
superbus, -a, -um = proud

superior, -ōris = higher, upper, previous
superō, -āre, -āvī, -ātum = I overcome
supersum, -esse, superfuī (+ dat.) (irreg.) = I survive
surgō, -ere, surrēxī, surrēctum = I rise, get up
suspicor, -ārī, -ātus sum = I suspect
sustineō, -ēre, sustinuī, sustentum = I hold up, hold back
sustulī: see *tollō*
suus, sua, suum = his (own), her (own), its (own) or their (own)
taberna, -ae, f. = inn, shop
taceō, -ēre, tacuī, tacitum = I am silent
tacitus, -a, -um = silent
tālis, -e = such
tam = so
tamen = however (not generally written first word in clause)
Tamesis, -is, m. (acc. sing.: *Tamesim*) = River Thames
tandem = at last
tangō, tangere, tetigī, tāctum = I touch
tantum (adverb) = only
tantus, -a, -um = so great
tēctus: see *tegō*
tegō, -ere, tēxī, tēctum = I cover, hide (trans.)
tēlum, -ī, n. = spear, missile
tempestās, -ātis, f. = storm, weather
templum, -ī, n. = temple
tempus, -ŏris, n. = time
teneō, -ēre, tenuī, tentum = I hold
tener, -era, -erum = tender
tepidus, -a, -um = warm
tergum, -ī, n. = back
terra, -ae, f. = land, earth
terreō, -ēre, -uī, -itum = I terrify
terror, -ōris, m. = terror
tetigī: see *tangō*
Teucrī, -ōrum, m. pl. = Trojans
theātrum, -ī, n. = theatre

timeō, -ēre, -uī = I fear
timor, -ōris, m. = fear
toga, -ae, f. = toga
tollō, -ere, sustulī, sublātum = I lift, raise
tot = so many
totiēns (or *totiēs*) = so often
tōtus, -a, -um (like *ūnus*) = whole
trādō, -ere, trādidī, trāditum = I hand over
trahō, -ere, trāxī, tractum = I drag
trāiciō, -ere, trāiēcī, trāiectum = I pierce
trāns (+ acc.) = across
trānseō, -īre, -iī, -itum (goes like *eō*) = I go across
trāxī: see *trahō*
tredecim = thirteen
trepidō, -āre, -āvī, -ātum = I tremble
trēs, tria = three
trīstis, trīste = sad, gloomy
Troia, -ae, f. = Troy
Troiānus, -a, -um = Trojan
tū = you (singular)
tuba, -ae, f. = war trumpet
tueor, tuērī, tūtus sum = I observe, protect, maintain
tulī: see *ferō*
tum = then, at that time
tumultus, -ūs, m. = uproar, riot
tumulus, -ī, m. = burial mound
tunc = then, at that time
turba, -ae, f. = crowd
turbō, -āre, -āvī, -ātum = I disturb
turpis, -e = foul, disgraceful
tūtus, -a, -um = safe
tuus, -a, -um = your (belonging to you (sing.))
ubĭ = when; where
ubĭ? = where?
Ulixes, -is, m. = Ulysses
ūllus, -a, -um (like *ūnus*) = any
ultimus, -a, -um = last, furthest
ultrō (adverb) = of one's own accord
umbra, -ae, f. = shadow
umerus, -ī, m. = shoulder

umquam = ever
ūnā (adverb) = together
unda, -ae, f. = wave
unde? = from where? (whence?)
ūndecim = eleven
ūndēvīgintī = nineteen
undique = from all sides
ūniversus, -a, -um = all together
ūnus, -a, -um (gen. sing.: *ūnīus*, dat. sing.: *ūnī*) = one, only one, one alone
urbs, urbis, f. = city
ut (+ indicative) = as; (+ subjunctive) = in order that, with the result that, etc.
ut prīmum = as soon as
uterque, utraque, utrumque (gen. sing. *utrĭusque*, dat. sing. *utrīque*) = each (of two)
ūtilis, -e = useful
ūtor, ūtī, ūsus sum (+ abl.) = I use
utrum...an = whether...or
uxor, -ōris, f. = wife
valē / valēte = farewell
valeō, -ēre, valuī, valitum = I am strong, healthy, able
valēns, valentis = strong
validus, -a, -um = strong
vallis (or *vallēs*), *vallis*, f. = valley
vāllum, -ī, n. = rampart
varius, -a, -um = various, different
vehementer = strongly, fiercely
vehō, -ere, vēxī, vectum = I convey
vel = or
vel...vel = either...or
velle: see *volō*
vēndō, -ere, vēndidī, vēnditum = I sell
venēnum, -ī, n. = poison
veniō, -īre, vēnī, ventum = I come
ventus, -ī, m. = wind
vēr, vēris, n. = spring
(verber), verberis, n. (only found in gen. and abl. sing., and in plural) = a flogging
verbum, -ī, n. = word

vērē (adverb) = truly, really
vēritās, vēritātis, f. = truth
vērō = indeed
vertō, -ere, vertī, versum = I turn (trans.)
vērus -a, -um = true
vester, vestra, vestrum = your (belonging to you (pl.))
vestis, vestis, f. = clothing
vetō, vetāre, vetuī, vetitum = I forbid
vetus, veteris = old
vēxī: see *vehō*
via, -ae, f. = road, street, way
vīcīnus, -a, -um = neighbouring
victor, -ōris, m. = victor
victōria, -ae, f. = victory
victōriam pariō = I win a victory
videō, -ēre, vīdī, vīsum = I see
videor, vidērī, vīsus sum = I seem
vīgintī = twenty
vīlla, -ae, f. = country house, villa
vincō, -ere, vīcī, victum = I conquer
vīnum, -ī, n. = wine
vir, virī, m. (irreg.) = man (as opposed to woman)

virga, -ae, f. = rod, stick
virgō, virginis, f. = maiden, girl
virtūs, virtūtis, f. = courage
vīs, pl. *vīrēs*, f. (irreg.) = force (in the sing.), strength (in the pl.)
vīsus: see *videō*
vīta, -ae, f. = life
vītō, -āre, -āvī, -ātum = I avoid
vitricus, -ī, m. = step-father
vīvō, vīvere, vīxī, vīctum = I live, am alive
vīvus, -a, -um = alive
vix = scarcely
vōbīs: see *vōs*
vocō, -āre, -āvī, -ātum = I call
volō, -āre, -āvī, -ātum = I fly
volō, velle, voluī (irreg.) = I wish, am willing
vōs = you (plural)
vōx, vōcis, f. = voice
vulnerō, -āre, -āvī, -ātum = I wound
vulnus, vulneris, n. = wound

English – Latin Vocabulary

(Including all words used in Books I, II and III, together with some additional, commonly-used words)

Ability (of intellect or character) = *ingenium, -iī*, n.

Able, I am = *possum, posse, potuī* (irreg.)

Absent, I am = *absum, abesse, āfuī*

Accord, of one's own = *sponte*

Accuse, I = *accūsō, -āre, -āvī, -ātum*

Accustomed, I am = *soleō, -ēre, solitus sum*

Across = *trāns* (+ acc.)

Add, I = *addō, addere, addidī, additum*

Advise, I = *moneō, -ēre, -uī, -itum*

Affair, matter = *rēs, reī*, f.

After (adverb) = *post*

After (conjunction) = *postquam*

After (preposition) = *post* (+ acc.)

Afterwards = *posteā*

Again = *iterum*

Against = *contrā* (+ acc.)

Agree, I = *cōnsentiō, -īre, cōnsēnsī, cōnsēnsum*

Alive = *vīvus, -a, -um*

All = *omnis, -e*

Allow, I = *permittō, -ere, permīsī, permissum* (+ dat.)

Ally = *socius, -iī*, m.

Almost = *paene*

Alone = *sōlus, -a, -um* (like *ūnus*)

Already = *iam*

Also = *etiam; quoque* (written *after* the word it emphasises)

Altar = *āra, -ae*, f.

Although = *quamquam* (+ indic.); *cum* (+ subj.); *quamvīs* (+ subj., if the concession is accepted only as a hypothesis)

Always = *semper*

Am, I = *sum, esse, fuī* (irreg.)

Amazed = *attonitus, -a, -um*

Amazed at, I am = *mīror, mīrārī, mīrātus sum*

Ambassador = *lēgātus, -ī*, m.

Ambush = *īnsidiae, -ārum*, f. pl.

Among = *inter* (+ acc.)

And = *et; ac* (not before vowels or *h*)*; atque; -que* (on end of word)

And...not = *nec; neque*

Anger = *īra, -ae*, f.

Angry = *īrātus, -a, -um*

Angry, I am = *īrāscor, īrāscī, īrātus sum* (+ dat. of thing or person)

Animal = *animal, animālis*, n.

Announce, I = *nūntiō, -āre, -āvī, -ātum*

Answer, I = *respondeō, -ēre, respondī, respōnsum*

Any = *ūllus, -a, -um* (like *ūnus*); *quī, qua, quod* (used after *sī* and *nē*)

Anyone, anything (pronoun) = *quis, quid* (used after *sī* and *nē*)

Approach, I = *appropinquō, -āre, -āvī, -ātum* (+ dat. or *ad* + acc.); *adeō, adīre, adiī, aditum* (goes like *eō*)

Area, region = *regiō, -ōnis*, f.

Arise, I = *orior, orīrī, ortus sum* (mixed conjugation, despite infinitive in *-īrī*)

Armed = *armātus, -a, -um*

Arms (weapons) = *arma, -ōrum*, n. pl.

Army = *exercitus, -ūs*, m.

Around = *circum* (+ acc.)

Arrival = *adventus, -ūs*, m.

Arrive, I = *adveniō, -īre, advēnī, adventum*

Arrow = *sagitta, -ae*, f.

Art = *ars, artis*, f.

As = *ut* (+ indicative)

As soon as = *simul ac/atque* (*ac* not used before vowels or *h*)*; ut prīmum*

Ashamed, I am: use *pudet* (impersonal: + acc. of person and gen. of cause)

Ask, I = *rogō, -āre, -āvī, -ātum*

At last = *tandem*

At the house of, among = *apud* (+ acc.)

At the same time = *simul*

Attack (noun) = *impetus, -ūs*, m.

Attack, I = *aggredior, aggredī, aggressus sum*; *oppugnō, -āre, -āvī, -ātum* (only used of towns and cities)

Avoid, I = *vītō, -āre, -āvī, -ātum*

Bad = *malus, -a, -um*

Band of men = *manus, -ūs*, f.

Bank = *rīpa, -ae*, f.

Barbarian (noun) = *barbarus, -ī*, m.

Barbarian = *barbarus, -a, -um*

Battle = *proelium, -iī*, n.; *pugna, -ae*, f.

Battle line = *aciēs, aciēī*, f.

Bear, I = *ferō, ferre, tulī, lātum* (irreg.)

Beard = *barba, -ae*, f.

Beautiful = *pulcher, pulchra, pulchrum*

Beauty = *fōrma, -ae*, f.

Because = *quod, quia*

Bed = *cubīle, cubīlis*, n.; *lectus, -ī*, m.

Before (adverb) = *ante*

Before (conjunction) = *antequam; priusquam*

Before (preposition) = *ante* (+ acc.)

Beforehand, previously = *anteā*

Began, I = *coepī, coepisse, coeptum* (defective)

Begin, I = *incipiō, -ere, incēpī, inceptum*

Beginning = *initium, -iī*, n.

Believe, I = *crēdō, -ere, crēdidī, crēditum* (+ dat.)

Best = *optimus, -a, -um*

Betray, I = *prōdō, -ere, prōdidī, prōditum*

Better = *melior, -us*

Between = *inter* (+ acc.)

Big = *magnus, -a, -um*

Bigger = *maior, -us*

Biggest = *maximus, -a, -um*

Bird = *avis, avis*, f.

Black = *niger, nigra, nigrum*

Blame (noun) = *culpa, -ae*, f.

Blood = *sanguis, sanguinis*, m.

Body = *corpus, -ŏris*, n.

Bold = *audāx, audācis*

Bone = *os, ossis*, n.

Book = *liber, librī*, m.

Booty = *praeda, -ae*, f.

Born, I am = *nāscor, nāscī, nātus sum*

Both…and = *et…et*

Boy = *puer, puerī*, m.

Brave = *fortis, -e*

Bravely = *fortiter*

Bread = *pānis, pānis*, m.

Break, I = *frangō, -ere, frēgī, frāctum; rumpō, -ere, rūpī, ruptum*

Breast = *pectus, pectoris*, n.

Bridge = *pōns, pontis*, m.

Brief = *brevis, breve*

British = *Britannus, -a, -um*

Brother = *frāter, frātris*, m.

Build, I = *aedificō, -āre, -āvī, -ātum*

Building = *aedificium, -iī*, n.

Burden = *onus, oneris*, n.

Burn, I (transitive) = *incendō, -ere, incendī, incēnsum*

Bury, I = *sepeliō, -īre, sepelīvī, sepultum*

But = *sed*

But…not = *nec tamen; neque tamen*

Buy, I = *emō, emere, ēmī, ēmptum*

By (with agent) = *ā, ab* (+ abl.)

By chance = *forte*

Call, I = *appellō, -āre, -āvī, -ātum; vocō, -āre, -āvī, -ātum*

Camp = *castra, -ōrum*, n. pl.

Can, I: use *possum* = I am able

Capture, I = *capiō, -ere, cēpī, captum*

Care (noun) = *cūra, -ae*, f.
Care for, I = *cūrō, -āre, -āvī, -ātum*
Careful = *dīligēns, -entis*
Carry, I = *portō, -āre, -āvī, -ātum;*
   ferō, ferre, tulī, lātum (irreg.)
Carry away, I = *auferō, auferre,*
   abstulī, ablātum (goes like *ferō*)
Carthaginian (adjective) = *Pūnicus,*
   -a, -um
Carthaginian (noun) = *Poenus, -ī*, m.
Catch sight of, I = *cōnspiciō, -ere,*
   cōnspexī, cōnspectum
Cause = *causa, -ae*, f.
Cause (to happen), I = *efficiō, -ere,*
   effēcī, effectum (*ut* + subj.)
Cautious, I am = *caveō, -ēre, cāvī,*
   cautum
Cavalry = *equitēs, -um*, m. pl.
Certain = *certus, -a, -um*
Certain, a (adjective) = *quīdam,*
   quaedam, quoddam;
   (pronoun) = *quīdam, quaedam,*
   quiddam
Change, I = *mūtō, -āre, -āvī, -ātum*
Charge, attack (noun) = *impetus,*
   -ūs, m.
Chief = *prīnceps, prīncipis*, m.
Children, offspring = *līberī, -ōrum*, m.
   pl. (only used to refer to the sons
   and/or daughters of a particular
   parent; for "children" in the sense
   of "young boys and girls", use
   puerī and/or *puellae*)
Choose, I = *legō, -ere, lēgī, lēctum*
Citadel = *arx, arcis*, f.
Citizen = *cīvis, cīvis*, c.
City = *urbs, urbis*, f.
City-state = *cīvitās, cīvitātis*, f.
Climb, I = *ascendō, -ere, ascendī,*
   ascēnsum
Close, I = *claudō, claudere, clausī,*
   clausum
Clothing = *vestis, vestis*, f.
Cohort = *cohors, cohortis*, f.
Cold (noun) = *frīgus, -oris*, n.

Collect = *colligō, -ere, collēgī,*
   collēctum
Column (of army) = *agmen,*
   agminis, n.
Come, I = *veniō, -īre, vēnī, ventum*
Come together, I = *conveniō, -īre,*
   convēnī, conventum
Command (noun) = *imperium, -ī*, n.
Commander = *praefectus, -ī*, m.
Companion = *comes, comitis*, c.
Compel, I = *cōgō, cōgere, coēgī,*
   coāctum
Complain, I = *queror, querī, questus*
   sum
Complete, I = *cōnficiō, -ere,*
   cōnfēcī, cōnfectum
Concerning = *dē* (+ abl.)
Condemn, I = *condemnō, -āre, -āvī, -*
   ātum
Conquer, I = *vincō, -ere, vīcī,*
   victum
Consul = *cōnsul, cōnsulis*, m.
Conversation = *sermō, -ōnis*, m.
Convey, I = *vehō, -ere, vēxī, vectum*
Corn = *frūmentum, -ī*, n.
Count, I = *numerō, -āre, -āvī, -ātum*
Country = *patria, -ae*, f.
Country house = *vīlla, -ae*, f.
Countryside = *rūs, rūris*, n.
Courage = *virtūs, virtūtis*, f.
Course = *cursus, -ūs*, m.
Cow = *bōs, bovis*, c. (irreg.)
Crime = *scelus, sceleris*, n.
Crowd = *turba, -ae, f.; multitūdō,*
   -inis, f.
Crown = *corōna, -ae*, f.
Cruel = *crūdēlis, -e*
Cultivate, I = *colō, colere, coluī,*
   cultum
Cure, I = *sānō, -āre, -āvī, -ātum*
Custom = *mōs, mōris*, m.
Cut, I = *caedō, -ere, cecīdī, caesum*
Danger = *perīculum, -ī*, n.
Dangerous = *perīculōsus, -a, -um*
Dare, I = *audeō, audēre, ausus sum*

Daughter = *fīlia, -ae*, f. (dat. and abl. pl. = *fīliābus*)

Day = *diēs, diēī*, m. (f. if an appointed day)

Dead = *mortuus, -a, -um*

Dear = *cārus, -a, -um*

Death = *mors, mortis*, f.

Death, I put to = *interficiō, -ere, interfēcī, interfectum*

Deceive, I = *fallō, -ere, fefellī, falsum*

Decide, I = *cōnstituō, -ere, cōnstituī, cōnstitūtum*

Deep = *altus, -a, -um*

Defend, I = *dēfendō, -ere, dēfendī, dēfēnsum*

Delay (noun) = *mora, -ae*, f.

Delay, I = *moror, morārī, morātus sum*

Delight, I = *dēlectō, -āre, -āvī, -ātum*

Deny, I = *negō, -āre, -āvī, -ātum*

Depart, I = *discēdō, -ere, discessī, discessum*

Deserve, I = *mereō, -ēre, -uī, -itum; mereor, -ērī, meritus sum*

Desire, I = *cupiō, -ere, -īvī, -ītum*

Desirous (of) = *cupidus, -a, -um* (+ gen.)

Despair, I = *dēspērō, -āre, -āvī, -ātum*

Despise, I = *contemnō, -ere, contempsī, contemptum*

Destiny = *fātum, -ī*, n.

Destroy, I = *dēleō, dēlēre, dēlēvī, dēlētum*

Die, I = *morior, morī, mortuus sum; pereō, -īre, periī, peritum* (goes like *eō*)

Difficult = *difficilis, -e*

Dine, I = *cēnō, -āre, -āvī, -ātum*

Dinner = *cēna, -ae*, f.

Disaster = *clādēs, clādis*, f.

Disgraceful = *turpis, -e*

Distinction = *dignitās, dignitātis*, f.

Divide, I = *dīvidō, -ere, dīvīsī, dīvīsum*

Do not! = *nōlī / nōlīte* (+ infin.)

Do, I = *faciō, -ere, fēcī, factum; agō, agere, ēgī, āctum*

Doctor = *medicus, -ī*, m.

Dog = *canis, canis*, c.

Doubt, I = *dubitō, -āre, -āvī, -ātum*

Doubtful = *dubius, -a, -um*

Down from = *dē* (+ abl.)

Drag, I = *trahō, -ere, trāxī, tractum*

Draw up, I = *īnstruō, -ere, īnstrūxī, īnstrūctum*

Dream (noun) = *somnium, -iī*, n.

Drink, I = *bibō, -ere, bibī*

Drive, I = *pellō, -ere, pepulī, pulsum*

Duty = *officium, -iī*, n.

Each (adjective) = *quisque, quaeque, quodque*

Each (pronoun) = *quisque, quaeque, quidque*

Eager about, I am = *studeō, -ēre, studuī* (+ dat.)

Eagle = *aquila, ae*, f.

Ear = *auris, auris*, f.

Easily (adverb) = *facile*

Easy = *facilis, -e*

Eat, I = *edō, ēsse* (or *edere*), *ēdī, ēsum* (irreg.)

Eight = *octŏ*

Eighteen = *duodēvīgintī*

Either…or = *vel...vel*

Eleven = *ūndecim*

Emperor = *prīnceps, prīncipis*, m.

Empire = *imperium, -iī*, n.

Encourage, I = *hortor,-ārī, -ātus sum*

End = *fīnis, -is*, m.

Enemy (personal) = *inimīcus, -ī*, m.

Enemy (of the state) = *hostis, hostis*, c. (usually used in plural)

Enough = *satis*

Enter = *intrō, -āre, -āvī, -ātum*

Escape, I = *effugiō, -ere, effūgī*

Even = *etiam*

Even if = *etsī, etiamsī*

Ever = *umquam*

Every = *omnis, -e*

Every day = *cotīdiē* (or *cottīdiē*)

Exile = *exsilium, -iī*, n.

Explore, I = *explōrō, -āre, -āvī, -ātum*

Eye = *oculus, -ī*, m.

Face = *ōs, ōris*, n.; *faciēs, faciēī*, f.

Faith = *fidēs, fideī*, f.

Faithful = *fidēlis, -e*

Fall, I = *cadō, -ere, cecidī, cāsum*

False = *falsus, -a, -um*

Fame = *fāma, -ae*, f.

Famous = *clārus, -a, -um*

Far away = *procul*

Farewell = *valē / valēte*

Farmer = *agricola, -ae*, m.

Fate = *fātum, -ī*, n.

Father = *pater, patris*, m.

Fatherland = *patria, -ae*, f.

Favour, I = *faveō, -ēre, fāvī, fautum* (+ dat.)

Fear (noun) = *timor, -ōris*, m.

Fear, I = *timeō, -ēre, -uī*

Feel, I = *sentiō, -īre, sēnsī, sēnsum*

Few = *paucī, -ae, -a*

Field = *ager, agrī*, m.

Fierce = *ācer, ācris, ācre; ferōx, ferōcis*

Fifteen = *quīndecim*

Fight (noun) = *pugna, -ae*, f.

Fight, I = *pugnō, -āre, -āvī, -ātum*

Fill, I = *compleō, -ēre, complēvī, complētum*

Find, I = *inveniō, -īre, invēnī, inventum*

Fire (flames) = *ignis, ignis*, m. (abl. sing.: *ignī* or *igne*)

Fire, a (i.e. a conflagration) = *incendium, -iī*, n.

First, at = *prīmō / prīmum*

Five = *quīnque*

Flame = *flamma, -ae*, f.

Flee, I (transitive) = *fugiō, -ere, fūgī, fugitum*

Fleet = *classis, classis*, f. (abl. sing.: *classī* or *classe*)

Flight = *fuga, -ae*, f.

Flower = *flōs, flōris*, m.

Fly, I = *volō, -āre, -āvī, -ātum*

Follow, I = *sequor, sequī, secūtus sum*

Food = *cibus, -ī*, m.

Foot = *pēs, pedis*, m.

Foot soldier = *pedes, peditis*, m.

For = *enim* (2nd word in clause); *nam; namque*

For a long time = *diū*

Forbid, I = *vetō, vetāre, vetuī, vetitum*

Force = *vīs*, f. (irreg.), used in singular

Force, I = *cōgō, cōgere, coēgī, coāctum*

Forces = *cōpiae, -ārum*, f. pl.

Forget, I = *oblīvīscor, oblīvīscī, oblītus sum* (+ gen. of person or + gen. or acc. of thing)

Fortify, I = *mūniō, -īre, -īvī, -ītum*

Fortunate = *fēlīx, fēlīcis*

Fortune = *fortūna, -ae*, f.

Forum = *forum, -ī*, n.

Fountain = *fōns, fontis*, m.

Four = *quattuor*

Fourteen = *quattuordecim*

Free (adjective) = *līber, -era, -erum*

Free, I = *līberō, -āre, -āvī, -ātum*

Freedom = *lībertās, -ātis*, f.

Friend = *amīcus, -ī*, m.

Friendship = *amīcitia, -ae*, f.

From = *ā, ab* (+ abl.)

From all sides = *undique*

From here, hence = *hinc*

From there, thence = *illinc*

Full = *plēnus, -a, -um* (+ abl. or gen.)

Furthest = *extrēmus, -a, -um*

Garden = *hortus, -ī*, m.

Gate = *porta, -ae*, f.

Gaul (the country) = *Gallia, -ae*, f.

Gaul (the person) = *Gallus, -ī*, m.

General = *imperātor, -ōris*, m.

Gift = *dōnum, -ī*, n.

Girl = *puella, -ae*, f.

Give, I = *dō, dăre, dedī, dătum*

Give back, I = *reddō, reddere, reddidī, redditum*

Gladly = *libenter*

Glory = *fāma, -ae*, f.

Go, I = *eō, īre, iī* (or *īvī*), *itum* (irreg.)

Go back, I = *redeō, redīre, rediī, reditum* (goes like *eō*)*; regredior, regredī, regressus sum*

Go down, I = *dēscendō, -ere, dēscendī, dēscēnsum*

Go forward, I = *prōcēdō, -ere, prōcessī, prōcessum; prōgredior, prōgredī, prōgressus sum*

Go in, I = *introo, -āre, -āvī, -ātum; ineō, -īre, iniī, initum* (goes like *eō*); *ingredior, ingredī, ingressus sum*

Go out, I = *exeō, exīre, exiī, exitum* (goes like *eō*); *ēgredior, ēgredī, ēgressus sum*

God = *deus, deī*, m. (irreg.)

Goddess = *dea, -ae*, f. (dat. and abl. pl. = *deābus*)

Gold = *aurum, -ī*, n.

Good = *bonus, -a, -um*

Goods, possessions = *bona, -ōrum*, n. pl.

Grass = *herba, -ae*, f.

Great = *magnus, -a, -um*

Greatly = *magnopere*

Greece = *Graecia, -ae*, f.

Greek = *Graecus, -a, -um*

Greet, I = *salūtō, -āre, -āvī, -ātum*

Grief = *dolor, dolōris*, m.

Ground = *humus, humī*, f.

Guard (noun) = *custōs, custōdis*, c.

Guard, I = *custōdiō, -īre, -īvī, -ītum*

Guest = *hospes, hospitis*, m.

Hall = *ātrium, ātriī*, n.

Halt, I = *cōnsistō, -ere, cōnstitī, cōnstitum*

Hand = *manus, -ūs*, f.

Hand over, I = *trādō, -ere, trādidī, trāditum*

Happens (that), it = *accidit, -ere, accidit* (impersonal: + *ut* + subj.)

Happens to: use *forte* (+ verb)

Happy = *laetus, -a, -um*

Harbour = *portus, -ūs*, m.

Hard = *dūrus, -a, -um*

Harm, hurt, I = *laedō, laedere, laesī, laesum; noceō, -ēre, nocuī, nocitum* (+ dat.)

Hate, I = *ōdī* (defective)

Hatred = *odium, -iī*, n.

Have, I = *habeō, -ēre -uī, -itum*

Head = *caput, -itis*, n.

Hear, I = *audiō, -īre, -īvī, -ītum*

Heavy = *gravis, -e*

Hello = *salvē, salvēte*

Help (noun) = *auxilium, -iī*, n.

Help, I = *iuvō, iuvāre, iūvī, iūtum; adiuvō, -āre, adiūvī, adiūtum*

Her (own) = *suus, sua, suum*

Here = *hīc*

Hesitate, I = *dubitō, -āre, -āvī, -ātum*

Hide, I = *cēlō, -āre, -āvī, -ātum*

High = *altus, -a, -um*

Higher = *superior, -ōris*

Hill = *collis, collis*, m.

Hinder, I = *impediō, -īre, -īvī, -ītum*

His (own) = *suus, sua, suum*

Hold, I = *teneō, -ēre, tenuī, tentum*

Home = *domus, -ūs*, f. (irreg.); homewards = *domum*; at home = *domī*

Honour = *honōs* (or *honor*), *honōris*, m.

Hope, I = *spērō, -āre, -āvī, -ātum*

Horse = *equus, equī*, m.

Horseman = *eques, equitis*, m.

Host = *hospes, hospitis*, m.

Hour = *hōra, -ae*, f.

House = *domus, -ūs*, f. (irreg.)

How? = *quōmodŏ?*

How…(exclamatory) = *quam* (+ adjective or adverb)

How great? = *quantus, -a, -um?*

How many? = *quot?*

How often? = *quotiēns?* (or *quotiēs?*)

However = *autem* (never written as first word in clause)*; tamen* (not generally written as first word in clause)

Huge = *ingēns, ingentis*

Hundred, one = *centum*

Hurry, I = *festīnō, -āre, -āvī, -ātum; contendō, contendere, contendī, contentum*

Husband = *marītus, -ī*, m.

I = *egŏ*

If = *sī*

If, whether = *num*

If...not = *nisi* (or *nī*)

Immediately = *statim*

Immortal = *immortālis, -e*

In = *in* (+ abl.)

In order to, in order that = *ut* (+ subjunctive)

In vain = *frūstrā*

Indeed = *vērō; quidem*

Infantry = *peditēs, peditum*, m. pl.

Inform, I = *certiōrem/certiōrēs faciō*

Inhabitant = *incola, -ae*, c.

Injustice = *iniūria, -ae*, f.

Inn = *taberna, -ae*, f.

Into = *in* (+ acc.)

Iron = *ferrum, -ī*, n.

Island = *īnsula, -ae*, f.

Italy = *Ītalia, -ae*, f.

Its (own) = *suus, sua, suum*

Join, I = *iungō, iungere, iūnxī, iūnctum*

Joke = *iocus, -ī*, m. (in pl. also *ioca, -ōrum*, n. pl.)

Journey = *iter, itineris*, n.

Joy = *gaudium, gaudiī*, n.

Judge = *iūdex, iūdicis*, c.

Jupiter = *Iuppiter, Iovis*, m.

Just, righteous = *iūstus, -a, -um*

Just as = *sīcut*

Kill, I = *necō, necāre, necāvī, necātum; occīdo, -ere, occīdī, occīsum; interficiō, -ere, interfēcī, interfectum; caedō, -ere, cecīdī, caesum*

Kind = *benignus, -a, -um*

King = *rēx, rēgis*, m.

Kingdom = *rēgnum, -ī*, n.

Kiss (noun) = *ōsculum, -ī*, n.

Knee = *genū, genūs*, n.

Know, I = *sciŏ, scīre, scīvī, scītum*

Know, I do not = *nesciŏ, -īre, nescīvī, nescītum*

Land = *terra, -ae*, f.

Lake = *lacus, -ūs*, m.

Language = *lingua, -ae*, f.

Last = *ultimus, -a, -um*

Laugh, I = *rīdeō, -ēre, rīsī, rīsum*

Law = *lēx, lēgis*, f.; *iūs, iūris*, n.

Lawful, it is = *licet, -ēre, licuit* (+ dat.; impersonal)

Lead back, I = *redūcō, -ere, redūxi, reductum*

Lead, I = *dūcō, -ere, dūxī, ductum*

Leader = *dux, ducis*, c.

Learn (find out), I = *cognōscō, -ere, cognōvī, cognitum*

Learn, I = *discō, -ere, didicī*

Leave, I = *relinquō, -ere, relīquī, relictum*

Left = *sinister, -tra, -trum*

Legion = *legiō, -ōnis*, f.

Leisure = *ōtium, -iī*, n.

Lest = *nē* (+ subjunctive)

Letter = *epistola* (or *epistula*), *-ae*, f.

Lie (be lying down), I = *iaceō, -ēre, iacuī, iacitum*

Life = *vīta, -ae*, f.

Lift, I = *tollō, -ere, sustulī, sublātum*

Light (noun) = *lūx, lūcis*, f.

Light, unimportant = *levis, -e*

Like, I = *amō, amāre, amāvī, amātum*

Lion = *leō, leōnis*, m.

Listen to, I = *audiō, -īre, -īvī, -ītum*

Little, a (adverb) = *paulum*

Live (inhabit), I = *habitō, -āre, -āvī, -ātum*

Live, (i.e. am alive), I = *vīvō, vīvere, vīxī, victum*

Long = *longus, -a, -um*

Look at, I = *spectō, -āre, -āvī, -ātum*
Look! = *ecce*
Lord = *dominus, -ī*, m.
Lose, I = *āmittō, -ere, āmīsī, āmissum*
Love = *amor, amōris*, m.
Love, I = *amō, amāre, amāvī, amātum*
Lower = *īnferior, -ōris*
Make, I = *faciō, -ere, fēci, factum*
Man (as opposed to woman) = *vir, virī*, m. (irreg.)
Man (person) = *homŏ, hominis*, c.
Magistrate = *magistrātus, -ūs*, m.
Maiden = *virgō, virginis*, f.
Manage, I = *gerō, -ere, gessī, gestum*
Many; *see* much
March, I = *contendō, contendere, contendī, contentum*
Marriage = *mātrimōnium, -iī*, n.
Marvellous = *mīrābilis, -e*
Master = *dominus, -ī*, m.; *magister, magistrī*, m.
Meanwhile = *intereā*
Merchant = *mercātor, mercātōris*, m.
Messenger = *nūntius, nuntiī*, m.
Middle = *medius, -a, -um*
Mind = *animus, -ī*, m.; *mēns, mentis*, f.
Missile = *tēlum, -ī*, n.
Mix, I = *misceō, -ēre, miscuī, mixtum*
Money = *pecūnia, -ae*, f.
Month = *mēnsis, mēnsis*, m.
Moon = *lūna, -ae*, f.
More (comparative of many) = *plūs, plūris* (neuter singular noun + gen.; or adjective in plural)
Moreover = *autem* (not first word in clause)
Most (superlative of much/many) = *plūrimus, -a, -um*
Mother = *māter, mātris*, f.
Mountain = *mōns, montis*, m.
Mouth = *ōs, ōris*, n.

Move, I (transitive) = *moveō, -ēre, mōvī, mōtum*
Much = *multus, -a, -um*
My = *meus, -a, -um*
Naked = *nūdus, -a, -um*
Name = *nōmen, nōminis*, n.
Near = *prope* (+ acc.)
Nearest = *proximus, -a, -um*
Neglect, I = *neglegō, -ere, neglēxī, neglēctum*
Neighbouring = *vīcīnus, -a, -um*
Neither...nor = *nec...nec; neque...neque*
Never = *numquam*
New = *novus, -a, -um*
Next = *proximus, -a, -um*
Night = *nox, noctis*, f.
Night, in the (adverb) = *noctū*
Nine = *novem*
Nineteen = *ūndēvīgintī*
No (adjective) = *nūllus, -a, -um* (like *ūnus*)
No longer = *nōn iam*; (i.e. not for a longer time = *nōn diūtius*)
Noble = *nōbilis, -e*
No one = *nēmō, (nēminem, nūllĭus, nēminī, nūllō)* c.
Nor = *nec; neque*
Not = *nōn*
Not even = *nē...quidem*
Not know, I do = *nesciŏ, -īre, -īvī, -ītum*
Not only...but also = *nōn sōlum... sed etiam*
Nothing = *nihil* (or *nīl*)
Now = *iam; nunc*
Nowhere = *nūsquam*
Number = *numerus, -ī*, m.
Obey, I = *pāreō, -ēre, -uī, -itum* (+ dat.)
Offer, I = *praebeō, -ēre, praebuī, praebitum; offerō, offerre, obtulī, oblātum* (goes like *ferō*)
Office, rank = *honōs* (or *honor*), *honōris*, m.
Often = *saepe*

Old (e.g. x years old) **annōs nātus,
-a, -um**
Old = **vetus, veteris**
Old man = **senex, senis**, m.
On = **in** (+ abl.)
On account of = **propter** (+ acc.); **ob**
(+ acc.)
On behalf of = **prō** (+ abl.)
On the next day = **postrīdiē**
Once (adverb) = **semel**
Once, once upon a time = **ōlim,
quondam**
One = **ūnus, -a, -um** (gen. **ūnĭus**, dat.
ūnī)
One, the...other, the = **alter...alter**
Only (adverb) = **modŏ, tantum,
sōlum**
On to = **in** (+ acc.)
Open (adjective) = **apertus, -a, -um**
Open, I = **aperiō, -īre, aperuī,
apertum**
Opportunity = **occāsiō, -ōnis**, f.
Oppress, I = **opprimō, -ere,
oppressī, oppressum**
Or = **aut; vel**
Orator = **ōrātor, -ōris**, m.
Order, I = **imperō, -āre, -āvī, -ātum** (+
dat.); **iubeō, -ēre, iussī, iussum**
Other (of two) = **alter, altera, alterum**
Other = **alius, alia, aliud**
Other (i.e. remaining) = **cēterī**
Ought, I = **dēbeō, -ēre, -uī, -itum**
Our = **noster, nostra, nostrum**
Out of = **ē, ex** (+ abl.)
Outcome = **exitus, -ūs**, m.
Outside = **extrā** (+ acc.)
Over = **super** (+ acc.)
Overcome, I = **superō, -āre, -āvī,
-ātum**
Overwhelm, I = **opprimō, -ere,
oppressī, oppressum**
Owe, I = **dēbeō, -ēre, -uī, -itum**
Ox = **bōs, bovis**, c. (irreg.)
Pain = **dolor, dolōris**, m.
Pain, I feel = **doleō, -ēre, doluī,
dolitum**

Parent = **parēns, parentis**, c.
Part = **pars, partis**, f.
Peace = **pāx, pācis**, f.
Penalty = **poena, -ae**, f.
Penalty, I pay the = **poenās dō**
People (population) = **populus, -ī**, m.
People (race) = **gēns, gentis**, f.
People (the common people) = **plēbs,
plēbis**, f.
Perhaps = **fortasse**
Perish, I = **pereō, -īre, periī, peritum**
(goes like **eō**)
Person = **homŏ, hominis**, c.
Persuade, I = **persuādeō, -ēre,
persuāsī, persuāsum** (+ dat.)
Philosopher = **philosophus, -ī**, m.
Pitch camp, I = **castra pōnō**
Pity, it moves to (impersonal) =
miseret (+ acc. of person and
gen. of cause)
Place (noun) = **locus, -ī**, m. (plural =
loca, -ōrum, n. pl., when this
refers to a region; **locī** refers to
individual places)
Place, I = **pōnō, -ere, posuī, positum**
Plain (noun) = **campus, -ī**, m.
Plan = **cōnsilium, -iī**, n.
Plan, I adopt a = **cōnsilium capiō**
Play, I = **lūdō, -ere, lūsī, lūsum**
Please, I = **placeō, placēre, placuī,
placitum** (+ dat.)
Pleases, it (impersonal) = **placet**
(+ dat.); **iuvat** (+ acc. of the thing
+ infin.)
Poem = **carmen, carminis**, n.
Poet = **poēta, -ae**, m.
Poor = **pauper, pauperis** (like **vetus**)
Pour, I = **fundō, -ere, fūdī, fūsum**
Power = **potestās, potestātis**, f.
Praise (noun) = **laus, laudis**, f.
Praise, I = **laudō, -āre, -āvī, -ātum**
Pray, I = **ōrō, -āre, -āvī, -ātum**
Prefer, I = **mālō, mālle, māluī** (irreg.)
Prepare, I = **parō, -āre, -āvī, -ātum**
Present, I am = **adsum, adesse,
adfuī**

Pretend, I = **simulō, -āre, -āvī, -ātum**
Prevent, I = **prohibeō, -ēre, -uī, -itum**
Price = **pretium, -iī**, n.
Priest(ess) = **sacerdōs, sacerdōtis**, c.
Prisoner = **captīvus, -ī**, m.
Proceed, I = **prōcēdō, -ere, prōcessī,
    prōcessum**
Produce, I = **ēdō, -ere, ēdidī, ēditum**
Prohibit, I = **prohibeō, -ēre, -uī,
    -itum**
Promise, I = **prōmittō, -ere, prōmīsī,
    prōmissum**
Proper, it is = **decet, decēre, decuit**
    (impersonal: + acc. of the person
    + infin.)
Proud = **superbus, -a, -um**
Province = **prōvincia, -ae**, f.
Punish, I = **pūniō, -īre, -īvī, -ītum**
Pupil = **discipulus, -ī**, m. / **discipula,
    -ae**, f
Put to death, I = **interficiō, -ere,
    interfēcī, interfectum**
Put to flight, I = **fundō, -ere, fūdī,
    fūsum; fugō, -āre, -āvī, -ātum**
Queen = **rēgīna, -ae**, f.
Quick = **celer, celeris, celere**
Quickly = **celeriter**
Quiet (noun) = **quiēs, quiētis**, f.
Raise, I = **tollō, tollere, sustulī,
    sublātum**
Rampart = **vāllum, -ī**, n.
Read, I = **legō, -ere, lēgī, lēctum**
Reason = **causa, -ae**, f.
Receive, I = **accipiō, -ere, accēpī,
    acceptum**
Recent = **recēns, recentis**
Recently = **nūper**
Rejoice, I = **gaudeō, gaudēre,
    gāvīsus sum**
Release, I = **solvō, -ere, solvī,
    solūtum**
Religion = **religiō** (or **relligiō**),
    -ōnis, f.
Remain, I = **maneō, -ēre, mānsī,
    mānsum**
Remaining = **reliquus, -a, -um**

Remember, I = **meminī, meminisse**
    (+ gen. or acc.; defective)
Reply, I = **respondeō, -ēre, respondī,
    respōnsum**
Report, I = **nūntiō, -āre, -āvī, -ātum**
Republic = **rēspūblica, reīpūblicae**, f.
    (both **rēs** and **pūblica** decline;
    may be written as two words)
Resist, I = **resistō, -ere, restitī** (+
    dat.)
Rest (noun) = **quiēs, quiētis**, f.
Return (noun) = **reditus, -ūs**, m.
Return (come back), I = **reveniō, -īre,
    revēnī, reventum**
Return (give back), I = **reddō,
    reddere, reddidī, redditum**
Return (go back), I = **redeō, redīre,
    rediī, reditum** (goes like **eō**);
    **regredior, regredī, regressus
    sum**
Reward = **praemium, -iī**, n.
Rich = **dīves, dīvitis** (like **vetus**)
Riches, wealth = **dīvitiae, -ārum**,
    f. pl.
Right (as opposed to left) = **dexter,
    dextra, dextrum** (or **dexter,
    dextera, dexterum**)
Right (as opposed to wrong) = **rēctus,
    -a, -um**
Right, it is (impersonal) = **oportet**
    (+ acc. and infin.)
Rise, I = **surgō, -ere, surrēxī,
    surrēctum**
River = **flūmen, flūminis**, n.
Riverbank = **rīpa, -ae**, f.
Road = **via, -ae**, f.
Rock = **saxum, -ī**, n.
Roman (adjective) = **Rōmānus, -a,
    -um**
Roman (noun) = **Rōmānus, -ī**, m.
Rome = **Rōma, -ae**, f.
Rule, I = **regō, -ere, rēxī, rēctum**
Run, I = **currō, -ere, cucurrī, cursum**
Rush, I = **ruō, ruere, ruī, rutum**
    (future participle = **ruitūrus**)
Sacred = **sacer, sacra, sacrum**

Sacrifice (noun) = *sacrificium, -iī*, n.
Safety = *salūs, salūtis*, f.
Sad = *trīstis, trīste*
Sad, I am = *doleō, -ēre, doluī, dolitum*
Safe = *tūtus, -a, -um*
Safety = *salūs, salūtis*, f.
Sail, I = *nāvigō, -āre, -āvī, -ātum*
Sailor = *nauta, -ae*, m.
Same = *īdem, eadem, ĭdem*
Savage = *saevus, -a, -um*
Save, I = *servō, -āre, -āvī, -ātum*
Say, I = *dīcō, dīcere, dīxī, dictum*
Say that …not, I = *negō, -āre, -āvī, -ātum*
Says, he/she/they (quoting direct speech) = *inquit / inquiunt*
Scarcely = *vix*
School = *lūdus, -ī*, m.
Schoolmaster = *magister, magistrī*, m.
Sea = *mare, maris*, n.
See, I = *videō, -ēre, vīdī, vīsum*
Seek, I = *petō, -ere, petīvī, petītum; quaerō, -ere, quaesīvī, quaesītum*
Seem, I = *videor, vidērī, vīsus sum*
Seize, I = *rapiō, -ere, rapuī, raptum; occupō, -āre, -āvī, -ātum*
Self (reflexive) = *sē*
Self (emphatic) = *ipse, ipsa, ipsum*
Sell, I = *vēndō, -ere, vēndidī, vēnditum*
Senate = *senātus, -ūs*, m.
Senator = *senātor, -ōris*, m.
Send, I = *mittō, -ere, mīsī, missum*
Sense, good = *prūdentia, -ae*, f.
Sensible = *prūdēns, prūdentis*
Serious = *gravis, -e*
Serve, I = *serviō, -īre, -īvī, -ītum* (+ dat.)
Set out, I = *proficīscor, proficīscī, profectus sum*
Seven = *septem*
Seventeen = *septendecim*
Several = *complūrēs, complūrium*
Shadow = *umbra, - ae*, f.

Shepherd = *pāstor, -ōris*, m.
Shield = *scūtum, -ī*, n.
Ship = *nāvis, nāvis*, f. (abl. sing.: *nāvī* or *nāve*)
Shop = *taberna, -ae*, f.
Shore = *lītus, lītoris*, n.; *ōra, -ae*, f.
Short = *brevis, breve*
Shortage = *inopia, -ae*, f.
Shoulder = *umerus, -ī*, m.
Shout (noun) = *clāmor, -ōris*, m.
Shout, I = *clāmō, -āre, -āvī, -ātum*
Show, I = *ostendō, -ere, ostendī, ostēnsum / ostentum*
Sick = *aeger, aegra, aegrum*
Side = *latus, lateris*, n.
Sign, signal = *signum, -ī*, n.
Silence = *silentium, -iī*, n.
Silent = *tacitus, -a, -um*
Silent, I am = *taceō, -ēre, tacuī, tacitum*
Silver = *argentum, -ī*, n.
Similar (to) = *similis, -e* (+ dat. or gen.)
Since = *cum* (+ subjunctive); *quoniam* (+ indic.)
Sing, I = *cantō, -āre, -āvī, -ātum; canō, -ere, cecinī, cantum*
Sister = *soror, -ōris*, f.
Sit, I = *sedeō, sedēre, sēdī, sessum*
Six = *sex*
Sixteen = *sēdecim*
Skill = *ars, artis*, f.
Skilled (in) = *perītus* (+ gen.)
Sky = *caelum, -ī*, n.
Slaughter (noun) = *caedēs, -is*, f.
Slave = *servus, -ī*, m.
Sleep (noun) = *somnus, -ī*, m.
Sleep, I = *dormiō, -īre, -īvī, ītum*
Slowly = *lentē*
Small = *parvus, -a, -um*
Smaller = *minor, minus*
Smallest = *minimus, -a, -um*
Smile, I = *rīdeō, -ēre, rīsī, rīsum*
Smoke = *fūmus, -ī*, m.
Smooth = *lēvis, -e*
So (adverb) = *tam* (used with adjectives and adverbs only)

So, to such an extent = **adeō** (used with verbs)
So, therefore = **itaque**
So, thus = **ita, sīc**
So great = **tantus, -a, -um**
So many = **tot**
So often = **totiēns** (or **totiēs**)
Soldier = **mīles, mīlitis**, c.
Some = **nōnnūllī, -ae, -a; aliqui, aliqua, aliquod**
Someone (pronoun) = **aliquis, aliquid**
Son = **fīlius, fīliī** (or **fīlī**), m. (irreg.)
Song = **carmen, carminis**, n.
Soon = **mox**
Sorry, I am: use **paenitet** (impersonal: + acc. of person and gen. of cause) = it repents
Sound = **sonitus, -ūs**, m.
Spare, I = **parcō, -ere, pepercī, parsum**
Speak, I = **loquor, loquī, locūtus sum**
Spear = **hasta, -ae**, f.; **tēlum, -ī**, n.
Speech = **ōrātiō, -ōnis**, f.
Speed = **celeritās, celeritātis**, f.
Spirit = **animus, -ī**, m.
Stand, I = **stō, stāre, stetī, stătum**
State = **cīvitās, -ātis**, f.
State, city = **rēspūblica, reīpūblicae**, f. (both **rēs** and **pūblica** decline, may be written as two words)
Step = **gradus, gradūs**, m.
Still = **adhūc**
Storm = **tempestās, -ātis**, f.
Story = **fābula, -ae**, f.
Street = **via, -ae**, f.
Strength = **vīrēs, vīrium**, f. pl. (irreg.)
Strong = **valēns, valentis; validus, -a, -um; fortis, -e**
Strong, I am = **valeō, -ēre, valuī, valitum**
Strongly = **vehementer**
Study, I = **studeō, -ēre, -uī** (+ dat.)
Stupid = **stultus, -a, -um**
Such = **tālis, -e**
Suddenly = **subitō**
Suffer, I = **patior, patī, passus sum**

Suitable = **aptus, -a, -um**
Summer = **aestās, -ātis**, f.
Sun = **sōl, sōlis**, m.
Supply (noun) = **cōpia, -ae**, f.
Survive, I = **supersum, -esse, superfuī** (+ dat.)
Suspect, I = **suspicor, -ārī, suspicātus sum**
Swear, I = **iūrō, -āre, -āvī, -ātum**
Sweet = **dulcis, -e**
Swift = **celer, celeris, celere**
Sword = **gladius, gladiī**, m.
Table = **mēnsa, mēnsae**, f.
Take (seize), I = **capiō, -ere, cēpī, captum**
Take up, I = **sūmō, -ere, sūmpsī, sūmptum**
Talk, I = **loquor, loquī, locūtus sum**
Task = **labor, labōris**, m.
Teach, I = **doceō, -ēre, docuī, doctum**
Tear (noun) = **lacrima, -ae**, f.
Tell (e.g. a story), I = **nārrō, -āre, -āvī, -ātum**
Temple = **templum, -ī**, n.
Ten = **decem**
Tender = **tener, -era, -erum**
Terrify, I = **terreō, -ēre, -uī, -itum**
Territory = **fīnēs, -ium**, m. pl.
Terror = **terror, -ōris**, m.
Than = **quam**
Thanks, I give = **grātiās agō**
That = **ille, illa, illud; is, ea, id**
Theatre = **theātrum, -ī**, n.
Their (own) = **suus, sua, suum**
Then = **deinde; inde; tum; tunc**
There = **ibĭ**
There, in that place = **illīc**
There, thither, to there = **eō**
Therefore = **igitur** (not generally written first word in clause); **itaque**
Thing, matter = **rēs, reī**, f.
Think, I = **putŏ, -āre, -āvī, -ātum**
Thirteen = **tredecim**
This = **hic, haec, hoc**
Thousand = **mīlle** (in plural **mīlia, -um**, n. pl.)

Threaten, I = *minor, -ārī, minātus sum* (+ acc. of thing and dat. of person)

Three = *trēs, tria*

Through = *per* (+ acc.)

Throw, I = *iaciō, -ere, iēcī, iactum*

Thus = *ita; sīc*

Time = *tempus, -ŏris*, n.

Tired = *fessus, -a, -um*

To, towards = *ad* (+ acc.)

To here, hither = *hūc*

To there, thither = *illūc, eō*

Today = *hodiē*

Together with = *cum* (+ abl.)

Tomorrow = *crās*

Tongue = *lingua, -ae*, f.

Tooth = *dēns, dentis*, m.

Top of, topmost = *summus, -a, -um*

Touch, I = *tangō, tangere, tetigī, tāctum*

Towards = *ad* (+ acc.)

Town = *oppidum, -ī*, n.

Treacherous = *perfidus, -a, -um*

Treachery = *perfidia, -ae*, f.

Tree = *arbor, -ŏris*, f.

Tribe = *gēns, gentis*, f.

Troy = *Troia, -ae*, f.

True = *vērus -a, -um*

Trumpet = *tuba, -ae*, f.

Trust, I = *crēdō, -ere, crēdidī, crēditum* + dat.; *cōnfīdō, -ere, cōnfīsus sum* (+ dat., or + abl. of things)

Truth = *vēritās, vēritātis*, f.

Try, I = *cōnor, cōnārī, cōnātus sum*

Turn, I = *vertō, -ere, vertī, versum*

Twelve = *duodecim*

Twenty = *vīgintī*

Twice (adverb) = *bis*

Two = *duŏ, duae, duŏ*

Type = *genus, generis*, n.

Under = *sub* (+ abl.)

Understand, I = *intellegō, -ere, intellēxī, intellēctum*

Unequal = *inīquus, -a, -um*

Unknown = *ignōtus, -a, -um*

Unless = *nisi* (or *nī*)

Untrue = *falsus, -a, -um*

Unwilling = *invītus, -a, -um*

Unwilling, I am = *nōlō, nōlle, nōluī* (irreg.)

Uproar = *tumultus, -ūs*, m.

Upset, I = *commoveō, -ēre, commōvī, commōtum*

Urge, I = *hortor, -ārī, -ātus sum*

Use, I = *ūtor, ūtī, ūsus sum* (+ abl.)

Useful = *ūtilis, -e*

Valley = *vallis* (or *vallēs*), *vallis*, f.

Victor = *victor, -ōris*, m.

Victory = *victōria, -ae*, f.

Voice = *vōx, vōcis*, f.

Wage (a war), I = *gerō, -ere, gessī, gestum*

Wait for, I = *exspectō, -āre, -āvī, -ātum*

Wake, I (transitive) = *excitō, -āre, -āvī, -ātum*

Walk, I = *ambulō, -āre, -āvī, -ātum*

Wall = *mūrus, -ī*, m.

Walls (fortified) = *moenia, moenium*, n. pl.

Wander, I = *errō, -āre, -āvī, -ātum*

Want, I = *cupiō, -ere, -īvī, -ītum; volō, velle, voluī* (irreg.)

War = *bellum, -ī*, n.

Warn, I = *moneō, -ēre, -uī, -itum*

Watch, I = *spectō, -āre, -āvī, -ātum*

Water = *aqua, -ae*, f.

Wave = *unda, -ae*, f.

Way (i.e. manner) = *modus, -ī*, m.

Way (i.e. road) = *via, -ae*, f.

We = *nōs*

Weapons = *arma, -ōrum*, n. pl.

Wear, I = *gerō, -ere, gessī, gestum*

Weather = *tempestās, -ātis*, f.

Weep, I = *fleō, flēre, flēvī, flētum*

Well = *bene*

Well-known = *nōtus, -a, -um*

What kind? = *quālis, -e?*

What? = *quid?*

When (conjunction) = *ubĭ*

When? = *quandŏ?*

Whenever = *cum* (+ perfect stem
  tense of indicative)
Where from? = *unde?*
Where to? = *quō?*
Where? = *ubĭ?*
Whether = *num*
Whether...or = *utrum...an*
While = *dum*
Who, which = *quī, quae, quod*
Who? = *quis?*
Whole = *tōtus, -a, -um* (like *ūnus*)
Why? = *cūr?*
Wicked = *scelerātus, -a, -um;*
  scelestus, -a, -um
Wide = *lātus, -a, -um*
Wife = *coniūnx, coniugis*, c.
Wife = *uxor, -ōris*, f.
Willing, I am = *volō, velle, voluī* (irreg.)
Willingly = *libenter*
Wind = *ventus, -ī*, m.
Wine = *vīnum, -ī*, n.
Winter= *hiems, hiemis*, f.
Wisdom = *sapientia, -ae*, f.
Wise = *sapiēns, sapientis*
Wish, I = *volō, velle, voluī* (irreg.)
Wish, I do not = *nōlō, nōlle, nōluī*
  (irreg.)
With = *cum* (+ abl.)
Within = *intrā* (+ acc.)
Without = *sine* (+ abl.)
Woman = *fēmina, -ae*, f.; *mulier,*
  mulieris, f.

Wonder at, I = *mīror, mīrārī, mīrātus*
  sum
Wood, forest = *silva, -ae*, f.
Word = *verbum, -ī*, n.
Work (noun) = *labor, labōris*, m.;
  opus, operis, n.
Work (business) = *negōtium, -iī*, n.
Work, I = *labōrō, -āre, -āvī, -ātum*
Worse = *peior, -us*
Worship, I = *colō, colere, coluī,*
  cultum
Worst = *pessimus, -a, -um*
Worthy (of) = *dignus, -a, -um* (+ abl.)
Wound (noun) = *vulnus, vulneris*, n.
Wound, I = *vulnerō, -āre, -āvī, -ātum*
Wretched = *miser, -era, -erum*
Write, I = *scrībō, -ere, scrīpsī,*
  scrīptum
Year = *annus, -ī*, m.
Yesterday = *herī*
Yield, I = *cēdō, -ere, cessī, cessum*
You (plural) = *vōs*
You (singular) = *tū*
Young person, man = *iuvenis,*
  iuvenis, c.; *adulēscēns, -entis*, c.
Your (belonging to you (plural)) =
  vester, vestra, vestrum
Your (belonging to you (singular)) =
  tuus, -a, -um

Index of subjects